THE GOSPEL OF GOD
A Journey Through Romans

CAM ARENSEN

ISBN# 979-8580-0045-0-1

Book layout & design: Blake Arensen
Cover photo: Azka Nurakli
Author photo: Brad Kerr

Scripture quotations unless otherwise indicated are from the English
Standard Version, copyright 2001 by Crossways, a publishing ministry of
Good News Publishers.

DEDICATION

This book is dedicated to Mr. Bob Hendry, Dr. Curtis Mitchell, Dr. Earl Radmacher, Dr. Ralph Alexander, Dr. Grant Howard, Dr. Ronald Allen and the many other excellent Bible teachers from whom I had the privilege of learning. I would be remiss if I did not add my own father (Ed Arensen) to the list. His lengthy series of messages on the Book of Acts, preached in the Kijabe mission station chapel services when I was in high school, gave me my first experience with the methodology as well as the power of expository preaching. Together these men passed on to me a reverence and love for the Scriptures and equipped me with the desire and tools to study it and communicate its truth effectively. While most of them are now with the Lord, their influence lives on.

TABLE OF CONTENTS

Acknowledgments

My thanks goes to those who helped along the way to bring this book into its final form. To Dave Petersen in Bend, Oregon for being the first to read through the manuscript and for his helpful comments. His perspective as a lawyer was invaluable. To Larry Kroon in Alaska for helping me wrestle with some of the more complex passages (like Romans 7!). To Suzi Malan in South Africa for her encouragement and her eye for details in the final proof reading process. Finally, to Kenya, thanks to my brother Shel Arensen for publishing help and to my nephew Blake Arensen for the cover design and layout. It has truly been an international undertaking!

Foreword

I was fresh in my faith. Just a week prior, I was liberated from an addiction to cocaine and Crown Royal – my biggest enemy had been my self-will. God gathered up my broken life and transformed me. I was now a new creation. The old was gone, and the new had begun. But this newly birthed young man needed to stand on the solid rock of truth, and God knew just what I needed.

My father told me that a noted preacher in the area had just finished preaching through Romans and that his recordings would give me some solid footing. This wise counsel shored up and shaped my faith. Those sermons gave me something to get my teeth into and to satisfy my hungry young appetite. I was blown away. That noted preacher was Cam Arensen. His passion poured out as he spoke. My spirit connected with Cam's spirit and the Spirit of God began to rinse and irrigate my soul. I played and replayed those tapes. Sometimes I would stand up and shout; other times, I would kneel and cry. But they were tears of joy as God was placing the steel of truth in my foundation.

Many years have passed, but I still revisit the notes and highlights in my first, well-worn bible. The pages of the Book of Romans are just a mess of color, and I owe that to Cam Arensen. When I heard that Cam was putting his teaching into print, my heart leaped for joy. But now my happiness is for many others like you. His crystal clear, sound exegetical approach to Romans makes it possible for you to walk in victory and discover the richness of our new-birth miracle.

Please read it, highlight it, and grab up some copies to share with others on this incredible journey. Many people cherry-pick from Romans 8 or jump into the "practical" section of chapter 12 and following. But Cam is spot on when he writes: "Any attempt we may make to apply and live by the teachings of Romans 12-

16 that is not firmly and squarely built upon the teaching and theological truths of the first 11 chapters is impractical."

Jump in now and enjoy <u>The Gospel of God: A Journey through Romans</u>. I trust the truth it contains will impact you as much as it has me.

Karl Clauson
Pastor: 180 Chicago Church
Host: Karl & Crew Mornings – Moody Radio Chicago

Introduction

Why another book on Romans? It's a fair question. Paul's letter to the Romans has been thoroughly explored, exegeted, discussed and debated by Christian scholars for almost 2,000 years. Everything you'd ever want to know about Romans has already been written and it's "out there" somewhere in the literature. The problem is, not everyone knows where to find it and not everyone is looking for it. Maybe a fresh look, a fresh face, a fresh approach will entice some new readers.

Who are the readers I have in mind? They are not the Biblical scholars who reside in seminaries and theological schools. This is not a critical commentary. Those already exist in abundance, and the scholars know how to find them. However, neither is this a "Romans lite" approach, with everything reduced to devotional soundbites. The readers I have in mind are the serious-minded Christians who show up in church every week with hearts and notebooks open, with a desire to hear God's words in a way that will impact their minds, engage their wills and change their lives. The chapters contained in this book originated as sermons preached to just that kind of audience.

My first serious introduction to the Book of Romans came when I was a high school senior at Rift Valley Academy, a school for missionary children in Kenya. We had required Bible classes as part of the curriculum. I shall always be grateful to Mr. Bob Hendry. He was a gifted Bible teacher who thought it was a worthwhile investment of his time to teach the Book of Romans to a class of a dozen high school boys on a school day, right after lunch. The first thing he did was introduce us to the outline of the letter. Our first assignment was to memorize that outline. Though it sounds uninspiring, it was in that outline and those classes that I was first introduced to the power of this letter and to Paul's Spirit-inspired logic as he laid out the gospel of Jesus Christ that is "the power of God for salvation to everyone who believes."

During my pastoral ministry of over 40 years, I had the opportunity to preach through the Book of Romans three times. The first time was to a small church in rural Alaska. I then preached it twice more to an international church in Abu Dhabi, the capital city of the United Arab Emirates. The last two times were separated by a gap of 17 years. Each time God used his Word to change lives. Each time God used his Word to change me, as fresh study not only brought new insights but also refreshed the fundamental truths expounded in Paul's letter. It reminded me once again of the solid faith ground on which I stand. When I preached it the second time in the church in Abu Dhabi, our congregation numbered more than 800, made up of people from over 50 nationalities. God's Word transcended cultures and spoke to the hearts of many in this diverse congregation.

As I was preparing to retire from Abu Dhabi, a member of our congregation named Karin de Toldi approached me. Karin and her family came from France. She said that she had been impacted by my messages on Romans, and asked if I would give her permission to translate them into French (using my sermon manuscripts and voice recordings). I gave her my blessing. She completed the project and then found a publisher in Quebec, Canada. These books (2 volumes) are now in print and the publisher is circulating them widely as part of book kits for pastors in Francophone Africa. When I tell people this story, the question inevitably comes back, "When are you going to publish the English version?"

Now I am retired and sitting in my study in Bend, Oregon, asking the Lord how he wants me to spend my time in this new season of life. The answer comes; "Put your Romans sermons into written form (in English!). Leave this as your legacy." So, whether the readers may be many or few (or just a dozen high school boys!), I will endeavor to obey this call.

Some words about my approach, and how the reader can get the best out of this book. Begin each reading with prayer, asking the Holy Spirit to be your teacher and to keep your heart and mind open to his truth. Then read the designated Scripture text (usually a paragraph in length) from your Bible before beginning to read the chapter in front of you. I will not reproduce the Scripture passage as a whole in the text of the book. However, I will refer frequently to sections of the text. These excerpts will be included as I refer to them. (Almost all quotes will be taken from the English Standard Version unless otherwise noted. When I do quote from another version it is usually the New International Version (NIV), 1984 edition.) When I quote the Biblical text, it is in italics with occasional underlining or bold print for emphasis. I have deliberately eliminated the verse numbers, so that they read more like what they are: a quote from a letter. I should point out that this is not a running commentary. I will not always go verse by verse. What I have endeavored to do in each chapter is what good homiletics practice teaches preachers to do: capture the main thought or idea of the text, show how or why I came to this conclusion (by frequent reference to the text and context) and then make an application to the reader. I will not attempt to answer every question that may arise. I will not make extensive quotes from other sources. I will not attempt complicated lessons in Greek grammar. However, I have studied the passage thoroughly in the original language and will make reference to it when doing so is important to the understanding of the passage.

Paul's letter to the Romans has been called one of the finest examples of legal reasoning in literature. Its impact rests in the "argument" or reasoning process of the writing. I have sought to capture and explain Paul's reasoning as he develops it. Thus, dipping in and out of this book at select places is not the way to get the best out of it. For example, skipping to chapter 12 because it contains your favorite verse is not the way to get the most out of Romans or of this book. You will benefit most from a systematic reading. You may also find it helpful to keep a notebook handy to jot down your thoughts and your questions. I can't promise to answer every question, but some of them will be answered as we move along. And if I don't answer them, well, you have something for your next study project!

One last word. In most commentaries, the author seeks to stay out of the picture and remove all personal references.

However, preaching is different. Good preaching is personal and can be enhanced by personal references and illustrations. I have decided to write as I preached, including personal references and illustrations and writing often in the first person. For these references to make sense to you as the reader, you need know a little bit about my life. I was born in Tanzania, the 3rd of 5 sons born to missionary parents. I grew up in Tanzania and Kenya, attending schools for missionary children. After graduating from high school, I relocated to the US for college and seminary. I married my high school sweetheart (also a child of missionaries) and following seminary, I followed God's leading into a life of service as a pastor/missionary, serving churches in Alaska, Kenya, California and Abu Dhabi until we retired in 2016. That is the broad outline and will help you make sense of the personal examples and illustrations I will insert from time to time.

Enough said! Let's begin.

1

The Journey Begins
Romans 1:1-17

Do you like to travel? Do you like to explore and discover new things? In this book, we are embarking on a voyage of discovery through the Book of Romans. We might think of it as a journey by boat up a long and winding river. It is a river with many twists and turns. The journey will at times surprise us, at times confuse us, and at times delight us. Parts of the journey will be difficult as we make our way through dense jungle thickets of theological truth. It will be a lengthy journey, but it is a very important journey. What we are searching for is incredibly valuable; we are not searching for the fountain of youth, but something far more valuable. It is the spring and source of eternal life.

Let us push off from shore and begin our voyage. The Book of Romans is the longest of Paul's Epistles. In this letter, Paul was writing to a church and a city that he had never visited. He knew many people in the church, as his list of personal greetings in the last chapter will attest. However, he does not know them as a congregation. Many scholars believe that it is this fact that explains the thoroughness with which he lays out the gospel message. He does not know what they know or do not know. Therefore he is not troubleshooting specific problems as he does in some of his other epistles. Rather he is laying out a thorough, comprehensive discourse on the fundamentals of Christian faith and doctrine, particularly the doctrine of salvation. It is this thoroughness that makes the epistle so valuable to us and so worthy of our study.

In this chapter we are going to cover the opening paragraph, verses 1-17. If you have not already done so, I encourage you to open your Bible and read this passage now and keep your Bible open. In this opening section, Paul introduces himself as the writer of the letter. He talks about his interest in the believers in Rome and his prayers for them as well as his desire and his plans to visit them in Rome.

In introducing himself, Paul also introduces his message. It is this message that defines the man and it is this message that will form the topic for his letter. He refers to this message as the gospel in verse 1: *"Paul, a servant of Christ Jesus, called to be an apostle, set apart for the gospel of God..."*

For Paul, his message defined him. He describes himself first as a servant or slave of Jesus Christ. He received a divine calling to be an apostle, a messenger of Jesus Christ. This calling set him apart and totally dedicated him to a single purpose: what he calls here "the gospel of God."

We'll come back to that phrase in a moment. He refers specifically to the gospel three more times in this opening section. In verse 9 he speaks of *"the gospel of his Son."* In verse 15 he says, *"I am eager to preach the gospel to you also who are in Rome."* In verse 17 he says boldly, *"I am not ashamed of the gospel..."*

Obviously this word, this message, is important to Paul. But what is this gospel? It means "good news" or a "message of good news." Originally, the word was used to refer to a proclamation of victory and triumph. When kings went out to war with their armies, the people of the city would wait with nervous anxiety to hear the outcome of the battle. Their future prosperity, status and possibly their very lives would hang on the result. Finally they would see the messenger approaching. Would he announce "bad news" of defeat and death? Or would he proclaim "good news" of victory and triumph?

As we trace Paul's use of the term, we find that he uses it to refer to the core and essential message of Christianity. This was what he was called and sent to proclaim. He was "set apart" for this task. So what is this gospel? What is this essential message? This is what Paul is going to explain and expound upon in the chapters to follow. This will be the subject of our study in this book.

In this opening section, Paul uses a number of words and

phrases that he does not take time to define or explain. He is like a chess player laying his pieces on the table, getting ready for a game. But in this opening paragraph, he does not elaborate on their purpose, their place or the strategy of the game he is about to play. He introduces words like "grace," "faith," "righteousness," and "salvation." These are the pieces he will use so powerfully as he develops his argument through the course of the letter. But just as he mentions them without explanation, I also will not explain them in this opening chapter. We will let Paul do the explaining as his letter progresses. What I do want to do is simply glean what we can about the gospel from Paul's introductory remarks.

The first thing we discover is that **God is the source of the gospel.** In verse 1, Paul calls it "the gospel of God." God is the originator of this "good news." This is God's message. This is absolutely pivotal in Paul's thinking. In Galatians 1:11-12, he says: *"For I would have you know, brethren, that the gospel which was preached by me is not according to man. For I neither received it from man, nor was I taught it, but I received it through a revelation of Jesus Christ."* This gospel is not the product of human ingenuity or imagination. It is not man's thought, evolved over centuries. This is a proclamation of good news straight from God himself.

The second thing we discover is that **this gospel was promised by God through the prophets.** Look at verse 1-2: *"the gospel of God, which he promised beforehand through his prophets in the holy Scriptures..."* This tells us that this message, this plan of God, was no afterthought. This is not God improvising when his other plans did not work out. The gospel is not Plan B. This was where he was headed and what he had in mind from the very beginning. From Genesis 3:15, where God promises that the seed of the woman will crush the head of the serpent, to the writings of Malachi, who promises that the *"messenger of the covenant in whom you delight, behold he is coming,"* (Malachi 3:1) this was God's plan. Now it was here. The messenger had come, the message of good news has been delivered, and Paul had given his life to proclaiming it.

The third thing we discover is that **the gospel is good news about a person.** It is the identity of that person that makes up a substantial and crucial part of the gospel. Paul makes this identity clear. He states that the gospel is the message and good news about "God's Son." This was a truth that the Jewish leadership rejected. They accused Jesus of blasphemy because he "claimed to be the Son of God." But this was an essential part of the Old Testament prophecy about the coming Messiah. In Psalm 2, one of the great Messianic Psalms, the Messiah, the Anointed One, was declared to be the Son of God and the kings of the nations were commanded to *"Kiss the Son..."* The Jewish leaders did not stumble over the fact that the Messiah would be called the Son of God. They stumbled over Jesus' claims that he was that promised Messiah, the Son of God.

Paul expounds on this Good News about the identity of this person. He was and is both human and divine. In verses 3-4 we continue to read: *"concerning his Son, who was descended from David according to the flesh and was declared to be the Son of God in power according to the Spirit of holiness by his resurrection from the dead, Jesus Christ our Lord..."*

This is essential to the gospel that Paul proclaimed; the two natures of the Messiah, human and yet divine; Son of David and Son of God. This identity was declared, demonstrated and proven once and for all by his resurrection from the dead. And now, lest we have any doubt about the One whom he is describing, he names him. **Jesus:** that is his human name, assigned to him by angels before his birth. **Christ:** that is his title. Christ or "Christos" as it is in Greek, is the Greek translation of the Hebrew word "Messiah", "the Anointed One." And finally his status: "our Lord."

The gospel is a message about a person. The identity of Jesus as the Messiah and the Son of God is central to the message. In fact, I don't think it is overstepping the mark to say that **Jesus is the message. Jesus is the gospel.**

The fourth thing we discover is that **the gospel is a powerful message.** This is what Paul tells us in verse 16: *"I am not ashamed of the gospel, for it is the power of God..."* That is a powerful statement! The Greek word is "dunamis." When the Swedish inventor, Alfred Nobel, invented a powerful new explosive force, he reached into the Greek language for inspiration and borrowed this word. He called his invention "dynamite." Raw, explosive power. But in fact, that word image is not really helpful. The idea behind this word is not explosive, destructive power. It is constructive power; the power to get things done, to accomplish one's purpose, and to fulfill one's objectives. And what is the objective of the power of God displayed in the gospel? It is the power of God *"for salvation to everyone who believes."*

I think a better analogy for the power of the gospel, is the power of the acorn. For one year, I pastored a small church in California near the town of Oakhurst. The most common trees in the area were oak trees. It is an inspiring exercise to stand with a tiny acorn in hand and look up at a towering oak tree. How does the one produce the other? What kind of power rests in the acorn which can produce such a mighty tree? And what must you do with the acorn to release its power? Set it on fire? Hit it with a hammer? Put it in a gun and pull the trigger? There is no flash or bang in an acorn. But plant it deep in soil, water it, and the power is released. It is the power of life. It is the power of growth. That is the kind of power that is in the gospel.

It is a power that changes lives. It is the power of God for salvation to everyone who believes. In verse 17, Paul lays out this acorn of God's power, in a kind of cryptic summary of the gospel. *"For in it (the gospel) the righteousness of God is revealed from faith for faith, as it is written, 'The righteous shall live by faith.'"* That's it. That is the kernel, the nugget, the acorn of the gospel message which we will be exploring and expounding throughout these chapters. I am not explaining Paul's words in this chapter, but simply laying them out in front of us. We are going to allow Paul to give the explanations in the chapters to follow.

I do want to make one very crucial point from this verse. It is the answer to the question I posed a moment ago. What must you do with this acorn to release its power? The answer is found embedded in these two verses. In verse 16, we read, *"The gospel is the power of God for salvation..."* What is the rest of that verse? *"For everyone who believes."* That's the key. That's what it takes to release the power of the gospel into your life "for salvation." You have to believe it. If you take a quick look at verse 17, you will see a word that is repeated. It is the word "faith." *"Faith from first to last…the righteous will live by faith."* You need to know that, in Greek, the word "faith" and the word "believe" are the same root word. In fact the only difference is that one is a verb and the other is a noun. Verse 16 tells us that the gospel is the power of God for salvation for everyone who believes. Then verse 17 tells us that it is by *"faith (belief), from first to last,"* and *"the righteous will live by faith (belief)."* It is faith, belief that releases the power of God into our lives for salvation.

Before I end this chapter, I want to come back to some other phrases and statements in this opening section. They are statements by Paul about his own motivation and commitment to the gospel. I find them immensely challenging. Let me quote them:

"Set apart for the gospel of God…God is my witness, whom I serve with my spirit in the gospel of his Son…I have often intended to come to you, in order that I may reap some harvest among you…I am under obligation both to Greeks and to barbarians, both to the wise and to the foolish…So I am eager to preach the gospel to you also who are in Rome…I am not ashamed of the gospel."

"Set apart…serving with a whole heart…obligated…eager… not ashamed…" I wonder how many of us can say the same? Are we eager to share the gospel? Do we carry a sense of obligation and indebtedness to the people we meet? Are we serving God with our spirit, our whole heart in proclaiming the gospel? If not, why not?

Could the flaw be that we are not convinced of the power of the gospel? Are we sometimes hesitant, even ashamed, at least a little bit, of the gospel? "You're not one of those 'born again' Christians are you?" How do you feel when someone says that to you?

What does it mean to be "ashamed of the gospel?" The Greek word Paul used has a rather specific meaning. It means to put confidence and trust in something, only to have it fail. The resulting emotion is a mixture of disappointment and embarrassment; disappointment, because the object of our trust has not performed as we expected and we have not received the desired outcome; embarrassment, because we now look foolish to those around us who have witnessed our discomfort. But notice what Paul says: *"I am not ashamed of the gospel."* Why not? Because it is the power of God; the power of God to accomplish his purpose; the power of God to bring salvation to everyone who believes. The gospel of God will not disappoint us or leave us embarrassed. When the gospel is shared and believed, it will accomplish God's purposes. **A powerful message is a powerful motivation.** Do we believe in the power of the gospel? Do we believe in it enough to be eager to share it? Do we believe in it enough to plant it, like an acorn, in another person's life, believing that, if it is met with faith, it will grow into a towering oak tree?

That is why I am eager to share these chapters with you. I am not ashamed of the gospel for it is *"the power of God for salvation for everyone who believes…"* A powerful message is truly a powerful motivation.

2

WHO NEEDS THE GOSPEL? CASE STUDY #1

Romans 1:18-32

Let's go on a field trip. As soon as we are ready we are going to enter (by way of our imaginations) through a pair of heavy wooden doors into a courtroom. We are going to need to be very quiet. Are you ready? Then let's go in. Quietly now, find yourself a place to sit near the back, where you can still see and hear what is going on.

What do we see? First of all, the judge is seated in his elevated chair at "the bench." In the courtroom we have entered, the judge is God himself. The Judge of all the earth is presiding.

The second key figure in the courtroom is the prosecuting attorney. We soon discover that in this courtroom, the prosecuting attorney is Paul, the renowned apostle.

In our next three chapters, we are going to sit in on three different cases. In each case, Paul, as the prosecuting attorney, is going to bring an individual, or a category of persons, before the court and argue the case against them.

In the first chapter, Paul introduced himself and his message. He called his message "the gospel," the good news. He summarized that message in a rather cryptic manner in verse 17:

"For in it (the gospel) the righteousness of God is revealed from faith for faith, as it is written, 'The righteous shall live by faith.'"

The title for this chapter is **Who Needs the Gospel?** Actually, that's the title for the next three chapters. In this chapter we are looking at Case Study #1. In the next two chapters we will consider two more case studies. Who needs the gospel? Or let me ask the question a different way. Paul tells us in verse 17 (as translated in the NIV translation) that *"in the gospel a righteousness from God is revealed, a righteousness that is by faith."* Who needs this righteousness from God that is by faith that is revealed in the gospel? Let me start off by making a presuppositional argument. If you have your own righteousness, you don't need this righteousness from God that is by faith. God is an absolutely fair and righteous judge. He will not condemn a righteous man or woman. He will not condemn the innocent. So, if you are righteous, if you are innocent, you do not need to fear the judgment of God. If your own righteousness is adequate, you do not need the righteousness from God that is by faith. You do not need the gospel.

Before we go further though, we need to take a closer look at this word "righteousness." The underlying idea is one of conformity to a norm or a standard. People are righteous when their personal and interpersonal behavior is consistent with an established moral and ethical standard. In Biblical terms, that standard is the Law of God, summarized in the Ten Commandments. When measured by the Law of God, by God's standard, does your lifestyle, your behavior, match up? Are you righteous, right, according to the Law of God? If you are ... then carry on as you are. You do not need the gospel. However, if your own righteousness, as measured by God's standard, is not adequate, then you need the gospel.

So, the judge is in place and the prosecuting attorney rises and begins to argue his first case. Who is the first person Paul brings before the court? I am going to refer to him by a rather old-fashioned word. The word is **pagan.** I debated a long time before choosing this word, as it has pejorative connotations and it is not my desire to offend unnecessarily. However, I have concluded that it is the best word. I am using it carefully according to a precise dictionary definition. Here is how **Merriam-Webster's Dictionary** defines it. "1. A follower of a polytheistic religion. 2. One who has little or no religion and who delights in sensual pleasures and material goods; an irreligious or hedonistic person."

That is the dictionary definition. Let me expand on **the description of the pagan.**

First, he is a person who is out of contact with God's written revelation. He may never have seen a Bible, either Old or New Testament. If he has seen one, he has probably never read it. If he has read it, he did so without any real interest or understanding. We might even expand this to say that this person has no "holy book." No Torah, no New Testament. This person has no word or book which says, "This is what God requires."

Secondly, if the pagan has a religion (some do and some do not), then he is an idolater, worshiping images of his own making; or he is an animist, worshiping the spirits of ancestors or of trees, rocks and other things.

Thirdly, the pagan is often a person who lives in open sin, pursuing his own pleasure. Generally speaking, no one would describe this category of person as "good." Listen to some of Paul's words of description:

"For the wrath of God is revealed from heaven against all ungodliness and unrighteousness of men, who by their unrighteousness suppress the truth." (v. 18)

"and exchanged the glory of the immortal God for images resembling mortal man and birds and animals and creeping things." (v. 23)

"Therefore God gave them up in the lusts of their hearts to impurity, to the dishonoring of their bodies among themselves..." (v. 24)

"They were filled with all manner of unrighteousness, evil, covetousness, malice. They are full of envy, murder, strife, deceit, maliciousness. They are gossips, slanderers, haters of God, insolent, haughty, boastful, inventors of evil, disobedient to parents, foolish, faithless, heartless, ruthless." (verses 29-31)

Do you get an idea of the kind of person who is now standing before God's court? This description covered a large segment of the world when Paul was writing. It covers a large segment of the world today. The case against such a person looks very strong. But wait just a moment. If you are thinking carefully, you may have discerned a possible line of defense for such a person. His defense is one of **ignorance.** "I didn't know any better. No one told me!" he might cry. If, by definition, the pagan has no written revelation from God, no "divine standard," then how can he be held accountable for living a sinful life, or for serving gods of wood and stone?

Paul moves quickly to challenge this line of defense. In fact, **the defense is removed** in the very first verse of the paragraph in verse 18: *"For the wrath of God is revealed from heaven against all ungodliness and unrighteousness of men, who by their unrighteousness suppress the truth."*

According to this verse, these people had "truth." What truth did they have? How did they know it? This is the argument Paul makes in verses 19-20.

"For what can be known about God is plain to them, because God has shown it to them. For his invisible attributes, namely, his eternal power and divine nature, have been clearly perceived, ever since the creation of the world, in the things that have been made. So they are without excuse."

The **first source of knowledge about God available to the pagan is found in Creation** – the world that God has made. The question then arises: how much can be known and deduced about God from the created world alone? I will be the first to admit that I am at a significant disadvantage in attempting to answer this question due to the fact that I have always had revealed truth about God. I was raised on the Bible from my earliest memory. I cannot filter out what I learned by looking at the creation and what I learned from God's written revelation. But I didn't write these words in verse 18. This is divine revelation, given by God through the Apostle Paul. God's assessment is that by looking at the creation, man has access to significant truth about God; truth about his power, truth about his divine nature, his "God-ness." These things can be "clearly perceived." But here is the key. What did the "pagan man" do with this truth? That is what verse 18 tells us. He *"suppressed the truth."* He held it down, pushed it away and ignored the truth about the one true Creator God.

Then the pagan did something else. He "exchanged" the truth. This is the thought Paul develops in verses 21-25:

"For although they knew God, they did not honor him as God or give thanks to him, but they became futile in their thinking, and their foolish hearts were darkened. Claiming to be wise, they became

fools, and exchanged the glory of the immortal God for images resembling mortal man and birds and animals and creeping things. Therefore God gave them up in the lusts of their hearts to impurity, to the dishonoring of their bodies among themselves, because they exchanged the truth about God for a lie and worshiped and served the creature rather than the Creator, who is blessed forever! Amen."

This is important to Paul's reasoning. Why do men worship idols? Common reasoning says that it is man's effort to find God; to please him as best they know how. God says, "No!" Men turn to the worship of idols in an effort to suppress the truth and to turn away from the true God. The idol worshipper is exchanging the truth about God revealed in Creation and replacing it with a lie. Now, how can I say that? How can I look at a man bowing down in worship to his idols and judge him? The simple answer is, "I can't." He may look perfectly sincere to me. But I didn't write this passage. This is God's assessment, not mine. God knows what is in a man's heart. God says that men and women do not worship idols out of ignorance, but in an effort to suppress the true knowledge of God that is available to them.

Furthermore, Paul makes a very important connection between this deliberate turning from the knowledge of God and the sinful lifestyle of the pagan. There is a particular phrase that is repeated three times in this text. The NIV translates it, *"God gave them over…"* The ESV translates it, *"God gave them up…"* It is used in verse 24, in verse 26 and again in verse 28. The phrase is actually a technical legal term meaning "to turn over to the authorities for judgment and punishment." We use similar language today, when we talk about "turning someone in" or "turning someone over to the police."

But notice what it is that God "gives them over" to. In each case, God gives them over to their sin. In verse 24, we read, *"<u>God gave them up</u> in the lusts of their hearts to impurity."* Do you see that? He gave them over to the sinful desires of their hearts!

Look at verse 26: *"For this reason <u>God gave them up</u> to dishonorable passions."*

Now look at verse 28: *"And since they did not see fit to*

16

acknowledge God, <u>God gave them up</u> to a debased mind to do what ought not to be done."

Paul then goes on to give that "laundry list" of sinful behaviors that we read earlier.

In each reference, God is actually giving them over to their sin. Get this! It is critical to Paul's argument. The sin itself becomes a means of God's judgment. The sinner may think he or she is getting away with something. "Look! No one is stopping me!" They do not realize that sin carries in it its own punishment and its own destruction.

My brother Jon loved ice cream. My mother used to make ice cream, and we had it for dessert regularly. But my mother always dished it up: two scoops each; never more. For Jon, that was never enough. Then one time when we were in the U.S. Jon was staying for a week or so with an elderly relative. In her freezer he discovered a full gallon container of ice cream. No one was looking. He got a spoon and started to eat right out of the container. It was good! He ate and he ate. Because there was no one to stop him, he just kept eating. He ate until he couldn't eat anymore. And then he began to feel sick. No one had to punish him. His "sin" became its own punishment. It was many months before he could look at a dish of ice cream again without feeling sick.

When we see someone who is practicing an openly sinful lifestyle, we must realize that they did not get that way over night. They didn't get there by accident. They didn't get there through ignorance. It has been a process of deliberate suppression of the knowledge of God that is available to them; of continued rebellion against the knowledge of God. Their arrival at that point of open wickedness is already a sign of God's wrath and judgment against them. One of the ways God punishes people is to simply take his hands off and let them experience the full effect of their sin. The epidemic of a whole variety of "addictions" in modern society is a testimony to the punishing nature of sinful behavior. It starts with an excessive indulgence of physical desire. It then becomes a perversion of natural human desire for that which is unnatural. And it then becomes a corruption of the mind itself; what Paul refs to as a depraved mind. Nothing is wrong anymore. Do what you want. There are no standards. Righteousness does not exist. Not only do they defy God's standards themselves, but they also applaud others who do so.

This process can be traced in the life of an individual. As I said earlier, the epidemic of various "addictions" in our society give testimony to this reality. Society now labels them as illnesses. The sufferers are seen as victims of something beyond their control. But every addiction begins somewhere with a choice that then becomes a series of choices. Like a python or boa constrictor, seemingly harmless indulgences take up residence. We wind them around our neck or shoulder. We admire the pretty scales and stroke the smooth skin. Then the python begins to squeeze. Too late, we realize that we have become trapped by our own sinful choices. Our pleasures have become addictions. Our "freedoms" soon become bondage.

I believe the same progression can also be traced corporately in the life of a family, of a community, of a culture and a nation. When people suppress the knowledge of God that is available to them and abandon his standards, God turns them over to their own excesses of evil. Families disintegrate. Cultures decay. Entire civilizations fall.

But the keynote of this message is that it does not come from ignorance. Even at the end of that depressing and self-destructive sequence, they are still acting against the witness of God in their own hearts. Do you see that still in verse 32? *"Though they know God's righteous decree that those who practice such things deserve to die, they not only do them but give approval to those who practice them."*

This is God's assessment, not mine. This gives us a clue to **a second source of knowledge which is available to the pagan**. Not only does the pagan have the knowledge of God revealed in the created world. **He also has an innate knowledge of God's righteous decrees embedded in his conscience.** Even at the end of this hideous downward spiral of sinful behavior, we are told that "they know God's righteous decree" yet they continue to sin against it.

One of the principles of God's judgment, of God's courtroom, is that God will judge each man or woman, boy or girl in accordance with the knowledge each one had. Based on that assessment, where does the pagan stand? This is the summary of the matter in Paul's own words in verse 20: *"For his invisible attributes, namely, his eternal power and divine nature, have been clearly perceived, ever since the creation of the world, in the things that have been made. So they are without excuse."*

That is the heart of the matter. *"They are without excuse."* **God has not left himself without a witness, both in creation and in the conscience of each man.** Everyone is responsible for what he/she does with that witness. Based on that witness, the pagan stands condemned. He is not condemned for ignorance; for what he did not know. The pagan is not condemned for rejecting a gospel he never heard. No, he is condemned because of what he did know and because he suppressed that knowledge to pursue his own sinful and rebellious path. He is without excuse. He stands condemned in God's courtroom.

Who needs the gospel? The pagan does! He is in desperate need of the gospel and the righteousness of God that is by faith.

What application shall we make of this chapter? My next line could be, "If you are a pagan..." But the reality is that pagans rarely pick up a book like this. If you are that rare person, and you believe that God will give you a free pass because you are ignorant of God's standards, I trust this chapter has shown you the error of your reasoning. You are accountable to God for what you know. And simply by reading this chapter, you now know more than you did before. You need the gospel! I urge you to keep reading to find out more.

But as I said, such a person is the exception. Most people who fall in this category rarely darken the door of a church (or even know what a church is) or voluntarily read a book about the gospel. That places the burden of responsibility squarely on the shoulders of those of us who know the gospel. If they will not come to us, then we must go to them. They desperately need the gospel. Their ignorance is no excuse. They have enough knowledge about God to condemn them, but they do not have enough knowledge to save them. That is the task that God has entrusted to us as his followers.

I am going to conclude by jumping ahead in Romans. It will be many chapters before we get there, but it is something we need to consider now. It is found in Romans 10. Verse 13 tells us, *"Everyone who calls on the name of the Lord will be saved."* That is the promise of the gospel. That is the Good News. And it is available to the people we have been describing in the second half of Romans 1. But notice the verses to follow:

"How then will they call on him in whom they have not believed? And how are they to believe in him of whom they have never heard? And how are they to hear without someone preaching? And how are they to preach unless they are sent? As it is written, 'How beautiful are the feet of those who preach the good news!'" (Romans 10:14-15)

One of the common objections raised to the gospel and its exclusive claims is the question: "What about the heathen (read "pagan") in Africa (or wherever) who has never heard?" My parents considered that very question. They answered it by spending over 40 years in Africa as missionaries, sharing the gospel message.

Who will tell them? We can. We must! May we echo the words of Paul from the first part of chapter 1: *"For I am not ashamed of the gospel, for it is the power of God for salvation to everyone who believes... So I am eager to preach the gospel to you also who are in Rome."*

Remember, Rome was a city filled with "pagans." May God give us that same eagerness to make the gospel known! May God give us beautiful feet!

3

WHO NEEDS THE GOSPEL?
CASE STUDY #2

Romans 2:1-16

I am happy to say that I have not spent much time in courtrooms during my life. However, I did have one experience in an Abu Dhabi courtroom many years ago. My car had been rear-ended in an accident. The man who was driving the car when the accident happened had departed the country by the time the case came up in court. It fell to me as the car owner to appear in traffic court. So I went to court. The pastor of the Arabic church volunteered to go with me to translate if necessary. Everyone who had a case that day entered the courtroom at the same time and had to sit there and wait for their case to be called. So there we sat as the judge and his helpers began their work. I leaned over and whispered to Pastor Adel to ask a question. There was an immediate pause in the proceedings. The judge said something in Arabic. The official translator then announced in English: "Talking in the courtroom is not permitted."

Properly rebuked, I sat back. I could see this was going to be a long morning. Fortunately I had brought along a copy of the day's newspaper. Holding it carefully and quietly in my lap, I began to read. There was another break in the proceedings. The judge said something else in Arabic. The translator announced: "Reading in the courtroom is not permitted."

I quietly put my newspaper away. This was really going to be a long morning! I sat back against the hard bench and tried to find a comfortable position. Before long there was another pause. Again the judge spoke. Again the translator announced: "Crossing legs is not permitted in the courtroom." By this time, I was sure I was going to be thrown in jail for bad courtroom behavior long before my case was even called! The rest of the morning I sat frozen in place, hardly daring to breathe. The story

21

has a happy ending. When my case was finally called, the driver of the other car admitted full responsibility, and the case was quickly dismissed. I escaped without being charged with any courtroom misbehavior.

I don't have a really good reason for relating that story, except to introduce the fact that we will once again be entering a courtroom in this chapter. We are entering God's courtroom to listen to the second of three court cases. The title of these three messages is **Who Needs the Gospel?**

This is Case Study #2. In Romans 1:17, Paul states that the gospel message reveals a *"righteousness from God that is by faith."* I would reiterate what I said in the previous chapter. If we have our own righteousness and our own righteousness is adequate, then we do not need a righteousness from God that is by faith. We do not need the gospel. So Paul, as prosecuting attorney, is bringing three groups before God's court to argue the case against them and to demonstrate their liability before God.

In the first chapter, we listened to Paul argue the case against the pagan; the man without the law of God who lives an openly sinful life. His one line of defense is that of ignorance. "I didn't know any better," he might plead. In the second half of chapter 1, Paul shows that the defense will not stand up in court. The pagan's sinful life style is not, in fact, a result of ignorance, but the result of deliberately suppressing the knowledge of God that is available to him in the creation and in his own conscience.

Today, as we take our places in the courtroom, we take a close look at the second defendant. To our surprise, this person looks pretty good. He is well dressed, well groomed, with a pleasant expression on his face. In fact he looks very good. We might wonder what he is doing in court at all. He looks just like your next-door neighbor, or even like the person who sat next to you in church last Sunday. In fact, he looks a lot like you!

Who is this man? We shall call him **the moral man.** This is the man who believes that he is right with God because he is pretty good. He has never murdered anyone. He pays his taxes. He tries to live by the Ten Commandments and the Golden Rule. And he even succeeds, at least more often than most people.

Let's listen in as the **moral man presents his case before God's court**.

The moral man's first defense is **I have high standards.** The moral man believes in high standards. The people Paul is addressing in this section were both Jews and Gentiles. Some had the law of God, referring to the Old Covenant (Testament) laws and code of behavior and ethics. Others had a law of right and wrong written in their hearts, their consciences. In either case, the moral man or woman is a person with high standards.

The second line of defense of the moral man is **I have good intentions.** Not only does the moral man have high standards, but he fully intends to live by them. But here is the problem. All too often, good intentions do not, in fact, result in corresponding actions. He fools himself into thinking that he is good because he intends to be good. Let me illustrate. It is New Year's Day. I stand in front of a mirror and realize that it isn't an entirely pretty picture. I need to lose about 20 pounds. So, I determine in my mind that I am going to go on a diet and start an exercise program. In my mind, I can see the pounds falling away. I can picture what I will look like. In fact, for a brief period I can even hold in my stomach and see what I would look like. That's the real me. All I have to do is eliminate all sugar and desserts and start jogging and riding a bike. Soon my mind is flooded with happy pictures of the "new me," the real me that will emerge from my new lifestyle. In fact, the vision is so real and makes me so happy, that I decide to reward myself with a snack; just one last chocolate bar before I start my new life – tomorrow!

The third defense of the moral man is **I have a good public image.** Because he is a person with high standards and good intentions, he makes a great effort to present that image to the rest of the world. When I was growing up, we used to tease our mother about her "rug dance." We had a large area rug just inside our door. It was there to catch the dirt and mud we were always tracking into the house. Because there were five of us boys in and out of the door throughout the day, the rug was always getting rumpled and pushed into odd angles of disorder. Whenever someone would knock and Mom would go to answer the door, she would stop just before she opened the door and do a little shuffle with her feet to straighten out the rug. You see, Mom wanted to present an image as a woman with straight rugs and a tidy house. Hence that little, last minute "dance." And so you and I often do a little shuffle to straighten out our image as we enter the public. We all do it. The problem comes when I begin to think that my public image is the real me.

The fourth source of confidence for the moral man is **I have good connections.** He comes from a good family. He associates with good people. His economic and social class is very respectable.

The fifth and final defense of the moral man is the thought: **God has been good to me.** Here is the logic. Life is good. I have a good job, a good family, good health. Things are going well. Surely this shows that God is pleased with me. If God is treating me well in the here and now, then surely I have nothing to fear when I face him in eternity.

The moral man takes all these things and stirs them together, and he comes away with a positive image of himself. He is a "good person." At least, in his own assessment, he is "better than" most other people. That brings us to a fundamental question. I would phrase it this way: **Does God grade on the curve?** When I was in school, I always used to relax when the teacher told us that he/she was going to grade on the curve. If you are not familiar with the concept, it is based on a standard bell curve of marks. Students are not graded against an absolute scale of 100% but against how they compare with their fellow students. The top 10% of the class will get A's, the next 20% will get B's, the next 40% will get C's, etc. I liked it, because grading on the curve meant I did not have to do my best. I only had to do better than my fellow students to get a good grade. Hence my question: Does God grade on the curve? Is being "better than" other people "good enough" in God's eyes and in God's courtroom?

With that background, let's go back into God's courtroom. Let's pick up where we left off last week, with that long list of sins and sinful behavior that Paul has laid at the feet of the pagan. Throughout that section, the moral man was sitting in the gallery and he was applauding: "That's right! You tell him, Paul! Go get him! Amen!" with each listing of the pagan's sins. But in verse 1 of chapter 2, Paul, the prosecuting attorney does a classic courtroom pivot. He turns and points straight at the moral man:

"Therefore you have no excuse, O man, every one of you who judges. For in passing judgment on another you condemn yourself, because you, the judge, practice the very same things." (Romans 2:1)

What does Paul mean when he says they *"practice the very same things?"* I don't think we need to conclude that this man is committing every one of the sins on that list, or that he does so with the same frequency or to the same extent. However, I believe he is committing the same fundamental error of suppressing God's truth and going in his own way; of failing to live up to the light he had.

As Paul goes on to build the legal case against the moral man, I want to reiterate what I said earlier. If your righteousness is sufficient to pass the test of God's courtroom, then you do not need the gospel or the righteousness by faith that God offers in the gospel. You can stand on your righteousness with nothing to fear. But before you decide to do that, you would be wise to know as much as you can about the righteousness that God requires. Does your righteousness measure up to God's standard? So, as Paul argues his case against **the moral man** let's listen carefully and glean what we can about God's standards and his criteria for judgment. There are several important principles sprinkled throughout this section.

First, **God's judgment is based on truth.** In verse 2 we read: *"We know that the judgment of God rightly falls on those who practice such things."* The NIV translates, *"Now we know that God's judgment against those who do such things is based on truth."* In this verse, he is referring back to God's judgment of the pagan in chapter 1. But a general principle is being laid out. **God's judgment is based on truth.** Human courts also attempt to base their rulings on the truth. In fact, most of the time in a courtroom is spent trying to arrive at "the truth." Witnesses are

25

called. They swear to "tell the truth, the whole truth and nothing but the truth." Evidence is presented. In the traffic court where I appeared, each case was accompanied by a file that contained a police report on the accident; the facts, the truth. In the human image of justice, the female figure representing justice is blindfolded. But God is not blind-folded. He knows all things, even before the prosecution and defense present their case. There will be no need to assemble the evidence or listen to witnesses. He knows the truth. He will make his judgments based on the absolute truth. There will be no mirages, no images, no erased tapes or missing evidence. Truth. When you stand before God, you will be judged by the truth. His judgments will be right because they are based on truth.

The second principle is that **God's judgment is based on deeds.** This is what we are told in verses 6-7: *"He will render to each one according to his works: to those who by patience in well-doing seek for glory and honor and immortality, he will give eternal life..."* The word "patience" can also be translated "persistence." That's the key to what Paul is saying. "By persistence in doing good." Real deeds, done every day, all day; not occasional righteous acts done to impress ourselves and others. Such occasional acts of righteousness are the moral equivalent of holding in my stomach when I stand in front of a mirror. I may like what I see, but is it the real me?

He says the same thing in verse 13: *"For it is not the hearers of the law who are righteous before God, but the doers of the law who will be justified."*

Please understand this and understand it well! High standards and good intentions are not what God is looking for. He will judge your deeds. He will judge what you have actually done, not what you intended to do. He will judge your achievements, not your aspirations. "Persistence in doing good." Will your righteousness pass that test?

At this point in Paul's argument, we need to pause and address an important question. Do these verses we have just read (v. 6-7, 13) teach a doctrine of salvation by works? Listen carefully, for my answer may surprise you. Yes, they do! But before you decide to take that road and attempt to ride your own righteousness into heaven, be sure you understand God's standards of judgment. Will your righteousness stand up to God's standards? It is not your intentions, your standards and your aspirations that God will judge, but your actual deeds; not your occasional deeds, but your consistent, everyday actions. I believe Paul's words in these verses are simply another way of saying that God, as a righteous Judge, will never condemn a righteous man. As such, salvation by works is theoretically possible. Now we must ask: Has any human being ever passed that standard and measured up to God's righteousness? That is another question entirely, which Paul will address in chapter 3. More importantly for our discussion right now is the question; do you measure up?

Before you answer that question, let's look at the third principle of God's judgment. **God's judgment will include all our secrets.** Look at verse 16: *"on that day when, according to my gospel, God judges the secrets of men by Christ Jesus."*

Do you have any secrets? The phrase reads literally, "the hidden things of men." Do you have any of those? Is there anything you do not want the rest of us to know about you? Is there a gap between the public image you portray and the hidden things of your private life, either past or present? Someone wise once said, "Everyone has three lives: a public life, a private life and a secret life." What we must understand is that it is not our public image that will be on trial before God. It is the real me, the real you, with all the secret and hidden things exposed. Are you ready to stand before God to be judged by that standard?

The fourth principle is also important. **God's judgment will not be based on favoritism.** Verse 11 states this clearly: *"For God shows no partiality."* This relates to the moral man's defense that he comes from good stock and belongs to good people. In Paul's case, the argument was, "I am a Jew!" as though a birth certificate and a passport or identity card was all that was necessary to secure entrance into heaven. There will be no concessions based on family name, who our friends were, or who we spent time with. God's judgment will be absolutely impartial, based on our deeds.

I want to take a moment to deal with a couple quick questions that arise from the text. What about the argument or line of defense Paul raised, that **God has been good to me?** Verse 4 addresses this matter succinctly: *"Or do you presume on the riches of his kindness and forbearance and patience, not knowing that God's kindness is meant to lead you to repentance?"*

This is a warning that we should not take God's kindness necessarily as a sign of his approval. God also shows his kindness to give us room and time to repent and turn to him. Let us not waste that opportunity or treat his kindness with contempt. We dare not erroneously assume that comfortable circumstances in this life equate to evidence that our eternal destiny is secure.

What about the issue that some people know more about God's standards than others? How can the Gentile be held accountable for not obeying a law he never read or heard? Paul takes a little more time on this question in verses 12-16:

"For all who have sinned without the law will also perish without the law, and all who have sinned under the law will be judged by the law. For it is not the hearers of the law who are righteous before God, but the doers of the law who will be justified. For when Gentiles, who do not have the law, by nature do what the law requires, they are a law to themselves, even though they do not have the law. They show that the work of the law is written on their hearts, while their conscience also bears witness, and their conflicting thoughts accuse or even excuse them on that day when, according to my gospel, God judges the secrets of men by Christ Jesus."

This passage clearly declares a fifth principle of God's righteous standard of judgment. We discovered this in the previous chapter. I reiterate it here. **God's judgment will be based on obedience or disobedience to the light one has received.** The Jews knew more of God's Law because they had the written revelation. They will be judged based on what they did with that knowledge. Did they obey it, or disobey it? The Gentiles did not have God's written Law. But they did have the law of God written in their conscience. They will be accused or defended based on whether they obeyed or disobeyed their own, innate, God-given sense of right and wrong. But what must be clearly understood, based on the gospel which Paul proclaimed, is that a day of judgment is coming when God will judge all men. Paul even says that the fact of this coming judgment is part of his gospel.

So we come back to our question. Who needs the gospel? Or let me put it more personally. Do you need the gospel? Do you need the righteousness that comes from God and is by faith? Once again, if your own righteousness is adequate, you don't need God's righteousness. If you are innocent, you do not need to fear God's court. But before you make that assessment, keep these thoughts in mind. God does not grade on the curve. Being "better than" is not "good enough" in God's courtroom.

The poet Robert Burns penned these lines: "O that God the gift would give us, to see ourselves as others see us." That, indeed, is a valuable gift. But there is a much more valuable gift that God has given us: "O that God the gift would give us, to see ourselves as he sees us." You see, others will not be our judge. God himself will be. When we stand before the court, it will not be the court of public opinion. It will be God's court. His judgment will be based on truth, based on deeds, without favoritism and taking into account the entire record, including our secrets. Are you ready to stand before God's court in your own righteousness, knowing that this will be the standard? Before you make that determination, let me point out the consequences if you get it wrong:

"Therefore you have no excuse, O man, every one of you who judges. For in passing judgment on another you condemn yourself, because you, the judge, practice the very same things. We know that the judgment of God rightly falls on those who practice such things. Do you suppose, O man—you who judge those who practice such things and yet do them yourself—that you will escape the judgment of God?" (Romans 2:1-3)

"But because of your hard and impenitent heart you are storing up wrath for yourself on the day of wrath when God's righteous judgment will be revealed." (2:5)

"But for those who are self-seeking and do not obey the truth, but obey unrighteousness, there will be wrath and fury. There will be tribulation and distress for every human being who does evil, the

Jew first and also the Greek (broadly used to refer to non-Jews)... "
(2:8-9)

Are you ready to take your chances and stand before God in your own righteousness, or do you, like me, need the gospel and the righteousness that comes from God by faith?

4

WHO NEEDS THE GOSPEL?
CASE STUDY #3
Romans 2:17-3:20

When I was a pastor in Alaska, our church participated in an evangelism training seminar. Part of the training involved going from house to house in our little town and using a survey to try and gain an opportunity to share the gspel with people. I can still remember it. It was in the fall, a cold day, but without any snow on the ground yet. We walked up the sidewalk to the first door and knocked. When the lady answered the door, we had hardly begun our introduction before she said, "I am a Lutheran." And she shut the door.

We moved on to the next door. A man answered our knock. As we started our preamble, he said, "I am a Baptist." And he shut the door. We went to the next house. "I am a Methodist," was her response before she also closed the door. And so it went up and down the street: "I am a Presbyterian, I belong to the Church of God, I am a Catholic..." and then the firm closing of the door.

This is the third chapter that addresses the same question: **Who Needs the Gospel?**

In Romans 1:17, Paul announced that *"In the gospel a righteousness from God is revealed, a righteousness that is by faith..."* The question is: Who needs this righteousness from God that is by faith? Who needs the gospel? I will repeat what I said in my introduction to the previous two chapters. If you have your own righteousness, and it is adequate to meet God's standards and criteria of judgment, then you don't need the gospel. You don't need the righteousness that comes from God and is by faith. So Paul has been bringing different people, or categories of people before God's court, seeking to demonstrate their legal standing before God – to show whether or not they need the gospel.

First he brought the Pagan Man before God's court; the man who has no written revelation from God and who lives an openly sinful life. His only defense is that of ignorance. In chapter 1 Paul demonstrated that ignorance is not a defense or an excuse. Even the pagan man has knowledge about God and a knowledge of right and wrong available to him in the Creation and in his own conscience, and he has chosen to suppress that knowledge.

Second he brought the Moral Man before God's court; this man has high standards, good intentions and a good public image. He is "better than" the pagan man and most other people as well. But Paul argues that when we stand before God, he will not judge us according to our standards, our good intentions or our public image. He is going to judge according to truth, according to our actions and according to our secrets. And God is not going to "grade on the curve." Being "better than others" is not "good enough" to pass the standards of God's courtroom.

Today we come to the third defendant in God's courtroom. We shall call him the **Religious Man.**

Let me pause at this point to make a brief comment. There is some discussion among Bible scholars on whether, in fact, the first and second sections of chapter 2 deal with two different kinds of people, or just one kind of person. From an interpretive point of view, I believe that Paul's words in chapter 2 are actually addressed primarily to just one group of people in his audience; the Jews. However, the Jews had two lines of defense that they were relying on as they entered God's courtroom. So Paul argues against both lines of defense. I have chosen to deal with them separately so we can see the distinction, but also because there are people today who might rely on one defense without the other.

What is **the religious man's defense?** Simply put, the religious man is depending on his religion to earn him acceptance with God and ensure his entrance into heaven. Romans 2:17-20: *"But if you call yourself a Jew and rely on the law and boast in God and know his will and approve what is excellent, because you are instructed from the law; and if you are sure that you yourself* *are a guide to the blind, a light to those who are in darkness, an instructor of the foolish, a teacher of children, having in the law the embodiment of knowledge and truth..."*

Let's look at that opening sentence. *"If you call yourself a Jew."* This is the first line of defense; the religious man believes that he is OK because he has **membership in the right religious group.** "I am OK because I am a Jew. I belong to the right religion or the right religious group." That was the same note we heard as we went door to door that afternoon in Palmer, Alaska. The only thing that differed was the label they used.

Now, don't get me wrong. I am not passing judgment on any of those denominations or church affiliations we heard cited that afternoon. Nor am I forming an opinion on whether or not the people behind those doors will or will not be in heaven. What I am saying is that if their only claim when they stand before God is, "I am a Lutheran, Baptist, Methodist or Catholic..." then there is a problem. A big problem.

The second defense of the religious man is that **he has the real truth from God.** For the Jews, it was the law, the Torah, the Old Testament Scriptures. Notice what he says: *"if you rely on the law... if you know his will and approve of what is excellent, because you are instructed from the law...because you have in the law the embodiment of knowledge and truth."*

Right doctrine, right teaching, truth...these things are deeply important to the religious man. They are so convinced of the truth they hold that they become teachers. *"You are sure that you yourself are a guide for the blind, a light for those who are in the dark, an instructor of the foolish, a teacher of children..."*

The religious man also **boasts in his special relationship to God.** Did you see that in verse 17? You *boast in God.* The NIV translates, *"You brag about your relationship to God."* "I am one of God's chosen people," the Jew would declare. Every religious man or woman does the same. Their religious group might differ, and they may claim different sources of "truth," but they believe that God will acknowledge them and give them special treatment because of their religious connections.

All of these claims to special status with God are often

condensed into powerful religious symbols or rituals. For the Jew it was circumcision; the sign of membership in the covenant community. "I have been circumcised!" the Jewish man would declare. This was the rite or ritual cutting of the flesh which identified the Jewish boys as members of God's chosen people. Almost every religious community has its equivalent: baptism, ritual washings or sacrifices, prescribed prayers, certain ways of dressing, marks on the body; there is a wide variety of symbols that the religious man uses to mark himself or set himself apart as one of the chosen.

So, do you have a clear picture of the religious man as he is about to appear before God's court? Membership in the right religious group, real truth from God, a special relationship with God, all captured in a symbolic ritual or symbol. How does Paul argue against such a man?

Let's look first at his claim to having real truth from God. *"You then who teach others, do you not teach yourself? While you preach against stealing, do you steal? You who say that one must not commit adultery, do you commit adultery? You who abhor idols, do you rob temples? You who boast in the law dishonor God by breaking the law. For, as it is written, 'The name of God is blasphemed among the Gentiles because of you.'"*

The first thing Paul points out is that **having the truth and even teaching the truth to others is no substitute for obeying the truth.** As with the moral man, having high standards and good intentions is no substitute for actual obedience. The Jews felt that with their religion came privilege. Paul's point is that with greater privilege comes greater responsibility. Because the Jews set themselves up as God's people who had the truth of God, the Gentile world was watching them with special care. The picture was not a pretty one. "Before you take pride in your Jewishness," Paul says, "look at your own history." The history of Israel was not a pretty story. Having the truth is no substitute for obeying it. Right doctrine is no substitute for right behavior. Orthodoxy is no replacement for orthopraxy.

The second thing Paul declares is that **external religious symbols are no substitute for obedience.** As noted before, for the Jews, that symbol was circumcision. Look at what Paul has to say about it in verses 25-27: *"For circumcision indeed is of value if you obey the law, but if you break the law, your circumcision becomes uncircumcision. So, if a man who is uncircumcised keeps the precepts of the law, will not his uncircumcision be regarded as circumcision? Then he who is physically uncircumcised but keeps the law will condemn you who have the written code and circumcision but break the law."*

As I said, the Jews were relying on their own religious symbol; that of circumcision. Different religions may have different symbols, but the reasoning remains the same. "I've been baptized…as an infant or otherwise…and I've got the certificate to prove it. I pray a certain number of times a day and in a certain way. I have done a pilgrimage to my religion's holy places." No matter what your symbols and rituals might be, God will look right past them and look into your heart. Rites don't make right. Religious rituals are no substitute for real righteousness.

That brings us to the third point Paul makes to the Jews. **External obedience to the letter of religious and moral law is no substitute for the internal obedience of the heart.** This is what Paul is driving at in verses 28-29: *"For no one is a Jew who is merely one outwardly, nor is circumcision outward and physical. But a Jew is one inwardly, and circumcision is a matter of the heart, by the Spirit, not by the letter. His praise is not from man but from God."*

Paul is taking a powerful hammer to the religious man's foundation. True religion, "true Jewishness" if you will, is about the heart, not simply external conformity to a written code of laws. I think our modern translations get it wrong when they capitalize the word "Spirit" here. I do not in any way deny the key role the Holy Spirit plays in salvation or sanctification. I just don't think it is what Paul is writing about here. He is stressing the "inwardness" of true righteousness: a circumcision of the heart and in the spirit of a man, not external conformity to a written code.

Was this not what Jesus said when he addressed the most religious people of his day: the scribes and the Pharisees? He took the standard of God's commandment against murder and applied it to anger and murderous thoughts. He took the standard of God's commandment against adultery and applied it to lustful thoughts and committing adultery in the heart. He accused the Pharisees of being like white-washed tomb stones, clean and pretty on the outside, but full of decay and corruption on the inside. He accused them of making a show of tithing the produce of their herb gardens while ignoring larger principles of justice and mercy in their dealings with the poor.

I remember reading the novel <u>Davita's Harp</u> by Chaim Potok about a young girl growing up in a home with a Jewish mother and a Gentile father in the middle of the 20th century. Her mother is a non-practicing Jew so little Ilana Davita grows up without understanding any of the Jewish ceremonies or religious practices. After visiting a synagogue one day, she is full of questions. She tries to get answers from a boy she knows. In explaining the various rituals he keeps saying "It's the law… Jewish law." His friends, however, snicker and mock the little girl for her ignorance and the naïve nature of her questions until she says, "Can I ask one more question…Is it the law that instead of helping you're supposed to laugh at someone who's trying to learn?" External allegiance to a religious standard is no substitute for the inner heart qualities of kindness, humility and gentleness that are the mark of the truly righteous.

Paul also touches on another very vulnerable point in the defense of the religious man. It is the question: Who are you doing it for? In raising this point, he is simply echoing the words of Jesus about the Pharisees in Matthew 23:5-7: *"They do all their deeds to be seen by others. For they make their phylacteries broad and their fringes long, and they love the place of honor at feasts and the best seats in the synagogues and greetings in the marketplaces and being called rabbi by others."*

Notice the contrast that Paul draws in the final sentence of this chapter (Romans 2): *"His praise is not from man, but from God."* True religion, the kind that God will honor and reward, is not done for man's praise, but for God's. Everything else is just a sham and a fraud that will not withstand the scrutiny of God when we stand before him. And so Paul concludes his argument against the Religious Man.

In a previous chapter as I was concluding my exposition on Romans 1 and Paul's argument against the Pagan Man, in my application I made the point that it was unlikely any true "pagans" would read this book, because pagans don't buy religious books or come to church. Today, as I apply this message and Paul's case against the Religious Man, guess where he is to be found? That's right! In churches, as well as in synagogues, mosques, and temples, and in the aisles of the religious section in bookstores. If you are going to take your stand before God, clothed in your religious robes, relying on your membership in the right religious group, carrying your code of religious ethics with you and clinging to your religious symbols or rituals, understand this. Membership alone is not enough. Holding the truth (even if it is the real truth) is no substitute for obeying the truth. Outward religious symbols or rituals (even if they are the right symbols and the right rituals) cannot atone for sinful actions. External conformity to a written code of ethics and religious behavior is no substitute for heart obedience. Man's applause and assessment of your conduct will matter not at all. Only God's condemnation or reward will be relevant on Judgment Day. Knowing this, will your righteousness, your religious righteousness, pass the test of God's judgment? Or do you, like me, need the righteousness from God which is by faith? Do you, like me, need the gospel?

Who needs the gospel? Three groups have now appeared before God's court: the pagan man, the moral man and now the religious man. I want to hit the fast forward button now to move to Paul's summary and conclusion. Romans 3:1-8 is actually a parenthesis in Paul's flow of thought. In this section, he takes up the questions he anticipates getting from the Jews in his audience. Is there any advantage to being a Jew? We are going to skip over that question and section for now, and pick it up when we come to the topic again later in the book.

For now, what is Paul's conclusion about the three groups he has prosecuted before the court? Listen as I read Paul's closing argument:

"What then? Are we Jews any better off? No, not at all. For we have already charged that all, both Jews and Greeks, are under sin..." (Romans 3:9)

Paul then goes on in 3:10-18 to string together a series of Old Testament quotations, taken mostly from the Book of Psalms:

As it is written: "None is righteous, no, not one; no one understands; no one seeks for God. All have turned aside; together they have become worthless; no one does good, not even one." "Their throat is an open grave; they use their tongues to deceive." "The venom of asps is under their lips." "Their mouth is full of curses and bitterness." "Their feet are swift to shed blood; in their paths are ruin and misery, and the way of peace they have not known." "There is no fear of God before their eyes."

Then, lest the Jews in his audience think that he is speaking only of the Gentiles, he adds these words in verses 19-20:

"Now we know that whatever the law says it speaks to those who are under the law, so that every mouth may be stopped, and the whole world may be held accountable to God. For by works of the law no human being will be justified in his sight, since through the law comes knowledge of sin."

That is rather inclusive and conclusive, is it not? "Every mouth silenced and the whole world held accountable to God." Who needs the gospel? Everyone needs the gospel!

Look at verse 20 again: *"For by works of the law no human being will be justified in his sight."* Or, as the NIV translates it: *"Therefore no one will be declared righteous in his sight by observing the law."* I need to point out that in the Greek text, there is no definite article in front of the word "law" in this verse like there is in verse 19. That opens up the possibility that Paul is not referring exclusively to "the Law" in the Old Testament, but to any law of right and wrong, including the law of conscience in every man. We might then paraphrase this verse: "Therefore, from all flesh, the entire human race, not one will be declared righteous in God's sight by law-keeping."

Who needs the gospel? Everyone needs the gospel! The pagan man, the moral man, the religious man. No one will pass the scrutiny of God's judgment by their own merits.

Then what hope is there? Let me give you just a teaser for where Paul goes next in the second half of chapter 3: *"But now the righteousness of God has been manifested apart from the law, although the Law and the Prophets bear witness to it - the righteousness of God through faith in Jesus Christ for all who believe."*

Someone might accuse me of being very negative in these opening chapters. I have to agree. I am guilty as charged. The sinfulness of men and the judgment of God are not easy subjects to elaborate on. In fact, it seems that not many do. I sometimes go to a "Sermon Central" website to see what other preachers have said on a passage. I have found lots of sermons on Romans 1, but very few on chapter 2 and the first half of chapter 3. In fact some modern day preachers have even purged the word "sin" from their vocabulary lest they offend modern sensibilities.

A man once came into my office. He was a follower of another religion, but he was attracted to Christianity and had many questions. He was especially attracted to Jesus and his teachings. He asked me, "Can you give me a book that includes only the positive sayings of Jesus? I don't want the things he said about judgment and condemnation. I only want the positive sayings."

I told him that I was not aware of any such book or compilation. But then I went on to say: "Even if I knew of the existence of such a book, I would not give it to you. Because it would not be the truth. It would be misleading. It is not given to us to be editors of God's words, to pick and choose only what we like and what makes us feel good. We need all the truth of God."

This reality was driven home to me once again in the preparation of these chapters. It particularly struck me as I studied one verse, which we actually considered in the previous chapter. Romans 2:16: *"On that day when, <u>according to my gospel</u>, God judges the secrets of men by Christ Jesus."*

Do you see what I see in that verse? The fact of the coming judgment of God is part of the gospel message! A quick survey of Paul's preaching in the Book of Acts certainly confirms that in Paul's own preaching. Note this summary in Acts 24: 25: *"And as he reasoned about righteousness and self-control <u>and the coming judgment,</u> Felix was alarmed and said, 'Go away for the present.*

When I get an opportunity I will summon you.'" If we turn Romans 2:16 around, we could logically render it: "My gospel declares that one day God will judge men's secrets through Jesus Christ." If we are not proclaiming and warning people that they will one day be judged by God, then we are not preaching a complete gospel! For if men do not understand the reality of coming judgment, they will have no reason to seek the mercy of God. If they do not know that they need the gospel, they will have no reason to listen to the gospel. If they don't know that they are lost and under the condemnation of God, they will have no sense of need to turn them to the Savior, the Lord Jesus Christ.

Who needs the gospel? I do! You do!

5
GOOD NEWS!
Romans 3:21-31

The Roman poet, Horace, once wrote an essay criticizing many of the plays that were being written and performed on the stages of ancient Rome. One criticism he made was that many playwrights would weave a very complicated set of problems in a play, and then solve them all in the final act by bringing one of the gods onto the stage to use his supernatural power to straighten everything out. This was Horace's concluding advice:

"Do not bring a god onto the stage unless the problem is one that deserves a god to solve it."

In the first two and a half chapters of the Book of Romans, Paul has been describing a problem. It is a problem that is shared by the entire human race. It is a sin problem. In these chapters, Paul has argued carefully to demonstrate the guilt of the pagan man, the moral man and finally, the religious man. We looked last time at his closing argument in chapter 3 and verse 19: *"so that every mouth may be stopped, and the whole world may be held accountable to God."*

We are sinners. We are guilty. What is more, this is no academic discussion. This is not simply a "fill in the blank" answer in a catechism book. Life is at stake. Eternity is at stake. Remember his words in 1:18: *"For the wrath of God is revealed from heaven against all ungodliness and unrighteousness of men."*

What is more, it isn't going to work to just double our efforts and try harder. Paul's statement in 3:20 is absolutely clear: *"For by works of the law no human being will be justified in his sight."*

Truly we have a problem. It is a problem without a human solution. It is time to bring God onto the stage.

That is exactly what Paul does in verse 21: *"But now the righteousness of God has been manifested apart from the law..."*

The NIV translates, *"But now a righteousness from God, apart from law, has been made known..."*

It is absolutely impossible to overemphasize the impact or significance of these words. It is an explosion of hope in the midst of great despair. It is a shaft of brilliant sunshine beaming down into a scene of unbearable darkness.

Let's look at the words carefully. *"A righteousness..."* This is a legal term. Paul is using legal language throughout. Righteousness signifies one's legal standing or status. The law has declared us guilty, but now this. A righteousness is available. It is *"from God."* It is both God-like in its character and has God as its source. A righteousness from God that is *"apart from law."* It does not depend on law or law-keeping. It has a completely different source. This right standing, this legal pardon from God's court *"has been made known."* The word means "to make plain, to reveal, to bring to light."

Wouldn't you like to know how you can have a righteous standing before God that does not depend on your efforts to do right or keep the law; a righteousness that comes from God himself? That is what is being offered; a life line to the human race, drowning in its own moral failure. It has been made known.

How can we have this righteousness? This *"righteousness from God,"* verse 22 tells us, is *"through faith in Jesus Christ,"* and it is for *"all who believe."* Let me quickly point out again that "faith" and "believe" are actually the same root in the Greek language in which Paul wrote. One is the noun, the other is the verb, but they carry the same nuance and meaning. To keep them lined up in our thinking as English speakers, I like to use the word "belief" rather than "faith." This *"righteousness from God"* is by *"belief in Jesus Christ for all who believe."*

Paul now pauses to make sure that his readers understand that he is talking about both Jews and Gentiles. *"There is no distinction."* No difference; no line of demarcation between the two. Why not? He reaches back to what he said in the earlier part of the chapter to reiterate the spiritual reality of both Jews and Gentiles; that all are without excuse, every mouth has been silenced, everyone stands convicted before God's court. And here is his summary; *"For all have sinned and fall short of the glory of God." (3:23)*

That verse requires some additional thought. *"All."* I think we get that. Rather a disturbingly inclusive word, isn't it? *"Have sinned."* This word looks into the past and is a summary statement of the moral realities of every human being. It is a reiteration of the Old Testament passages Paul quoted earlier in the chapter. *"None is righteous, no, not one..."* This is a clear description of God's assessment of every man's moral state.

However, the past is not our only problem. We continue to *"fall short."* This is in the present tense, describing our ongoing failure to live up to what God desires for us and requires of us. What do we fall short of? *"The glory of God..."* Genesis tells us that we were made in the image of God, to enjoy him and to reflect his glory. But through sin, both the sin of Adam and Eve and our own continued sinning, we have utterly failed and continue to fail to fulfill that purpose for which we were created. It is a failure shared by Jew and Gentile alike.

So what is the answer to our dilemma? Paul now returns to his description of the righteousness from God by believing in Jesus Christ. Continuing in verse 24: *"...and are justified by his grace as a gift, through the redemption that is in Christ Jesus."* Grammatically, Paul is continuing his description of what happens to those who believe in Jesus Christ. They are *"justified freely,"* as a gift!

That word "justified" is one that we need to take a closer look at. It comes from the same root as "righteousness." Righteousness in this context refers to our legal standing in God's courtroom. "Justified" is also a legal term and it means "to declare someone righteous," or to "declare a defendant's legal status as righteous before the court." "To justify" means to declare someone right or righteous in the eyes of the law. It is the opposite of "to condemn," which means to declare someone guilty and liable to the penalties of the law. Once again, it is a legal term and relates to one's legal standing under the law and before the court.

There are three descriptive words or phrases to explain the basis upon which we are declared righteous before God's court.

The first is an adverb. *"Freely."* We are justified "without cost, as a free gift, without paying." The second is a phrase, *"by his grace."* This is God's grace. God is the judge, and he is showing us kindness, mercy, unmerited generosity. On what basis? *"Through the redemption that came by Christ Jesus."* The word "redemption" means to set someone free, with the implication of the paying of a price or fee. Here we once again find ourselves in the courtroom. There are two ways a defendant can be justified in a court of law. He can be justified by being found innocent of the charges against him. Or he can be justified through the paying of the penalty the law has assessed against him for his crimes. Either way, the court declares that the defendant can walk out a free man. In our case, someone else has paid our penalty. That someone is Jesus Christ. "We owed a debt we could not pay. Jesus paid a debt he did not owe so that we could go free." That is redemption. That is the basis on which we can be justified, or declared righteous in God's court.

Paul continues to elaborate on his legal argument in verse 25-26: *"whom God put forward as a propitiation by his blood, to be received by faith. This was to show God's righteousness, because in his divine forbearance he had passed over former sins. It was to show his righteousness at the present time, so that he might be just and the justifier of the one who has faith in Jesus."*

In these verses, Paul is both elaborating on the gospel and defending God's righteousness. Two very similar questions arise in the mind to challenge the justice of God and the righteousness of his court. How could God, as a righteous judge, let the sins of Old Testament believers go so long unpunished? On what basis were they spared the wrath of God against their sins? Think of Abraham, of Moses, of David. Men of faith, yes, but sinners nonetheless. On what basis were their sins overlooked? By faith, yes! But no payment had been offered for their sin; no penalty had been required. And what is more, even in the present time, how can God be both just and the justifier of sinful people? The answer to that question lies in the cross of Jesus Christ and in his blood shed on that cross. God put Jesus forward. He "presented him" as the NIV translates, putting him on public display before the universe as a "propitiation." Propitiation is not a word we hear or use every day, is it? It means a sacrifice whereby the righteous requirement of God's law and God's courtroom was fulfilled and satisfied. The barrier of our sin that separated us from God was removed. God demonstrated his justice by punishing sin. Only the punishment fell on Jesus Christ. The innocent died in place of the guilty. This happened so that God could maintain his righteousness and the justice of his courtroom, and still justify or declare righteous everyone who believes in Jesus.

Paul then quickly moves to wrap up his legal argument, particularly as it relates to both Jews and Gentiles in his audience: *"Then what becomes of our boasting? It is excluded. By what kind of law? By a law of works? No, but by the law of faith. For we hold that one is justified by faith apart from works of the law. Or is God the God of Jews only? Is he not the God of Gentiles also? Yes, of Gentiles also - since God is one—who will justify the circumcised by faith and the uncircumcised through faith. Do we then overthrow the law by this faith? By no means! On the contrary, we uphold the law."*

Jew and Gentile are alike condemned before God. That is the conclusion of the first half of chapter 3. Jew and Gentile alike can be justified by faith and only by faith. That is Paul's point in the second half of the chapter. Does this truth nullify the law and the rest of the Old Testament Scriptures? No! It is in fact the fulfillment of the law and the whole message of the Old Testament. This takes us back to the summary of the gospel that Paul gave all the way back in Romans 1:17: *"For in it (the gospel) the righteousness of God is revealed from faith for faith, as it is written, 'The righteous shall live by faith.'"* Or as the NIV translates: *"in the gospel a righteousness from God is revealed, a righteousness that is by faith from first to last, just as it is written: 'The righteous will live by faith.'"*

The last phrase is, in fact, a quote from the Old Testament, found in Habakkuk 2:4 as well as in Genesis 15:6.

This, then, is the gospel. After over two chapters of "bad news" about the sinfulness of men and the coming judgment and wrath of God, the glorious light of the gospel is now shining. *"But now the righteousness of God has been manifested apart from the law, although the Law and the Prophets bear witness to it— the righteousness of God through faith in Jesus Christ for all who believe…and are justified by his grace as a gift, through the redemption that is in Christ Jesus."* Right standing before God as a free gift. Good news doesn't get any "gooder" than that!

How do we receive this gift? It should be clear by now. By faith. Remember, faith is belief. Belief has to have an object. Faith as an abstract entity has no real value. I recall seeing something on the internet inviting people to submit stories in which "faith" had played a significant role. It was an interfaith site. The presupposition was that any "faith," no matter what the object, was a powerful force. This is totally contrary to Biblical revelation. Belief must have the right object. More specifically, faith must be placed in the right person, or it is nothing more than the foolishness of positive thinking. According to our text, the object of our belief (the belief that brings salvation) is twofold. It is belief in the person of Jesus Christ; Jesus as Messiah, the anointed Messenger of God. And it is belief in "propitiation by his blood" according to verse 25. That means it is not enough to believe in Jesus as a historical person, or as a great moral teacher or even as a prophet. In fact, it is not even enough to believe in Jesus as the Messiah and the Son of God as portrayed in Scripture. We must also believe in and put our trust "in his blood" as the sacrifice of atonement for our sins. This is what we must believe if we would be "justified by belief in Jesus."

It is here that we must face the vital distinction between my role as the writer and you as the reader. My role is to declare the truth as clearly and as powerfully as I can under the anointing of the Holy Spirit. I have sought to do that. I don't think I can make the gospel any clearer than I have in this chapter. But when I have done all that is within my power as a writer, there is something I cannot do. I cannot believe for you. That is something that only you can do. And so I leave you with this simple question.

Do you believe in Jesus Christ? Do you believe in his blood, shed for you on the cross? Do you believe that his blood was a sufficient payment (propitiation) to satisfy the demands of God's justice?

If you do, then you have been… *"justified by his grace as a gift, through the redemptions that is in Christ Jesus."*

I think that is **Good News!**

6

FATHER ABRAHAM HAS MANY SONS
Romans 4

"Father Abraham had many sons. Many sons had Father Abraham." You may be familiar with those words. They are from an old camp song that was once popular with children and young people. The popularity of the song rested on its chorus and the actions that set us all to dancing around the campfire. But as nonsensical as most of the song is, the opening words do contain a seed of very important Biblical truth that is found in Romans chapter 4. Here is the question that is raised and answered in this chapter: Who are Father Abraham's sons and daughters? In this chapter we will be considering the entirety of Romans 4, as it consists of a single unit of thought. I hope you have taken the time to read the chapter through.

Who are the sons and daughters of Abraham? Why is this an important question and why does it arise in the Book of Romans? Paul is elaborating on his message: the gospel. The central truth of the gospel is that *"a righteousness from God is revealed that is by faith."* In the first three chapters of Romans Paul carefully developed his argument, addressing the question: **Who needs the Gospel?** The answer to that question, of course, is that everyone needs the Gospel. *"For all have sinned and fall short of the glory of God."* In this matter of needing the Gospel, there is *no distinction* between Jew and Gentile.

This declaration might well have caused the Jews among Paul's readers to bristle. "What? No difference between Jews and Gentiles? We are children of Abraham! Why do we need this righteousness from God that is by faith?" And so Paul turns to the story of Abraham to make the argument that right standing with God is now, and has always been, by faith and that this is the basic premise of the life story of Father Abraham.

Verse 1 says, *"What then shall we say was gained by Abraham, our forefather according to the flesh?"* Or as the NIV translates: *"What then shall we say that Abraham, our forefather, discovered in this matter?"* In the rest of the chapter, Paul uses a kind of circular logic, like spokes in a wheel that all come back to the same central point. Justification is by faith.

In the first spoke of the wheel, Paul points out that **justification is by faith apart from works.** In verses 2-3 we read, *"For if Abraham was justified by works, he has something to boast about, but not before God. For what does the Scripture say? 'Abraham believed God, and it was counted to him as righteousness.'"*

This quotation is taken from Genesis 15:6, when God affirmed his covenant with Abraham. *"Abraham believed God, and it was counted to him as righteousness."* There it is! The principle of justification by faith is found all the way back in the Book of Genesis. This Scripture is at the very heart of the Old Testament record. Central to Paul's argument is this word "counted" or as the NIV translates, "credited." Paul uses this word 11 times in this chapter alone. It is a word taken from the financial or bookkeeping world. It means to calculate and count something as either a debit or a credit. It was also used in the legal world. Evidence and actions can be counted either for or against a person in his standing before the court. They can be "entered into the record." Using this language, Paul uses this Scripture to argue that God took Abraham's faith in the promises of God and credited it to his account as "righteousness."

Paul then continues: *"Now to the one who works, his wages are not counted as a gift but as his due."*

Paul's reasoning makes sense, doesn't it? Imagine that you have worked hard all month. At the end of the month, your boss comes by your desk or work station. He says to you, "I want you to come to my office. I have a special gift I want to present to you." You enter his office with a sense of excitement and anticipation. With a great flourish, he hands you a check. When you look at it, you realize that the check is simply the amount of your monthly salary. How do you feel? If you're like me, you would be quick to say, "Gift? This is no gift! I earned this!" This is Paul's point. Did Abraham earn his right standing with God? If he did, then he has something to boast about. But the Scripture says that Abraham's right standing with God was credited to him as a gift.

Verse 5 is one of the most amazing verses in the Bible. *"And to the one who does not work but believes in him who justifies the ungodly, his faith is counted as righteousness..."*

This is truly radical! Abraham is here identified as one who "did not work." What does that mean? It means that he did not rely on his own works, his own righteous deeds, and his own right actions for his standing before God. Instead, he believed (trusted) in a God who *"justifies the ungodly."* This phrase alone, taken in isolation, almost seems to make God an accomplice in evil; an unjust judge. But it must be taken in the context of Paul's words at the end of chapter 3. Because of Jesus and his death, his propitiation, his "sacrifice of atonement," God can be both just and the justifier of those who put their faith in Jesus Christ, even though they are sinners. God is the one who "justifies the ungodly" (and that includes all of us) when we stop our own striving and trust in him. When we do that, God sees our faith and credits it to our account as righteousness. We have right standing before his court. We are **justified by faith apart from works.**

The second spoke in the wheel is that we are **justified by faith in spite of our sins.** This, too, he demonstrates from the Old Testament Scriptures. This time, he quotes from another Jewish hero, King David in verses 6-8, quoting from Psalm 32: *"...just as David also speaks of the blessing of the one to whom God counts righteousness apart from works: 'Blessed are those whose lawless deeds are forgiven, and whose sins are covered; blessed is the man against whom the Lord will not count his sin.'"*

This is the reverse side of the bookkeeping logic. The word "count" in verse 8 is the same bookkeeping word we have seen earlier. Faith is "counted as righteousness" and our sins are not "counted" against us. Our sins will never again appear in the debit column of our legal record. They have been erased.

The third spoke in Paul's wheel is that the Old Testament

saints were **justified by faith apart from circumcision.** Here Paul continues to keep the Jews in his audience firmly in mind. They would have been quick to argue for the necessity of circumcision in order to achieve right standing with God, so Paul goes back to the Old Testament account. He argues simply from the chronology of the story of Abraham. When does the Scripture say that *"Abraham believed God and it was counted to him as righteousness?"* It was in Genesis chapter 15. When did God institute circumcision? It was in chapter 17, by chronology, 13 years later. Abraham's faith and his justification in God's sight preceded circumcision. Listen to Paul's logic: *"Is this blessing then only for the circumcised, or also for the uncircumcised? For we say that faith was counted to Abraham as righteousness. How then was it counted to him? Was it before or after he had been circumcised? It was not after, but before he was circumcised. He received the sign of circumcision as a seal of the righteousness that he had by faith while he was still uncircumcised. The purpose was to make him the father of all who believe without being circumcised, so that righteousness would be counted to them as well..."* Once again, the key ingredient was not circumcision. It was faith.

Finally, the fourth spoke in the wheel is that **justification is by faith apart from the law.** Paul picks up this line of reasoning in verse 13-14: *"For the promise to Abraham and his offspring that he would be heir of the world did not come through the law but through the righteousness of faith. For if it is the adherents of the law who are to be the heirs, faith is null and the promise is void."*

So Paul has hammered home his argument based on the Old Testament Scriptures and stories. The principle of justification by faith is laid out. Justification by faith, apart from works, in spite of sin, apart from circumcision, and apart from the law. To the person who argues, "But I am a child of Abraham!" Paul now again addresses the question: Who are the true children of Abraham?

Here is Paul's conclusion. It is first seen in verses 11-12: *"The purpose was to make him the father of all who believe without being circumcised, so that righteousness would be counted to them as well, and to make him the father of the circumcised who are not merely*

51

circumcised but who also walk in the footsteps of the faith that our father Abraham had before he was circumcised..."

Paul follows up this conclusion in verses 16-17: *"That is why it depends on faith, in order that the promise may rest on grace and be guaranteed to all his offspring—not only to the adherent of the law but also to the one who shares the faith of Abraham, who is the father of us all, as it is written, 'I have made you the father of many nations'—in the presence of the God in whom he believed..."*

The children of Abraham are those who have the same faith Abraham had. They are those who are justified by faith, just like Abraham was. It was one of the rallying cries of the Reformation: Sola Fide! Faith alone! *"For in the gospel a righteousness from God is revealed, a righteousness that is by faith from first to last... But now a righteousness from God, apart from law, has been made known, to which the Law and the Prophets testify... This righteousness from God comes through faith..."* This is not a denial of the Old Testament Scriptures. It is, in fact, a fulfillment of them. The faith principle is fundamental to the Scriptures from Genesis to Revelation.

Before he leaves this vital topic, Paul takes some time in the final verses of this chapter to expound on the nature of faith, using the story of Abraham as an example and an illustration. The first thing we learn is that **faith must have the right object.** I must stress again what I have emphasized before. This is not faith in faith, or faith as an abstract energy. Faith, saving faith, must have the right object. As we consider Abraham's example, we find that **his faith was in God. He believed God.** We see this back in verse 3 in the quote from Genesis 15. *"Abraham believed God..."* We see it again in verse 17: *"In the presence of the God in whom he believed..."*

Going on a little further, we find that **he believed in the character and power of God.** This is found in the second half of verse 17: *"...the God...who gives life to the dead and calls into existence the things that do not exist..."*

Finally, and this is important, we find that **he believed in the promises of God.** We see this in verse 18: *"In hope he believed against hope, that he should become the father of many nations, as he had been told, 'So shall your offspring be.'"*

The key to that verse is found in the phrase: *"as he had been told..."* The same point is found again in verse 20-21: *"No unbelief made him waver concerning the promise of God, but he grew strong in his faith as he gave glory to God, fully convinced that God was able to do what he had promised."*

Notice the emphasis in those verses on the promises of God and what he said. I believe that, in some cases, faith can go awry here. We get ourselves in trouble when we misunderstand or misapply the promises of God. In Abraham's case, he had a very specific promise from God and he believed that God would fulfill his promise. Abraham believed in God, he believed in his character, his power and his promises. Paul uses the story of Abraham and the birth of Isaac to illustrate these points:

"In hope he believed against hope, that he should become the father of many nations, as he had been told, 'So shall your offspring be.' He did not weaken in faith when he considered his own body, which was as good as dead (since he was about a hundred years old), or when he considered the barrenness of Sarah's womb. No unbelief made him waver concerning the promise of God, but he grew strong in his faith as he gave glory to God, fully convinced that God was able to do what he had promised. That is why his faith was 'counted to him as righteousness.'"

This is a great story of faith in action; of faith in God under difficult circumstances. It is a story of faith that did not waver.

Before we leave this topic of faith, I want to make a few comments about **the content of faith.** While the nature of faith and its object remains the same, we find that there is a difference between the believers of the Old Testament and believers today when it comes to the content of faith. What was the content of Abraham's faith? He believed the promises of God: that God was going to give him a son; that through that son would come many descendants and even many nations; from those many descendants would come one particular descendant, through whom all the nations of the world would be blessed. Abraham believed God, and over the years, the promises were fulfilled; first through the birth of Isaac in his old age; then through the birth of many descendants and the whole nation of Israel.

Finally through the birth of that one special descendant or seed, the Messiah, the Christ, through whom God would bless the nations of the world. Abraham believed that it would happen, and his belief was credited to his account as righteousness. He was justified in God's sight by his faith.

What about believers today? What was the content of the faith required for Paul's readers in Rome and for our faith today? Let's look at verses 23-25: *"But the words 'it was counted to him' were not written for his sake alone, but for ours also. It will be counted to us who believe in him who raised from the dead Jesus our Lord, who was delivered up for our trespasses and raised for our justification."*

What do we believe? The object of our faith is the same. We *"believe in him…"* The same God Abraham believed in. But our content is more specific and more complete. We *"believe in him who raised from the dead Jesus our Lord."* Why is belief in Jesus and particularly in his resurrection so important? Paul is circling back to the truth of Jesus as the "propitiation" or "the atoning sacrifice" which he raised in chapter 3. *"He was delivered up for our trespasses…"* Do you believe that? He died for your sins and mine. But he did not remain in the grave. By the power of God – the same power that gave life to Sarah's womb so many years before – Jesus was raised to life. The resurrection is essential to the Gospel, because, as Paul states here, *"he was raised for our justification."* We might also translate; *"he was raised because of our justification"* or, *"he was raised on account of our justification."* Just as it was our sin that caused his death, so it was our justification that made possible his resurrection.

Think of it this way. When Jesus was on the cross, the sins of the world were laid on him. He bore our guilt. He cried out on the cross: *"My God, my God! Why have you forsaken me!"* Our sin caused that awful separation between God the Father and God the Son, because a holy God cannot associate with sin. Jesus was separated from the Father and then he died. He dismissed his spirit and his soul was separated from his body. The Righteous One died on behalf of the unrighteous. But then on the third day he was raised from the dead *"on account of our justification."*

His resurrection was the proof that his suffering and death had satisfied the wrath of God against our sins. The ransom payment had been accepted. We can now be justified before God's court by believing in the death, burial and resurrection of Jesus.

Who are the true descendants of Abraham? They are those who share the faith of Abraham. Abraham believed in a descendant, a promised Seed, the Messiah who would come. We believe in Jesus, the Messiah who came, who died and who rose again. Believe in him, and your faith will be credited to you as righteousness.

Father Abraham has many sons and daughters. I am one of them. Are you?

7

SINCE WE'VE BEEN JUSTIFIED
Romans 5:1-5

My earliest memories of Christmas took place in Tanzania, where my parents were missionaries. We lived on a remote mission station a day's drive from the nearest town, so shopping opportunities were non-existent. Even when we did make it to town, there wasn't much to buy that interested little boys. So one of the highlights of our Christmas each year was the package my Grandmother used to send from America. When the box would arrive in the weekly mail bag, we were dying to open it. But of course we had to wait until Christmas. Finally the great moment would arrive. The string and the tape would be cut away and the box opened. Inside we would find an enticing array of individually wrapped smaller packages.

I would like you to imagine that we have received a package from heaven from our Heavenly Father. This package is a free gift that has been identified. It is the gift of **justification by faith.**

We already know something about this gift. God has declared us to be righteous in his sight as an absolutely free gift. All we have to do is receive this gift by believing in Jesus and his death and resurrection. That is the big package. But as we open this big package, we find there are additional benefits or gifts included in it. Let's open and take a look at some of those gifts included in the gift of justification by faith.

Romans 5:1 begins with the words, *"Therefore, since we have been justified through faith, we have..."* In this chapter we are going to look at four additional benefits or gifts we receive when we are justified by faith.

"Therefore, since we have been justified by faith, we have peace with God through our Lord Jesus Christ."

Here is the first additional benefit: **We have peace with God.**

Peace with God! What a wonderful gift! What does it mean? It is important that we are clear on this, because there can be some misunderstanding here. We sometimes hear Christian preachers who say that Christians are the only ones who have "peace" and that followers of all other religions do not have "peace." But then I have read testimonies of people who have converted to other religions who say that the thing that attracted them to that religion was that they found a sense of peace. Who is right? Do Christians, followers of Christ, have a corner on the market in this matter of peace?

We need to understand that Paul is not referring to a feeling of peacefulness or a sense of peace. He is not referring to an emotional state at all. Peace with God is a standing; a position before God. It is a status of relationship with God that states that between me and God there is not a state of war, hostility, and alienation, but there is a state of peace, of friendship, and of alliance.

The nations of the world have sadly and all too often declared war on one another. Such a declaration means that a state of active hostility exists. When the soldiers of one side encounter the soldiers of the other side, they will shoot and shoot to kill. When the nations become weary of the fighting or one side gains the upper hand and the other side surrenders, treaties are negotiated and there comes a declaration of peace. It is a factual statement of a new status between the two nations; a status of peace rather than hostility and enmity.

This is the kind of peace that Paul is talking about; an objective, factual, positional relationship. You see, before we were justified by faith, the Bible teaches that we were in a state of enmity with God. We were in rebellion. We were at war with God. Look at Romans 5:10: *"For if while we were enemies…"* We were God's enemies! Because of our rebellion and sin, we were under God's wrath, and we could only fear his hostility and his judgment. However, now we have peace with God.

I am not saying that there are no feelings involved, but this peace is above and beyond feelings. It is a legal position and a status of our relationship with God. We are at peace with him.

In this sense, then, the Christian preachers are correct; followers of Christ are the only ones who have peace with God, because this state comes only as a result of having been justified by faith in Jesus. Apart from being justified by faith, we remain at enmity with God, because our sin has not been dealt with. Peaceful feelings may come and go; ebb and flow. Others may claim to have such feelings. But the testimony of Scripture is that only those who have been justified by belief in Jesus have peace with God.

This reality is expanded in the first part of verse 2; *"through him we have also obtained access by faith into this grace in which we stand."* The word "grace" occurs more frequently in Romans 5 than in any other chapter of the Bible. In this verse it is used to describe our standing. We stand in the status of those who have been recipients of God's divine, unmerited favor and kindness. We were under God's wrath. That was our standing before. But now we stand as recipients of God's favor and kindness. I believe this is simply a different way of describing our state of being at peace with God. How did we gain access to our new standing? Through Jesus Christ and by belief (faith) in him. This belief has given us access to this new standing; a standing as a recipient of God's favor; a standing of being at peace with God.

But that is not all. Let's look at the second additional benefit we have received since we have been justified through faith. Look at the rest of verse 2: *"And we rejoice in hope of the glory of God."* There it is! **We have hope for the future.** It is a very specific and magnificent hope. It is the hope of the glory of God.

Think with me. Where have we seen that phrase, "the glory of God" before? Do you remember? That's right! In Romans 3:23: *"For all have sinned and fall short of the glory of God"* From the very beginning of the human race, all the way back in Genesis 1 we learn that while man was created from dirt, he was destined for glory. He was crafted from the earth, but made in the image of God, to reflect and share his glory forever. But sin marred the image, and ever since that fateful day when Adam and Eve sinned in the Garden of Eden, every human being has "fallen short of the glory of God." But now here is hope! Hope that because of

Christ's death for our sin, and the righteousness from God that is by faith, we can be restored to the glory for which we were intended. There is hope that we shall one day fulfill our destiny and become the people God intended us to be. We shall one day fulfill the glory of God; be worthy of it and experience it in all its fullness. Since we've been justified, what a future lies before us!

But there is still more here in our text. Look at verse 3a: *"Not only that, but we rejoice in our sufferings…"* Here is a third additional benefit we receive when we are justified by faith. **We can rejoice in our sufferings.** The word for "sufferings" here is rather inclusive. It covers physical suffering. It can also refer to emotional and spiritual stress that can be caused by either external or internal pressures. It covers the whole gamut of human sufferings, whatever their source. Now, how can we rejoice in our sufferings? We can rejoice because we recognize that they have a positive purpose and promise a positive outcome. That is what Paul says in the rest of the verse: *"…knowing that suffering produces endurance, and endurance produces character and character produces hope."*

Let's take this apart. *We know that suffering produces endurance.* Let me first take an axe to a horrible little tree that has grown up in the minds of many Christians. The King James Version translates this, "tribulation worketh patience." Maybe you've heard preachers who say: "Be careful not to pray and ask God for patience. Because tribulation worketh patience, so if you ask God for patience he'll send you tribulation." Have you ever heard that? Well, put it out of your mind. That is not what this passage is teaching. It is a different word for patience. When most people talk about praying for patience, they mean self-control and the ability to keep their cool and to be gentle and understanding in their reactions to life's stressful situations. There is a very different word for that in the Greek language. You are safe to pray for that! That is not what is in view here. This word means endurance or perseverance; the ability to "remain under" and "bear up under" tough circumstances; to keep going when the going gets tough. It is the quality of spiritual endurance and it is a quality that is developed through suffering.

As followers of Christ, we must be ready for the long haul. The Christian life is a marathon, not a sprint. We are going to need endurance. Where does that come from? *Suffering produces endurance.* Are you suffering as you read this? Maybe it is financial difficulty; maybe it is emotional. Maybe it is related to your family, your job or your health. If you are suffering, you can rejoice. God has a good purpose and he promises a good outcome if you will "keep on keeping on." Keep on trusting God and keep on doing the right thing. If you "remain under" the trial and "bear up" under it, you will learn perseverance and you will grow in spiritual strength and stamina. Don't throw up your hands in despair when life is difficult. Regard the difficulties as a prescribed set of spiritual calisthenics designed to make you strong.

Let's go on. *Endurance produces character.* We learn something here about the Christian life. We are not promised that it will be easy. We are not promised that God will take away the struggle and make things smooth. We are not even told that we will have fewer struggles than we had before we trusted in Christ. Rather we are told that God has an entirely different agenda than we do. He is developing something in us called "character." What is character? Do you have it? The word Paul uses here is a rather difficult word to translate into English. It has the idea of not only undergoing a test, but also passing that test. There is an expression that is often used in throwing down a challenge to someone in some form of competition; "Let's find out what you're made of." In that sense, character is what you and I are made of. It is what is left after the testing is over; what is real and what is just pretend and bluster. We can say we believe a lot of things. We can say we trust God. But when the suffering comes, what then? What are we made of?

And so, when we have gone through times of testing and suffering and our faith has stood the test, we have increased our endurance and we have been molded and shaped in our character. This, in turn, produces something else. It produces hope; the increased confidence that our faith is genuine, that God is real, that we are his children, and that we shall experience his glory.

Charles Finney was a famous American evangelist of the 19th century. He once wrote a letter describing how many people had responded to the invitation at one of his evangelistic crusades. He then added these words: "We shall see how many of them are genuine." That is what hard times and suffering do for us. They prove the genuineness of our faith.

And hope does not put us to shame. (verse 5). This is the same word Paul used in Romans 1:16 when he declared that he was "not ashamed of the Gospel." It is a word that combines elements of disappointment and embarrassment that come from trusting in something that did not happen and believing something that did not come true.

I was always a fan of Charles Shultz and his cartoon strip "Peanuts." One of the recurring themes he revisited every Halloween was the story of Linus. Linus believed in the "Great Pumpkin" who would descend on the pumpkin patch at Halloween, bearing gifts for all the children who believed in him and stayed up to wait for him. Linus would stay up every Halloween night, waiting beside the pumpkin patch. And every Halloween, he went home disappointed and embarrassed because the Great Pumpkin never showed up. Linus had a hope which disappointed him. Paul tells us that our hope in God, a hope based on our justification by faith, is a hope which will not disappoint us and embarrass us. God will fulfill his promises to us.

There is one more additional benefit or gift for us to unwrap from this passage. The second part of verse 5 says, "*...because God's love has been poured into our hearts through the Holy Spirit who has been given to us.*" The fourth additional benefit we find here is that **we have God's love in our hearts.**

This is the first mention of the Holy Spirit in Romans since a passing reference to him in the opening paragraph. We are told first that "he has been given to us." The assumption of this passage is that everyone who has been justified by faith has received the gift of the Holy Spirit. And what is his ministry? One aspect of it is to flood our hearts with the love of God. I believe this refers to a subjective experience of God's love. God pours out his love into our hearts by the Holy Spirit, assuring us of his great love.

This is tied to the earlier sequence in the passage. When we are in the midst of struggles and suffering, one of the things that keeps our hope alive is the sense of the love of God. In my own experience, it is when I have gone through the greatest crises in my life that I have been most dependent on and most aware of the ministry of the Holy Spirit in my life. His consistent message to me during those times has been: God loves you! God loves you!

Well, there is still more to come. We are only half way through this wonderful paragraph. But we are going to save the rest for the next chapter. That is already a wonderful list of benefits, is it not? Since we have been justified by faith we have peace with God…we have hope for the future…we have joy in the midst of our suffering…and we have a deep, Spirit-given sense of God's love flooding our hearts.

No wonder God called his message the gospel: the Good News!

8

THE GREATEST LOVE STORY EVER TOLD
Romans 5:6-11

From the beginning of time, the world has been fascinated by love stories. Music, art and literature from every culture celebrate the theme of love. The title for this chapter is: **The Greatest Love Story Ever Told.**

This love story is one that is traced and told throughout the Scriptures, from Genesis to Revelation. It is highlighted, focused and concentrated in the passage we are studying in this chapter: Romans 5:6-11. It is part of a longer story which began in verse 1. It is a story that elaborates on the benefits of being justified by faith. The chapter opens with the words, *"Therefore, since we have been justified by faith, we have..."* In the previous chapter we looked at the first five verses, and four different benefits we receive when we are justified by faith. We have peace with God, we have hope for the future, we have joy in our sufferings, and we have the love of God poured out into our hearts.

It is to this last theme that Paul turns in the rest of this paragraph. As we study this portion of Romans, I would raise the question: What makes this the greatest love story ever told? I would like to offer three answers to this question taken from these verses. I will present each of the three answers in the form of a rhetorical question.

Here is the first one: **Could there be any less likely candidates for love?** Even as I pose that question, we should be swept by the realization that this is a different kind of love story. Normally love stories focus on the lovable qualities of the person loved: beauty, strength, courage, nobility of character. All of these are attributed to the persons loved. But when we examine these verses, we find that this is not the case. Could there be any less likely candidates for love?

Let us look at how the human race is described in these verses. I hope you have taken the time to read the passage in your Bible. If not, please do so now. The first description is found in verse 6: *"while we were still weak..."* The NIV translates: *"when we were powerless..."* There are two ways this adjective is used according to the lexicons. It is used to describe a state of helplessness in light of circumstances; trapped and unable to help ourselves. The second use is to describe someone who is morally weak and incapable of doing good. Both uses are actually true and relevant to this verse. This is the doctrine that theologians refer to as the doctrine of man's depravity. Morally weak and incapable of doing or sustaining any good course of action and hence helpless and trapped; unable to help ourselves. It is not a pretty picture!

But that is not all. Later in the same verse, Paul describes us as *"ungodly."* This is the word Paul used back in Romans 4:5 as he states that God *"justifies the ungodly."* It is a word that describes someone who lives his life without regard for God or his standards; someone who is ungodly and impious.

In verse 8, Paul refers to us all as *"sinners."* This is the same root as the word used in Romans 3:23 where we are told that *"all have sinned."* This is the noun, describing people who consistently miss the mark and fail to live up to God's standards.

Verse 10 then adds to the description by calling us God's *"enemies."* We are, by our very nature from birth, in a state of both passive and active rebellion against God and his rule over our lives.

What is the consequence and culmination of all this bad news? In verse 9 Paul talks about *"the wrath of God."* This phrase takes us all the way back to Romans 1:18 where Paul states that *"the wrath of God is revealed against all the ungodliness and unrighteousness of men..."*

It is not a pretty picture! When we look at the human race and see ourselves as God sees us, through the prism of his righteousness and holiness, we are morally powerless, spiritually bankrupt, miserable failures, active rebels against God and richly deserving of God's wrath. **Could there be any less likely candidates for love?**

That brings us to the second point in this sermon, also put in the form of a question: **Could there be any greater measure or demonstration of love?** The measure and demonstration of God's love is the dominant theme of these verses. The measure of God's love is clearly stated repeatedly. It is found in verse 6: "*Christ died for the ungodly.*" It is there again in verse 8 most clearly: "*But God shows his love for us in that while were still sinners, Christ died for us.*"

Verse 9 also makes a clear reference to Christ's death when Paul states that "*we have now been justified by his blood.*" And verse 10 makes it clear once again: "*we were reconciled to God by the death of his Son.*" This is the ultimate measure of love, is it not? Jesus said it himself: "*Greater love has no one than this, that someone lay down his life for his friends.*" (John15:13) This is truly the final and ultimate measure of love: to die for the one loved. Abraham Lincoln, in his famous Gettysburg address, paid tribute to the patriotism of the Union's fallen soldiers and their love of country when he referred to the "last full measure of devotion." You cannot give more than life itself. That is how much God loved us; how much Christ loved us. Christ died for us!

The full impact of this "greatest love story" comes through, however, when we put the first two points of this sermon together. The uniqueness of this love story is seen when we compare "the candidates for love" and "the measure of that love." This is what Paul points out in verses 7-8: "*For one will scarcely die for a righteous person—though perhaps for a good person one would dare even to die—but God shows his love for us in that while we were still sinners, Christ died for us.*"

I recall once browsing through the entertainment system during a long flight looking for a movie to watch. I settled on a film called "Dave." The premise of the film is rather far-fetched. The president of the United States is struck down by a massive stroke. Rather than announce the fact to the public, his Chief of Staff and others behind the scenes identify a man who has a striking resemblance to the president. In fact he makes a living appearing at events in which he impersonates the president. They move this man, named "Dave" into the White House and coach him on how to behave so that they can carry on as though nothing has happened until they can put their own plans for succession into place.

Like I said, it was rather far-fetched as this rather naïve but good-hearted man takes on the ceremonial and public roles of the president. One of the characters in the film is a Secret Service agent assigned to protect the president. Because he is so close to the action, he is brought in on the secret. Early in the film there is a scene in which Dave is talking with this agent about his job. As his responsibilities are described, Dave asks him, "So you are ready to take a bullet for the president?" "Yes, sir!" the agent responds. Dave thinks about that for a few seconds and then asks, "Would you take a bullet for me?" There was a long and uncomfortable silence as the question went unanswered.

As the story goes on, Dave finds ways to escape the evil conspirators, and even use the powers of the presidency to do some very good things for the country. In fact, he proves that he is a better man than the president he is impersonating. As the story winds down, and Dave is about to leave the White House and step back into his own anonymous life, there is one final scene when Dave says good bye to the Secret Service agent. As Dave turns to walk away, the agent says softly: "I just want you to know, I would take a bullet for you."

It was a moving, "feel-good" moment in the story. But here is the thing. That is as far as our human imaginings can take us. That is as far as we can project the power of human "love" traveling. Because Dave was a "good man," the agent was now willing to die for him. That is powerful. But as powerful as that is, God's love takes up where human love leaves off. The greatest measure of his love was spent and expended on those who were least deserving! *"While we were still weak (powerless), Christ died for the ungodly... While we were still sinners, Christ died for us... While we were God's enemies, we were reconciled to him through the death of his Son."* This is how God demonstrated his love. It is the greatest love story ever told! The full measure of devotion was expressed toward those who were most unworthy and undeserving. Jesus Christ took the bullet for you and for me. He did it because he loved us. He did it when we were least deserving.

There is an upside-down theology that has invaded the church and infiltrated much Christian preaching and writing and music lyrics. It comes from the human self-esteem movement. It is a teaching that looks at the cross of Christ and concludes, "The death of Christ on the cross demonstrates that we are worth dying for." I am sorry, but that is not what the Scripture teaches! The Scripture teaches that we were unworthy, but Christ loved us enough to die for us anyway. John Newton, the hymn writer had it right: "Amazing grace! How sweet the sound, that saved <u>a wretch like me.</u>"

There is a very subtle, but essential distinction between Biblical teaching and the modern purveyors of self-esteem. Christ did not die for us because we were valuable. We weren't. We were worthless. But now we have value because Christ died for us. The value lies in Christ, and in his love for us, not in us. And to him goes all the glory! We are saved by grace and grace alone! I said in the previous chapter that Romans 5 uses the word "grace" more often than any other chapter in the Bible. The word "grace" does not occur in the particular verses we are looking at in this chapter, but I believe that these verses represent one of the most powerful manifestations and descriptions of grace to be found anywhere in Scripture. When we were powerless…when we were sinners…when we were God's enemies…Christ died for us. That is grace. **Could there be any less likely candidates for love? Could there be any greater measure or demonstration of love?**

This takes us to our third point, also phrased as a question: **Could there be any greater result or benefit from love?** As we turn to this question, I would point you back to the dominant theme statement of the whole paragraph in verse 1: *"Therefore, since we have been justified by faith…"* That is the overall result or benefit we have received from the love of God that was demonstrated on Calvary. **We have been justified by faith.** We have been declared righteous in God's sight and before his courtroom by belief in Jesus. In the closing verses of this paragraph, Paul expands our understanding of justification by describing the benefits we have received in two additional ways.

First we are told that because of Christ's great love **we shall**

be saved. This is one of those phrases that was once a standard in the vocabulary of evangelical Christians. "Have you been saved?" we would ask each other. We would give our testimonies and say, "When I was saved..." We may have overused the language. It may have become a cliché. It may be misunderstood and even offend people. But let us never lose this word and the glorious truth it declares. It is grounded in the Scriptures. Paul uses the expression twice here: first in verse 9: *"Since, therefore, we have now been justified by his blood, much more <u>shall we be saved by him from the wrath of God.</u>"* He repeats it again in verse 10: *"we shall be saved by his life!"* To understand this language, we must understand what it is that we are being saved from. Paul makes it clear, does he not? *Saved from God's wrath.* God's wrath against sin has been revealed from heaven. That is what Paul told us in Romans 1:18. Now we are told that *"since we have been justified by his blood, we shall be saved from God's wrath."* It is interesting that Paul uses the future tense. God's wrath, his judgment against sin is something coming, both on the sinful world and on sinful people. How will we be saved from God's wrath? How will we escape? Through Christ and faith in his blood! By being justified by faith.

That brings us to a second way of describing what happened to us when we were justified through faith: **we were reconciled to God.**

"For if while we were enemies we were reconciled to God by the death of his Son, much more, now that we are reconciled, shall we be saved by his life. More than that, we also rejoice in God through our Lord Jesus Christ, through whom we have now received reconciliation." (Romans 5:10-11)

The word "reconciled" describes a change in relationship. It means to change from being an enemy to being a friend. Here Paul is not so much adding new truth as he is bringing us back full circle to where he began this paragraph. *Therefore, since we have been justified by faith, we have peace with God through our Lord Jesus Christ.* Being reconciled to God is another way of describing the state of being at peace with God. We were at war. Now we are at peace. We were God's enemies because of our sin. Now he declares us to be his friends.

There is an interesting phrase in the Old Testament that expresses this reality of our alienation from God. It is found in the Book of Leviticus. This is what it says in chapter 26, verses 27 and 28: *But if in spite of this you will not listen to me, but walk contrary to me, then I will walk contrary to you in fury and I myself will discipline you sevenfold for your sins.* "To walk contrary." The point that struck me is that it is a two-way alienation. When we walk contrary to God, then he walks contrary to us. This was our status. We were God's enemies. But now we have been reconciled to God. We have peace with God. Could there be any greater result or benefit from love?

Truly, this is the greatest love story ever told. **Could there be any less likely candidates for love?** We were powerless, ungodly, sinners, enemies of God. **Could there be any greater measure or demonstration of love?** Christ died for us. **Could there be any greater result or benefit from love?** We have been reconciled to God. We shall be saved from God's wrath.

That leads me to a simple and very personal question. Are you part of this love story? Have you received the free gift of salvation? Have you been justified by belief in Jesus? It is a step that is so simple it is hard. We keep thinking there has to be more to it. But there isn't. You simply have to call on the name of the Lord and the simple act of calling out to him in faith will be credited to your account as righteousness. You will be justified. You will be reconciled to God.

Let me close this chapter by adding two words of application for all who are already participants in this love story. You have been justified by faith and been reconciled to God. First of all, with great privilege comes great responsibility. In 2 Corinthians 5, Paul uses this same language of reconciliation to God and this is what he says, beginning in verse 17: *"Therefore, if anyone is in Christ, he is a new creation. The old has passed away; behold, the new has come. All this is from God, who through Christ reconciled us to himself and gave us the ministry of reconciliation; that is, in Christ God was reconciling the world to himself, not counting their trespasses against them, and entrusting to us the message of reconciliation. Therefore, we are ambassadors for Christ, God making his appeal through us. We implore you on behalf of Christ, be reconciled to God."*

To those who have been reconciled to God, God has entrusted the ministry and the message of reconciliation; of pleading with the world around us to be reconciled to God. Are we faithfully discharging that responsibility?

Finally I would call our attention to the final verse in this wonderful paragraph in Romans 5:11: *"More than that, we also rejoice in God through our Lord Jesus Christ, through whom we have now received reconciliation."*

What does it mean to *"rejoice in God?"* It is another of those Greek words that is hard to reproduce precisely in English. It means to boast and be proud of something; to be happy and take joy from something; to exult and celebrate something. This particular word has been a common thread in the first chapters of Romans. We first find it back in Romans 3:27, where Paul says, *"Then what becomes of our boasting? It is excluded."* Paul makes the same point in Romans 4:2: *"For if Abraham was justified by works, he has something to boast about – but not before God."* Now in chapter 5, Paul has used the very same word three different times but it is translated "rejoice." In verse 2, *"We rejoice in hope of the glory of God."* In verse 3, *"...we rejoice in our sufferings."* And now, here in verse 11: *"We also rejoice in God through our Lord Jesus Christ."*

It is not a matter of whether we boast, rejoice and exult or not. It is a matter of whether or not we are boasting, rejoicing and exulting in the right things. We do not boast or take pride in our own deeds and our own righteousness before God. As the Scripture tells us, *"All our righteousness is as filthy rags."* (Isaiah 64:6) But we can, in fact we are called on, to rejoice and exult in God who has reconciled us to himself. Our joy, our boast is not in us or in what we have done for God, but in him and what he has done for us.

I love the words from the song <u>How Deep the Father's Love for Us</u> by Stuart Townend.

"I will not boast in anything
No gifts, no power, no wisdom

But I will boast in Jesus Christ
His death and resurrection.
Why should I gain from His reward?
I cannot give an answer,
But this I know with all my heart
His wounds have paid my ransom."

9
GRACE ABOUNDS!
Romans 5:12-21

There is something fundamentally and drastically wrong with the world and the human race. As I write this chapter (spring, 2020) our world is being rocked by the Coronavirus. While this may be considered a "natural" crisis, it has pushed to the background several ongoing man-made disasters. Reports out of Syria are calling for help as over 2 million people are caught between the opposing Syrian and Turkish forces. Rare good news out of South Sudan trumpets the signing of a peace deal – but calls our attention to the fact that over 400,000 people have died in a civil war that has been largely ignored by the international media. Recently the US came perilously close to war with Iran. North Korea continues to develop its nuclear capability. Meanwhile our political leaders cannot agree on anything and spend their time and energy criticizing the "other side of the aisle." That is just a very brief summary of the news today. By the time this book is published, these crises may all be "old news," but there will be a new set of crises to report.

Every week, every day the news media are filled with alarming reports of war, violence, genocide, greed, crime, and man-made disasters. The headlines come from all over the world. No nation or race or part of the world has a monopoly on bad news. It is everywhere. Where did all this evil come from? What is wrong with us? (Hold onto that question for a moment).

Near the back of almost every newspaper there is a section entitled "Obituaries." An obituary is a notice of someone's death. It usually carries a brief synopsis of the life and history of the person who has died. Every year, The Times newspaper in London publishes a book which includes a collection of all the obituaries that appeared in their pages during the year. It is a big, thick book. Someone once loaned me a copy. It was rather fascinating to page through it, scanning the pages. What struck me was this simple, universal fact of human existence. People die. Not just some people. Not just poor people. Not just old people. Not just sick people. Everyone dies. In the book were the rich and the famous; world leaders, business leaders, significant artists and performers. The rich, the strong, the smart. People with every human resource at their disposal. Yet they still died. In spite of all man's advances in technology and medicine and science, the ratio is still the same: one out of one, 100 out of 100, a million out of a million. Everyone dies.

Why? Why does everyone die? Why is there so much evil in the world? Who got us into this mess?

In Romans 5:12-21, Paul gives us the Biblical answer to these questions. But more importantly, he not only tells us who got us into this mess, but he tells us who can get us out.

If you haven't already done so, take a moment to read the text. As you do so, you will not need me to tell you that this is a rather difficult passage. Yet is also a very important passage. The British preacher, Dr. Martyn Lloyd-Jones describes it as both the most difficult section in the Book of Romans and the most important. He believed it to be the key to the whole Epistle. In his series of sermons on Romans, he devoted fourteen sermons to this one paragraph – over 200 pages. (And you thought I was long-winded!) This paragraph is the key Bible passage on the subject of original sin and what is referred to as the imputation of sin. These are topics that have stirred considerable debate and discussion. I pulled an old book off my shelf: Strong's Theology. When I was in seminary, my wife used to come home and find me in my study, sitting in my chair, sound asleep, with this book spread across my chest. Dr. Strong spends 70 pages of very small print discussing the doctrine of imputation and original sin. Most of the discussion centers around the interpretation of this paragraph.

One of the reasons this passage and the doctrine it presents are difficult is because many of us have been raised in cultures and societies that stress individualism and the importance of the individual. But in Romans 5:12-21, we are introduced to the truth of one man whose actions had the gravest of consequences on all of his descendants. In addressing the question of how we got into the mess we're in, Paul looks back at the history of the first man, Adam. Adam was created by God. As Adam walked around in the Garden of Eden, we were all "in Adam."

What exactly does that mean? There are various theories. Theologians debate a rather subtle distinction between what is called a "federal headship" theory and a "natural headship" theory. Under the "federal headship" theory, Adam is seen as a figure-head or representative in an almost governmental sense. As the first man, he was our head, our representative; the father of the human race. He acted as our representative.

The "natural headship" theory goes a step further and proposes that all of us were actually "in Adam" physically or seminally. For support for this theory, they go to Hebrews 7, where the writer speaks of Levi being in the loins of his ancestor Abraham when Abraham paid the tithe to Melchizedek. I would suggest that we leave the resolving of that debate to the theologians. What is clear in this passage is that, because he was the first man, Adam's actions had real and serious consequences that affect us all.

What were his actions and how do they affect us? We are all familiar with the story of Adam and Eve in the Garden of Eden. God placed the first man and woman in a perfect environment and gave them full access to the garden and its fruit with only one restriction. Do not eat from the Tree of the Knowledge of Good and Evil. We know what happened. The Serpent tempted Eve. She disobeyed and ate from the fruit of the forbidden tree, and then she gave it to Adam and he ate.

Look at how Paul characterizes Adam's actions here in Romans 5:18. He speaks of *"one trespass."* The word trespass means literally "to fall beside" or to "go out of bounds." In verse 19 Paul speaks of *"one man's disobedience."* One clear and specific command, and Adam, the first man, our father, our representative, disobeyed it. What were the results? Paul lists several of them.

First, **sin entered the world.** In verse 12 we read *"Therefore, just as <u>sin came into the world</u> through one man."* Sin invaded.

Before that there was no sin in the world. Adam and Eve lived in a perfect Paradise. But when they disobeyed, sin invaded. But that is not all. Through their sin **death entered the world.** As we read in the rest of verse 12: *"and death through sin."* This builds off the same verb. Sin invaded, and, slipping in on its coattails, death invaded too. God had warned that this would happen. *"Do not eat of the tree...for on the day you eat of it, you will surely die."* They ate and they died. They died spiritually that very day in the sense that they were separated from God. Physical death also entered that day, and the process of dying began.

Physical death didn't just enter. The third result Paul refers to is that **death spread to all men.** Still in verse 12, *"...and so death spread to all men..."* Death permeated the human race, like a poison gas filling a room with its deadly fumes. No one escaped. In fact there is a kind of "Times Obituary" found in the fifth chapter of Genesis. It is a genealogical record, but in addition to the "begetting" each entry in the record ends with the same words; "and he died."

Now, why did that happen? What is the cause and effect? That brings us to the last phrase of the verse and the most difficult to interpret and understand: *"...because all sinned..."* What does this phrase tell us? The tense of the verb makes it clear that this is looking at one very specific act of sin that took place at a point in time. When did all sin? We "all sinned" when Adam sinned because we were all "in Adam." At that moment in time, we all suffered the consequences of Adam's disobedience as sin invaded. With sin came death. Death spread to every one of Adam's descendants.

The interpretation is supported by Paul's logic in the next two verses: *"for sin indeed was in the world before the law was given, but sin is not counted where there is no law. Yet death reigned from Adam to Moses, even over those whose sinning was not like the transgression of Adam, who was a type of the one who was to come."*

What is the logic? Paul is referring to the time period between Adam and Moses. During this time, there was no written code of laws. Men were sinning during that time, but because there was no written code to hold them accountable, the sin was not taken into account. However, everyone during that time period still died. They died, even though they did not sin in the same way that Adam did. They did not break a command, since they didn't have specific commands to break. Why did they die? Judicially speaking, they died, not because of their own sin, but because they, being "in Adam," were implicated in the sin of Adam. They inherited death from Adam.

Let's talk families and inheritance for a moment. We all come from families. With our family identity comes a family inheritance. There may be physical property, financial wealth, heirlooms, and so on, that may be included in that inheritance. There are also genetic and physical attributes that we may inherit. A bald head, blue or brown eyes, a big nose, a high or low IQ; all of these might be family attributes that are passed on from generation to generation. Then there are less tangible or visible things: a family value system, a coat of arms, a code of honor, a family reputation and community status might all be part of our inheritance.

All of us are members of Adam's family. What is our inheritance from him? Let me just read some additional selections from this paragraph that continue to document our inheritance.

Verse 15: *"…many died through one man's trespass…"*

Verse 16: *"The judgment followed one trespass and brought condemnation."*

Verse 17: *"…because of one man's trespass death reigned through that one man…"*

Verse 18: *"…as one trespass led to condemnation for all men…"*

Verse 19: *"…by the one man's disobedience the many were made sinners…"*

That is quite an inheritance, isn't it? Sin, death, condemnation. It is not a pretty picture. That is the human dilemma. That is how we got into the mess we are in. So what is the answer? Who can get us out of this mess?

At the end of verse 14, Paul introduces a key concept. He says that Adam is *"a type of the one was to come."* What does he mean by that? Adam is described as a picture, a foreshadowing of the one to come. Paul is referring to Christ. In fact Jesus is referred to in 1 Corinthians 15:45 as the last Adam in contrast to the first Adam. How is Adam a type of Christ? Certainly not in the matter of disobedience or sin! He is a type in this matter of being a representative or head of all who are "in him." This is the truth upon which Paul will build his argument in the rest of this passage. So far it is all bad news. The whole human race was "in Adam" when he sinned and as such, we inherited a sin nature, death and condemnation. Sin invaded and with sin came death and death spread to all men. That is how we got into the mess we are in. That is the historical and the theological explanation for the universality of sin and evil and the universality of death. All sinned. All died. And still, all sin and all die.

What is the solution? The solution is to join a new family with a different head or representative. The solution is to join a new family with a different inheritance. We need to find a way to be adopted into the family of the second Adam. Look at how Paul compares and contrasts the inheritance of the members of the family of the last Adam with that of the inheritance we received from the first Adam.

Beginning in verse 15: *"But the free gift is not like the trespass. For if many died through one man's trespass, much more have the grace of God and the free gift by the grace of that one man Jesus Christ abounded for many. And the free gift is not like the result of that one man's sin. For the judgment following one trespass brought condemnation, but the free gift following many trespasses brought justification. For if, because of one man's trespass, death reigned through that one man, much more will those who receive the abundance of grace and the free gift of righteousness reign in life through the one man Jesus Christ. Therefore, as one trespass led to condemnation for all men, so one act of righteousness leads to justification and life for all men. For as by the one man's disobedience the many were made sinners, so by the one man's obedience the many will be made righteous."*

There is both comparison and contrast here; like and not like; same, but different. The comparison lies in the fact that the act of the one influenced the many. Just as the disobedient act of the first Adam resulted in death for all men, so the obedience of Jesus Christ, the last Adam, in submitting to the will of the Father and going to the cross, results in life for all who are "in Christ." That is the comparison.

What about the contrast? How is the gift "not like" the trespass? The first point of contrast lies in the actions of the first Adam and the last Adam: disobedience versus obedience. The second point of contrast highlights that there is a difference in result. The result of the first Adam's act of disobedience was all negative. The result of the second Adam's obedience is all positive. Instead of sin, righteousness; instead of condemnation, justification; instead of death, life. Instead of death reigning, we shall reign in life through Jesus Christ. Instead of sin reigning, grace reigns. The third point of contrast that Paul makes is the "how much more" kind. He looks at God's grace in Christ and he contrasts it to the effects of Adam's sin, and he says "how much more, how much greater!" God's grace in Christ is far greater than man's sin and condemnation in Adam. Look at verse 15 again, this time from the NIV: *"...how much more did God's grace and the gift that came by grace of the one man, Jesus Christ, overflow to the many."* He makes a similar point in verse 20: *"But where sin increased, grace increased all the more."*

God's grace in Christ is greater than man's sin in Adam. God's grace trumps man's sin.

So, whose family are you in? We are all born into the first Adam's family. We didn't get a choice about that. But we have to be adopted into Christ's family, the family of the second Adam. We do get a choice about that. We became members of the family of the first Adam by being born. To get into the family of the last Adam, we have to be born again. We can be born again by believing in Jesus Christ and his death and resurrection. We can be born again by calling out to him in faith and thus being justified by faith.

There is a great deal in this section of Scripture that is hard to understand. There is truth here that is puzzling and even troubling. The good news is that we don't have to understand it to believe it. The declaration is clear. In Adam all sinned, all die, all are condemned. In Christ all are made righteous, all are made alive, all are justified. Are you still "in Adam?" Or are you "in Christ?" Who is your representative? Whose family do you belong to? The last Adam is greater than the first Adam. God's grace trumps man's sin.

The Greek word for "grace" in this passage is used interchangeably with the Greek word for "gift". All you have to do with a gift is accept it! And the result of accepting that gift? It is beautifully summarized verse 21, the final verse of this chapter:

"...so that, as sin reigned in death, grace also might reign through righteousness leading to eternal life through Jesus Christ our Lord."

10

WHAT DO YOU RECKON?

Romans 6:1-11

"What do you reckon?" That may sound like a strange question. It brings to my mind a line from some old cowboy movie, as the hero shifts his lump of chewing tobacco from one cheek to another, squints at the tracks in the ground in front of him and drawls, "What do you reckon?" His buddy responds, also looking at the tracks, "I reckon they must be about two hours ahead of us."

We don't seem to often use the word "reckon" anymore. But I want to pose the question anyway: What do you reckon? In this chapter I intend to make a case that what you reckon is absolutely vital to your Christian life and your walk with God.

This is the first of three chapters covering Romans chapter 6. In the first five chapters of Romans, Paul has made some truly remarkable, even radical statements. Here are a few examples.

Romans 3:21-24: *"But now the righteousness of God has been manifested apart from the law, although the Law and the Prophets bear witness to it— the righteousness of God through faith in Jesus Christ for all who believe. For there is no distinction: for all have sinned and fall short of the glory of God, and are justified by his grace as a gift, through the redemption that is in Christ Jesus."*

Romans 3:28: *"For we hold that one is justified by faith apart from works of the law."*

Romans 4:5: *"And to the one who does not work but believes in him who justifies the ungodly, his faith is counted as righteousness."*

Romans 5:20: *"Now the law came in to increase the trespass, but where sin increased, grace abounded all the more."*

Now, at this point, Paul, in his mind's eye, can see the hands going up all over the audience. It is as though he is reading the thoughts of his readers, and anticipating their questions and objections to what he has written, and so he stops to address some of those questions. This introduces the first of several lengthy parentheses or detours in the letter, in which Paul departs from his main argument to address questions about what he is saying. Chapter 6 records the first detour. Chapter 7 represents the second one. One of the reasons I believe these two chapters represent departures from Paul's main line of thought is that it would be possible to read from the end of Romans chapter 5, straight on into the opening words of chapter 8, and not miss a beat in the development of Paul's presentation of the gospel message. But we will save that until we get to chapter 8. For now, let's follow Paul on the first detour. (Note: when I say that these two chapters represent parentheses in Paul's argument, I do not mean to imply that they are less important!)

The first question that Paul addresses can be phrased this way: **Does justification by faith encourage us to continue in a sinful lifestyle?** Paul will spend all of chapter 6 dealing with this question. Let us look at how Paul poses the question: *"What shall we say, then? Are we to continue in sin that grace may abound?"*

It is a logical question, is it not? In fact, in his commentary, the British preacher, Dr. Martyn Lloyd-Jones goes so far as to say that unless people ask this question, then we probably have not preached the true gospel. We have not clearly proclaimed the radical nature of justification by grace through faith. I mean, it's perfectly logical: if it is true that *"...where sin increased, grace abounded all the more,"* then let's keep on sinning! Let's give God even more room and scope to demonstrate his grace. We will actually be doing God a favor!

So if it is a logical question, what is the answer? Paul first gives a very strong negative. "By no means!" No way! And he goes on to show us why. In the first paragraph of this remarkable chapter, Paul puts forward his first answer to the question. Here it is: **The believer's union with Christ makes a life of continued sin unthinkable.**

The person who asks this question has failed to understand some basic truths about the gospel. The gospel does proclaim justification by faith alone. The gospel does teach that by believing in Jesus and his death for our sins and his resurrection, we can be declared righteous in God's sight as an absolutely free gift of grace. It is a once-and-for-all transaction before God's court by which our faith is reckoned to our account as righteousness before God. But that is not all the gospel declares. The gospel also teaches us the great truth of **our union with Christ**.

Look at verse 2: *"By no means! How can we who died to sin still live in it?"* I would encourage every Christian to commit this verse to memory. It is a very strong weapon to have in your mental and spiritual arsenal when you encounter temptation. Everything else Paul says in this paragraph is encapsulated in this short verse. Having laid down this basic premise, Paul goes on to expand the logic behind it.

The first reality is that **we (believers) have been united with Christ.** Paul presents this reality using the language or metaphor of baptism. Verse 3 says, *"Do you not know that all of us who have been baptized into Christ Jesus were baptized into his death?"*

The Bible uses the word baptism or baptized in two different ways. First there is a literal use of the word to describe the ordinance of water baptism; to be dipped or immersed in water as an initiation rite, signaling a person's entrance into Christ and the Christian life, and identifying him/her as a follower of Jesus Christ. But closely allied with the act of water baptism is a deeper reality of which water baptism is only a symbol. That is the reality that when we put our faith in Jesus, we are actually united with Christ. Paul uses the word in this way in 1 Corinthians 12:13: *"For in one Spirit we were all baptized into one body—Jews or Greeks, slaves or free."*

One of the things that happens to us when we place our faith in Christ and we are justified by faith is that the Holy Spirit baptizes us into Christ and into Christ's Body, the church. We become part of him. We are, forever after, "in Christ." Think back to Romans 5, and the distinctive realities of being "in Adam" and being "in Christ." This is one of the great, underlying truths and realities of the Gospel. We have been "baptized into Christ Jesus." We are united with him. We are "in Christ."

There is another word here that adds to our understanding. This is found in the language Paul uses in verse 5: *"For if we have been united with him in a death like his, we shall certainly be united with him in a resurrection like his."*

According to one Greek dictionary, the word Paul uses for being united means, "to be closely associated in a similar experience—to be like, to be one with." The word "if" here can also be translated "since." "Since we have been united with him like this…"

I want to emphasize that this reality of our union with Christ is true of all believers. It is our birth right by virtue of our second birth through faith in Jesus. We are united with Christ. It is not an "experiential truth." That is, it is not something we necessarily feel or experience with our five senses. This is something that has happened to us by virtue of our new position. That is why Paul uses the language of knowing: Don't you know? Are you ignorant of this great truth, this great spiritual reality? Did you know that as a follower of Jesus, you are united with Christ? This is an integral part of the gospel message.

This great truth of our union with Christ has some very dramatic additional implications. **Since we are united with Christ, we died with him.** This is the first point Paul makes in verse 3: *"Do you not know that all of us who have been baptized into Christ Jesus were baptized into his death?"* When we were united with Christ, what is true of him became true of us. He died and we were baptized (or united with him) in death. His death became our death.

Not only that, but **since we are united with Christ, we were buried with him.** That's what the first part of verse 4 tells us: *"We were buried therefore with him by baptism into death."* In these verses, the symbol of water baptism and the spiritual realities portrayed are so closely allied that it is impossible to separate them. The act of water baptism is a graphic picture of burial, as the person being baptized is buried into the water. Christ died. What do you do with a dead person? You bury him. So Christ was buried. Since we are "in Christ" we died with him and we were also buried with him; spiritually when we were born again and symbolically when we were baptized.

Now this has some profound implications for us as Paul goes

on to point out. He tells us that since we are united with Christ and we died and were buried with Christ, then **the body of sin has been rendered powerless.** We must follow Paul's words carefully here in verse 6: *"We know that our old self was crucified with him in order that the body of sin might be brought to nothing, so that we would no longer be enslaved to sin."*

There are two phrases in this verse which must be contrasted and clarified. The first is the phrase "our old self," or as the KJV says "our old man." This phrase refers to the old, unregenerate self; the person we were before we came to Christ. That old man was crucified and nailed on the cross with Christ, and he was taken down from the cross and buried with Christ. The implication of the death of the old self is that "the body of sin" might be done away with. This second phrase, "the body of sin" refers to the sin nature which still resides in us as long as we live in this dying, mortal body; this body and this nature we inherited from Adam. This "body of sin" has been "brought to nothing." The translators struggle with this phrase. Some say "destroyed," some say "done away with." My own preferred translation would be "rendered powerless," or "rendered ineffective." The old nature (or "body of sin") no longer has the power to tyrannize or rule over us as it once did. *"That we would no longer be enslaved to sin."*

This is what Paul repeats in verse 7: *"For one who has died has been set free from sin."* That is a difficult verse to grasp fully, but the conclusion is clear; through our union with Christ in his death, we have been freed from the grip and tyranny of sin.

So far, Paul has been dealing with one side of the truth of our union with Christ; what we have been freed from. But there is even more glorious truth here. Remember, we are united with Christ. What is true of him is now true of us. He died. He was buried. But he didn't stay dead. He didn't stay buried. This is where Paul's whole argument is headed. Look back at verse 4: *"We were buried therefore with him by baptism into death, in order that, just as Christ was raised from the dead by the glory of the Father, we too might walk in newness of life."*

It is found again in verse 8-10: *"Now if we have died with Christ, we believe that we will also live with him. We know that*

Christ, being raised from the dead, will never die again; death no longer has dominion over him. For the death he died he died to sin, once for all, but the life he lives he lives to God."

Christ didn't stay in the tomb. He walked out alive! What's more, when he walked out alive, we walked out with him. Because of our union with Christ, we too may live a new life, a resurrection life; a life that is dead to sin and alive to God and his will and power and purpose in us.

Continue in a life of sin? No way! It is unthinkable!

Paul goes on to make a very specific application. There is actually a cluster of them in verses 11-14. We are only going to look at one of them here and save the others for the next chapter. This brings me back to the question with which I opened this chapter. **What do you reckon?**

Look at verse 11: *"So you also must consider yourselves dead to sin and alive to God in Christ Jesus."*

The King James Version translates it this way: *"Likewise reckon yourselves to be dead indeed unto sin, but alive unto God."* **What do you reckon?**

This is the very first command or use of the imperative verb form in the entire Book of Romans. Up until now, the whole letter has been describing what God has done; his work of grace in loving us and sending Christ to be the sacrifice for our sin and then justifying us when we place our faith in him. In this verse, we find the very first command directed toward us as Christ's followers. And what is it? "Reckon." "Consider." "Count." Have we seen this word before? Actually we have. It is the same word that is used back in Romans 4 where we are told that God took our faith and "reckoned" it or "counted" it, or "credited" it to us as righteousness. It means to take into account, figure it out, factor it in, add it up. Use your head and your logic. Think! Calculate! Understand!

What shall we reckon? Reckon yourself to be dead to sin but alive to God. Take into account the new reality that you have been removed from Adam and his influence, effect and inheritance. You are now united with Christ. The person you used to be is dead yet you are alive; a new person, living a new life in the sphere and influence of God. Continue in a life of sin? No way! *"How can we who died to sin still live in it?"* **The believer's union with Christ in his death, burial and resurrection makes a life of continued sinning unthinkable.**

I conclude with three questions for you as the reader to consider.

1. Have you been united with Christ? Have you put your faith in him as Savior and Lord?
2. Did you know that you have been united with Christ? Has anyone ever explained to you that you are now "in Christ" and what is true of him is true of you?
3. Are you reckoning this to be true and are you living like one who has been united with Christ; as one who is dead to sin and alive to God?

When I was pastoring our little church in Nairobi, Kenya, Florence (names changed for privacy) was one of our most faithful worshipers and workers. She was there every Sunday like clockwork. But her husband, Samuel, rarely came. He was not a believer and loved the good life on weekends too much to waste a Sunday coming to church. I visited numerous times in their home and drank lots of tea. Samuel was always very polite. He listened to our message. But he simply liked his old life too much to make a commitment to Christ.

Then one day Florence called me. "Pastor, please come for another visit. Samuel has been saved!" I went to visit. What a different home it was! For some who come to Christ, the changes are gradual. For Samuel, it was dramatic, as though someone had turned on a light switch. His face glowed with the love of Christ.

"What changed your mind about following Christ?" I asked.

He thought for a moment and then answered: "I realized that what I would gain by following Christ was far more valuable than anything I was giving up." He went on. "Now when my friends call me up and want me to go partying with them on weekends, I just tell them that the old Samuel is dead. The new Samuel doesn't enjoy those things anymore."

What do you reckon? Reckon yourself to be dead to sin but alive to God in Christ Jesus.

11

A NEW ALLEGIANCE, A NEW OBEDIENCE
Romans 6:12-14

Does the doctrine of justification by grace through faith encourage us to continue in a sinful lifestyle? This is the pressing question that Paul is addressing in Romans 6. In the first five chapters of Romans, Paul lays out the great themes of the gospel. It is a radical message that men can be "justified freely by God's grace," and that "where sin increased, grace increased all the more."

This leads Paul to address a logical question. He phrases it this way in Romans 6:1: *"What shall we say then? Are we to continue in sin that grace may abound?"* Does the doctrine of justification by faith encourage us to continue sinning?

Let me phrase the question a little differently by introducing some theological language. The two words I want to contrast and compare are "justification" and "sanctification." The word "justification" is one that we have already been considering in the first five chapters of Romans. It is a legal word, borrowed from the world of courts and courtrooms. It means "to declare someone righteous." It is an act of a judge or someone in legal authority who considers all the evidence and the law and its implications and demands and then makes an authoritative declaration that a person has right standing in the eyes of the court. All charges have been dismissed, all obligations met.

The word "sanctification" means "to make righteous or holy." While justification has to do with one's status and legal standing, sanctification has to do with one's conduct and behavior. Sanctification is a process by which the follower of Christ becomes holy and righteous in thoughts, words and actions. It is important to keep these two terms and concepts clear in our minds; justification = declared righteous; sanctification = made righteous. Now let me rephrase the question Paul is wrestling with in Romans 6. **Does justification by faith make sanctification unnecessary or unimportant?** Does the fact that we are declared righteous before God's court as a free gift of grace mean that we can now continue living any way we please?

In the previous chapter we looked at the first answer to this question, and we found that **the believer's union with Christ makes a life of continued sin unthinkable.** What we discovered in Romans 6:1-11 is that, as believers, we have been united with Christ in his death and his resurrection. Because of our union with Christ, what is true of Christ is now true of us. He died. We died with him. He rose from the dead. We rose from the dead with him.

Paul then issued this exhortation; the first command in the entire Book of Romans, in Romans 6:11. *"So you also must consider (reckon) yourselves dead to sin and alive to God in Christ Jesus."* Realize who you are. Understand your new identity. Take it into account. Let it soak into your mind and seep down into your actions.

I always enjoyed the opportunities I had over the years to go back to Kenya (where I grew up) to visit. Each time we did, there would come a time when I would borrow a car from one of my brothers. I would settle myself behind the steering wheel. But before starting the car, I would take a few minutes to do some reckoning. Here is how it went. "I am in Kenya now. In Kenya, people drive on the left side of the road. If I want to stay alive, I must remember where I am and act accordingly!" I had to reckon my new reality. Then I had to live out that new reality in my actions and reactions as I drove out onto the street. Then the next thing I would usually do is turn on the windshield wiper when I meant to use the turn signal, because it was on the wrong side of the steering column! Sometimes our reckoning can take a while to work its way down into our doing. But this is what Paul is calling us to do in verse 11; to constantly feed into our consciousness the new reality (that we are "in Christ" and therefore dead to sin and alive to God) until that begins to control every aspect of our lives.

Paul then follows this overarching command with three more commands. I think it is very interesting that after five and a half chapters with no commands, we suddenly run into this little nest full of commands in the middle of chapter 6. I would also point out that we will not see another command until we get to Romans 12, so we'd better pay attention to these.

Verse 12: *"Let not sin therefore reign in your mortal body, to make you obey its passions."*

The grammatical form of these commands in the original language is very important. For example, the command we found in verse 11 to "consider (reckon) yourselves dead to sin and alive to God" is in the present imperative verb form. This is used to express the need for continuous or repetitive action. "Constantly reckon yourselves…"

The form in verse 12 is also in the present imperative, but with the negative attached to it. The use of this construction means we must stop and desist from something we are presently doing. We can translate it, "Stop letting sin reign…" Sin has been reigning. This was the reality of our previous life. Now we live under a new reality. The metaphor of "reigning" is significant in Paul's letter. Remember that Paul was writing to the believers in Rome. *"To all those in Rome…,"* he wrote in Romans 1:7. Rome was the capital of an empire that extended over Europe, the Middle East and North Africa. It was where the emperor ruled. Politics, power, pomp and circumstance were a daily part of life for all who lived in Rome. Who is in power? Who is out of power? Who exercises authority? Paul borrows this language to teach us spiritual truth. The word for "reign" is simply the verb form of the word for "king." Who is acting as king? Who is the emperor?

Paul has used this language before. Back in Romans 5:12-21, Paul used this same word several times. We were told that through Adam, sin invaded and with sin came death. Death spread and we are told that death "reigned" and that "sin reigned in death" over all men who are in Adam. That is the natural man's condition. Sin reigns. Sin is his king, his ruler, his sovereign. But when we trust in Christ, all that changes. We have changed kings and kingdoms and families. We are no longer "in Adam." We are "in Christ." The first thing that needs to happen when we "reckon" that new reality to be true is that we must stop letting sin reign in our mortal body. We must stop obeying the old king.

The rest of this verse gives us further insight into what it means to obey the old king. It means to obey the evil desires that are part of our inheritance in Adam. Stop letting sin reign *"in your mortal body to make you obey its passions."* This is our present dilemma. We have a new nature, but we still live in mortal bodies with the remnant of our old nature attached. We still have strong passions; desires of the flesh that pull us toward evil. We must stop obeying those desires. We must stop letting sin reign over us.

The second of the three commands is found in verse 13: *"Do not present your members to sin, as instruments for unrighteousness."* Once again, this is a present imperative with a negative. It can also be translated, "Stop what you are doing. **Stop offering the members of your body to sin**, as instruments for unrighteousness." Paul is using interesting language and metaphor here. The word is "members", referring to the various parts of the human body; hands, feet, ears, eyes. The word "instruments" is very broad in its usage. It is used, for example, to describe a farmer's implements or a black smith's tools. One of the most common uses, especially in the plural as it is here, is to describe the weapons of a soldier.

Paul is inviting us to think of the various parts of our bodies as tools or weapons. Let's do something. Hold up your hand in front of you so you can see it. Open it and close it. It is a marvelous piece of engineering, isn't it? It is incredible in its dexterity and the diversity of tasks it can perform. Now clench it into a fist. Imagine it smashing into someone's face and the damage it could do. Now open it, and picture it backhanding someone across the face. Picture it forming an obscene gesture to insult someone. Imagine it reaching out to pick up that pornographic magazine off the news stand in the airport, or clicking on that enticing website on the internet. A tool, an implement; how have you used your hand this week? Where has it been?

Let's think about another member of the body. Put out your tongue. Not far; just enough so you can see it. It isn't very big, but I am told it is actually the strongest muscle in the body. But that is not where its real power lies. Picture your tongue spitting out profanity and foul language when you're angry. Imagine it smoothly spilling out lies. Listen to it calmly and sarcastically shredding another person's reputation through gossip. What a tool for evil! James describes it as a spark that can set a whole forest on fire.

Paul says that is what has been happening. That was the old reality when sin reigned. But now he says to us, "Stop! Stop offering your members as tools for doing evil." That is the negative side of Paul's teaching. That is what we are to stop doing. Instead he goes on to state it positively; what we are to do instead. This brings us to the third command, found in the second part of verse 13: *"But present yourselves to God as those who have been brought from death to life..."* Here we are back to the first part of the chapter, aren't we? We died with Christ. We also rose from the dead with Christ. *"Reckon yourselves to be dead to sin, but alive to God."* That is our new reality. Reckon it to be true, and as one who has been brought from death to life **present yourselves to God.** We have a new identity. We belong to a new family and a new kingdom. Present yourself to your new king, to God himself.

Once again, the use of tenses is intriguing here. There are two common ways for expressing a command in Greek. There is the present tense, which describes continuous, repeated, ongoing action. There is another tense that describes an urgent call to action; do it now! Which tense do you thing Paul uses here? I think most of us would guess the present tense for continuous action. However, Paul throws us a curve here; a bit of a surprise. He uses the tense to describe urgent, point in time action. Offer yourselves to God. Point in time. Urgent. Do it now.

Maybe a couple of illustrations will help us understand what Paul is calling for here. One is the picture of a soldier who is enlisting in the army and reporting for the first time to his commanding officer. He is presenting himself, offering himself to his commander, and with that act, he is placing himself under authority and accepting his responsibility to obey the officer's commands. That act of presenting himself is a very significant act which influences everything that follows. Or maybe, picture a person who has just become a citizen of a new country. After a long and complicated immigration process, she now stands before an official and is required to pledge allegiance to her new nation. It is a tremendously significant moment, as she takes upon herself the responsibilities of a citizen of her new nation.

I believe this is what Paul is calling on us to do. Yes, there will be a daily outworking of the new reality, a daily reckoning of the new identity and the new authority. But Paul is here calling for an initial acknowledgment and acceptance of one's new responsibilities and of one's new allegiance and submission to a new king and a new kingdom. I wonder if you have ever made such a commitment or taken such a stand?

The rest of the verse is a follow-up. The verb is not repeated, but Paul simply adds additional understanding to the scope of the command. It completes the symmetry of Paul's thought and also puts more specifics to the command for what we are doing when we "present ourselves." *"Present the members of your body to God as instruments for righteousness."*

Hold up your hand again. Now imagine it gently comforting a crying child, holding your spouse's hand, wiping away a friend's tears, giving someone a reassuring pat on the shoulder, preparing a meal for a sick friend, writing an encouraging note, picking up your Bible. What a tool! What a valuable implement for service to God!

Put your tongue out again. Picture it now in prayer, giving someone a sincere compliment, telling the truth, expressing an apology, teaching a children's Bible class, sharing Christ with a friend. What a tool! What a valuable and powerful implement for service to Christ!

That is the key. Offer yourself and every part of your body to God for service to him. Paul's clinching argument for all of this is expressed in verse 14: *"For sin will have no dominion over you, since you are not under law but under grace."*

We need to understand. The purpose of salvation, of justification, of redemption is not just to set us free from the penalty of sin, but also to set us free from the dominion or tyranny of sin in our lives. Paul says this in all confidence; if you have been justified by faith, sin is no longer your master. You have been set free! You have changed kings and kingdoms. You are not under law anymore. You are under grace. We will examine that statement more fully in the next chapter, but for now, just think of it as a statement or description of the old kingdom of sin, death and the dread of the law as contrasted to the new kingdom of God; a kingdom of grace and new life and of freedom from the tyranny of sin.

Once again, I close with three sets of questions. First, do you belong to this new family? Have you placed your faith in Jesus Christ as Savior? Have you been united with him by faith?

Second set of questions: As a member of this new kingdom and this new family, do you realize what it means? Have you understood and reckoned with this new reality, and have you presented yourself in allegiance to your new King and your members to him as instruments of righteousness?

When I was in high school, I attended a school for missionary children at Kijabe, Kenya. One Sunday evening for our young people's meeting, they held a campfire service. I don't remember the name or identity of the speaker. I do remember that he quoted the words of Jim Elliot, one of the missionaries who died at the hands of the Auca Indians in Ecuador: "He is no fool who gives up what he cannot keep to gain what he cannot lose." I also remember that the speaker challenged us to pray and to offer our lives to God as a kind of blank check for him to fill in. I remember bowing my head and saying to God: "Whatever you want me to do, Lord, I will do it. Wherever you want me to go, I am willing to go. Whatever you want me to be, I will be. I submit my will to you as Lord and King of my life." Have you ever prayed such a prayer and made such a commitment?

Final question: Maybe you have made such a commitment to the Lord. You have reported for duty. If you have, then this is my question for you: Is your life, in its present form, consistent with that commitment you made? How about this past week? Sometimes, old habits die hard, just like turning the windshield wipers on when you mean to put on the turn signal! If that's the case, you need to confess that to the Lord, receive his forgiveness and be restored to fellowship. Then you need to come back and present yourself once again in submission and allegiance to your new King.

12

CHOOSE YOUR MASTER
Romans 6:15-23

In this chapter we are considering Romans 6:15-23. In the entirety of chapter 6, Paul has been dealing with the same question or objection to the doctrine of justification by grace through faith. That is the question: Does justification by faith encourage us to continue in a life of sin?

As we look at this final section, it is fair to ask: Is this simply a repetition of what Paul has said in the first half of the chapter, or is Paul introducing something new? I think it is actually both.

First, it is a repetition in the sense that he is dealing with the same basic question of justification by faith and its effects; does the outrageous and radical nature of free grace encourage us to continue in sin?

Secondly, we shall find that Paul will make the same application and challenge to us as Christ's followers when he urges us to present the members of our bodies as servants to God.

Thirdly, I would make the point that because the second half of the chapter is repetitious in many respects, we should keep in mind that the Bible often repeats things for the sake of emphasis. It is one way of saying, "THIS IS IMPORTANT! DON'T MISS IT!"

But I would also point out that while there is much about the second half of this chapter that is repetitious, there are some subtle differences; slight changes in nuance and language which enhance our understanding of the overall message of the chapter.

The first subtle difference I want to highlight is in the way the question in verse 15 is worded: *"What then? Are we to sin because we are not under law but under grace?"* At first glance, this may look like a simple repetition of verse 1: *"What shall we say, then? Are we to continue in sin that grace may abound?"* But there is a slight difference in nuance. The form of the verb for "sinning" is different. In verse 1 it is present, continuous action; continual sinning as a pattern and lifestyle. In verse 15, it is in a form that describes the possibility of occasional acts of sin. In verse 1, Paul is asking the question whether continuing in sin were actually somehow meritorious. Won't we be doing God a favor because we are giving him more scope to demonstrate grace? In verse 15, Paul is reflecting instead the attitude that sin is no big deal. Since we are under grace and not under law, what is the harm in the occasional sin now and then? After all, we can always confess it afterwards, right?

So we first find that the form of the question is slightly different. The second subtle difference lies in the fact that there is a slightly different metaphor underlying Paul's choice of words in this section. In the first half of the chapter, Paul used the language of kings and kingdoms and ruling authority. Who is king? Who is the emperor in your life? Is sin still reigning or have you presented yourself in service to your new King?

In this last paragraph, Paul uses a slightly different word picture. He uses the language of slaves and slavery. Once again, it was a picture that would have had a vivid impact on his readers. Historians estimate that over half of the population of the Roman Empire consisted of slaves. There were many different classes of slaves, from common laborers to household slaves to well-educated slaves who served as tutors and mentors for the children of wealthy households. But regardless of their classification, a slave was still a slave and owed absolute allegiance and obedience to his or her master. So while the first half of Romans 6 calls us to allegiance to a new king, the second half calls us to obey a new master.

With that overview and comparison between the two sections of the chapter, let's take a closer look at how Paul develops his thought. After raising the question in verse 15, Paul answers it with the same vehement negative he used in verse 2: *"By no means!"* God forbid! No way!

Paul then goes on to state a universal principle in verse 16. *"Do you not know that if you present yourselves to anyone as obedient slaves, you are slaves of the one whom you obey, either of sin, which leads to death, or of obedience, which leads to righteousness?"*

This verse is really the heart of this section. If you get nothing else out of this section, hear what Paul is saying in this verse. The point that Paul is making is that there is no middle ground. There is no third option. There is no neutral position. We are either slaves to sin, which leads to death, or we are slaves to obeying God, which leads to righteousness.

It is my observation that many in the world, even many Christians, are not really convinced of this fact. We want to believe there is a third alternative. Imagine that life is a multiple choice question on an exam:

I want to be…
> **a. A slave to sin**
> **b. A slave to God**

We don't like the way that question is made up. We want more choices. But what Paul is saying is very clear. There are only two choices. You are a slave of one or the other. Make your choice. We might ask if Paul is the only one who puts the alternatives in such stark terms. How about Jesus himself? In John 8:34, Jesus says, *"I tell you the truth, everyone who practices sin is a slave to sin."* That is pretty black and white, isn't it?

We must understand this. Sin is not a benign, harmless, leisure-time activity. It is a tyrant, and when we yield to sin, we are obeying it. It is easy to recognize this point in others' lives and in society. The epidemic of addictions and addictive behavior provide multiple illustrations. What we are not so aware of is the tyranny of sin in our own lives in things like pride, the pursuit of fame or others' approval, the "me first" mentality. We may think we are asserting control over our own lives and declaring our "freedom," but in fact, when we serve self, we are serving sin. We do not choose whether to be a slave or not. We only choose which master we wish to serve. Having laid out this basic principle, Paul then goes on to contrast the two masters and the consequence of the two paths.

Let's consider first the description of the person who is **a slave**

to sin. Paul has this to say in verse 20: *"For when you were slaves to sin, you were free in regard to righteousness."* You weren't bothered by trying to live up to God's standards. You didn't struggle against sin. You just let it happen. Do what feels good. Do what everyone else is doing. That sounds pretty good, doesn't it? But that is not the whole story. Look at what he adds in verse 21: *"But what fruit were you getting at that time from the things of which you are now ashamed? For the end of those things is death!"*

What Paul is telling us is basic truth. Every path leads somewhere. Before you choose a path, choose a destination. The path of being "free in regard to righteousness" leads somewhere. There is fruit or consequences of choosing that path. One of them is shame. "Things you are now ashamed of!" That's where serving sin ends up. A fruitless life of shame. And the final result? Death.

In contrast to being a slave to sin, Paul lays down the alternative: **a slave to righteousness and a slave to God.** This is what he describes in verses 22-23. *"But now that you have been set free from sin and have become slaves of God, the fruit you get leads to sanctification and its end, eternal life. For the wages of sin is death, but the free gift of God is eternal life in Christ Jesus our Lord."*

What a difference in paths and in destinations! Slaves to God; fruit or benefits that lead to holiness (or sanctification) and the end result of eternal life. What a contrast between the two masters!

This the basic reality that Paul is laying down. There are but two masters. We are slaves of one or we are slaves of the other. We are either slaves of sin, or we are slaves to God. Before you make your choice, carefully consider the two options and where they lead. Let's look now at how Paul applies this basic reality in the heart of this section, in verses 17-18:

"But thanks be to God, that you who were once slaves of sin have become obedient from the heart to the standard of teaching to which you were committed, and, having been set free from sin, have become slaves of righteousness."

I want to point out something here. Paul did not know these people to whom he was writing. He had no first-hand knowledge of their everyday lives. He could not say this based on personal observation of their behavior. Yet he says, with all confidence,

"You have been set free from sin and have become slaves to righteousness."

How did Paul know this? He knew it because it is true of every true believer, every true child of God. Because this is, first and foremost, a positional truth. It is something that is true because we are "in Christ" as we learned in previous chapters.

Let's turn to a parallel passage in 1 Corinthians 6:19-20: *"Or do you not know that your body is a temple of the Holy Spirit within you, whom you have from God? You are not your own. For you were bought with a price."* In these verses, Paul is not telling us what we act like. He is telling us who we are and who we belong to. Only at the very end of verse 20 does he tell us how to behave: *"So glorify God in your body."*

Paul is doing the same thing in the passage in front of us in Romans 6. You were a slave to sin, but God redeemed you and set you free. This is what God has done for you. Now here is the application in verse 19: *"I am speaking in human terms, because of your natural limitations. For just as you once presented your members as slaves to impurity and to lawlessness leading to more lawlessness, so now present your members as slaves to righteousness leading to sanctification."*

Here is the final command in this chapter (and the last one we will see until chapter 12!) It is simply a repeat of the command we saw back in verse 13 in the same call to urgent action. We are slaves of righteousness and of God. That is our new identity. Now it is time to start acting like one. It is time to start serving him, to start presenting our members to him as slaves to righteousness.

Should we go on sinning because we are not under law, but under grace? No way! How could we even ask such a question? Don't we realize who we are? Don't we realize who our new master is? Don't we realize where the two paths ultimately lead?

A couple of questions before I conclude. Who is your master? Remember, there are only two options. If you are a follower of Christ, if you have been justified by faith, if you have been born again into the family of God, then the answer to that question is clear. God is your Master.

But that leads to the follow-up question. Have you lived this past week as though God were your master? Remember, in the previous chapter we talked about our hands and our tongues as examples of members of our body that we can use to either serve sin or to serve God. What have you done with your hand this week? What about your tongue? Or let's extend the thought. What about your eyes? How have you used them this week? How about your ears? What have you deliberately chosen to put into your ears? We have a choice. We can offer the members of our bodies in service to impurity and ever increasing wickedness. Or we can offer them in service to God and to righteousness leading to holiness and sanctification.

As I was preparing this chapter, I also happened to be reading in my devotions in the Book of Deuteronomy. In that book, there is the record of the final words of God through Moses, prior to Israel's entry into the Promised Land. There are many wonderful promises of blessings they can expect from God under their covenant agreement with God. But then there is a warning in Deuteronomy 29:19: *"When such a person hears the words of this oath, he invokes a blessing on himself and therefore thinks, "I will be safe, even though I persist in going my own way." This will bring disaster..."* (quoted from NIV)

The words brought me up short. Was this not the Old Testament equivalent of a believer today who says, "Shall I sin because I am not under law but under grace?" "I will be safe, even though I persist in going my own way." Is that what you've been saying to yourself? Is that the lie you've been telling yourself? God warned, "This will bring disaster." In Paul's words in Romans 6, there is also an implied warning. Let us not abuse the covenant of grace. We have been set free from sin. Why serve the old slave master any longer? Why keep doing the things that led to shame and eventually to death? We have been saved to serve our new Master, the Lord Jesus Christ.

And lest you chafe against the language of slave and master, I offer you the words of Thomas Cranmer, the English Reformer who died in the flames as a martyr for his faith. He described God as the one "whose service is perfect freedom."

I have always loved the traditional songs of Christmas, because they include such great gospel content. One particular song by Charles Wesley began to resonate in my mind as I was writing the conclusion to this chapter.

"Come, Thou long expected Jesus, Born to set Thy people free." Set us free from what? The next line answers the question: *"From our fears and sins release us."* Jesus didn't come to set us free **to** sin. He came to set us free **from** sin. The second verse of the song also echoes themes from Romans 6. *"Born Thy people to deliver, Born a Child, and yet a King; Born to reign in us forever, Now Thy gracious kingdom bring. By Thine own eternal Spirit, Rule in all our hearts alone; By Thine all-sufficient merit, Raise us to Thy glorious Throne."*

13

WE'RE FREE!

Romans 7:1-6

In the time period in which Paul wrote the Book of Romans, every child raised in a devout Jewish home came to recognize very early the presence of a very significant influence in his life. From earliest memory he heard it recited in his home and in his synagogue. It became the chief text in his school. He learned to read from it. He memorized long portions of it. It was part of his racial and family as well as his religious identity.

The influence to which I am referring is the Torah, the Law of God, as it was recorded by Moses in the first five books of the Jewish Scriptures. Paul was no exception. In his own writings he tells us: *"as touching the Law, I was a Pharisee."* In other words, he was trained in a school of theological thought which held the Law in highest esteem and he had studied it with the greatest vigor and seriousness.

With this background in mind, it is highly significant then when we read Paul making statements like these: *"But now the righteousness of God has been manifested apart from the law." (3:21).* Or, *"For we hold that one is justified by faith apart from works of the law." (3:28).* Or, even more significantly, *"You are not under law but under grace."(6:14)*

In the first five chapters of Romans, Paul has presented the doctrine of justification by faith. At the conclusion of chapter 5, it is as though Paul could see hands going up all over his audience with questions or objections to what he had just said. And so he stopped, and in chapters 6 and 7 he deals with those questions and objections. The first question he addressed in chapter 6 was this: Doesn't justification by faith encourage people to continue in a sinful lifestyle or to treat sin lightly? Paul's answer to that question is a forceful, "No way!"

Before we move on to chapter 7, I want to point out a connection here to the earlier chapters. As I said, chapters 6 and 7 represent a lengthy parenthesis in the letter as he departs from his main line of logic to deal with objections and questions. Yet the two chapters are quite distinct in their subject matter. It is also worth noting that, in their content, these two chapters actually line up remarkably well with Paul's logic from the earlier chapters. You may remember that in those chapters, Paul was dealing with the question: Who needs the Gospel? We looked at three different case studies as Paul brought different categories of people before God's court and argued the legal case against them. The first person he brought before the court was the "pagan man;" the man who lived an openly sinful life without any regard for the law of God. It struck me that these are the people who might be inclined to think that if they can be justified by grace through faith, then "let's keep on sinning!" Or at least others might make that argument: Paul, if you tell the pagan that he can be saved by just believing in Christ and if God truly "justifies the wicked" as you said in Romans 4:5, then what's to stop him from just continuing in sin? That is the objection Paul has answered in chapter 6.

But you may recall that Paul then proceeds to bring two more categories of people before God's court; the moral man and the religious man. In both cases, these were Jews; people who had the law, knew the law and honored the law of God. These were the people who were most likely to object to Paul's statements that it was possible to be justified by faith "apart from observing the law." It is to their objections that Paul turns in chapter 7.

"Paul, what do you mean by these statements about the law? How can you, as a former Pharisee, taught by the best Jewish rabbis, say these things? And if we are saved by faith apart from the law, then what is the relationship between the follower of Christ and the law?" If you have read the Book of Acts, you know that this was a burning and divisive issue in the early church. It comes up again and again in the epistles of the New Testament. It was, and remains, an important and difficult topic. As a result, Romans 7 is an important and difficult passage. We are going to spend three chapters working our way through it.

In this chapter, we are going to focus on just the first 6 verses and the title of the chapter is: **We're Free!** Let's take just a moment to reread the entire text so it is fresh in our minds.

"Or do you not know, brothers—for I am speaking to those who know the law—that the law is binding on a person only as long as he lives? For a married woman is bound by law to her husband while he lives, but if her husband dies she is released from the law of marriage. Accordingly, she will be called an adulteress if she lives with another man while her husband is alive. But if her husband dies, she is free from that law, and if she marries another man she is not an adulteress. Likewise, my brothers, you also have died to the law through the body of Christ, so that you may belong to another, to him who has been raised from the dead, in order that we may bear fruit for God. For while we were living in the flesh, our sinful passions, aroused by the law, were at work in our members to bear fruit for death. But now we are released from the law, having died to that which held us captive, so that we serve in the new way of the Spirit and not in the old way of the written code." (Romans 7:1-6)

Paul first introduces his specific target audience for this section of the letter; *"those who know the law."* As I said, these are the Jews in his audience who previously relied on their observance of the law for their right standing with God. He then uses the Jewish, or Biblical law of marriage to draw an analogy and make his point, which is that death ends a legal relationship. A woman is bound to her husband as long as he lives. But when he dies, she is free. She can marry another man without penalty and without stigma. The death of her husband has set her free from the law of marriage.

Now Paul makes his application in verse 4, and it is a twist in logic. *"Likewise, my brothers, you also have died to the law through the body of Christ."* Did you catch the twist? In the case of marriage, it is the husband who dies, setting the wife free. In the matter before us, it is the believer (the wife in his analogy, if you will) who dies. But the principle holds true (at least by analogy) that death severs the legal relationship. *"You have also died to the law through the body of Christ."* In making this point, Paul is going back to chapter 6 and the truth of our union with Christ. When we put our faith in Jesus Christ and are justified by faith, we are "baptized into Christ" or united with Christ. What is true of him is true of us. He died. We died with him. And when we died, our legal relationship with the law was changed. When we died with Christ, we were not only set free from sin and death; we were also set free from the law.

Let's take a moment to think back on the realities of life in the "old marriage" under the law. What was life like back then? Here is Paul's description in verse 5. *"For while we were living in the flesh, our sinful passions, aroused by the law were at work in our members to bear fruit for death."*

That was the old reality. The phrase "living in the flesh" is referring to the pre-conversion, pre-Christian life. In this life, the law is described as arousing "sinful passions." Sin is so deeply entrenched in us, that the law's effect is to stir it up. It is universal among Adam's descendents, is it not? Tell a child not to stick a fork in the electric socket, and what does he want to do? He may never have even thought of doing it before! But now? He has a great desire to do it. Law stirs up sinful passions. Say "No!" and the Adamic nature says, "Yes!" Tell him, "Don't!" and the son of Adam says, "I will!"

There's another phrase in this verse: These passions *"bear fruit for death."* If we put this back into the context of the marriage analogy, the fruit can be seen as the children of the old marriage. And the reality was a cruel one. There were none! This was a marriage that only produced miscarriages or still-born children. It is a picture of barrenness and futility.

We also find that in the old marriage we were in bondage. If we look at verse 6, we find that the law is described as something which *"held us captive."* The law was an unrelenting master. We could not keep it, yet we could not escape its demands.

Finally, we find that the law, at its very best, was an external standard which only produced external conformity. At the end of verse 6, Paul speaks of the *"old way of the written code,"* or as the KJV translates it: *"the oldness of the letter."* As I read those words of Paul, I am taken back to all that Jesus said in the Sermon on the Mount. There Jesus went beyond the letter of the law and external conformity to a legal standard and, in doing so, penetrated to the matters of the heart. "You want to talk of murder? Let's go deeper and talk about anger in the heart. You want to speak of adultery? Let's go to the heart of the matter and talk about lust. You want to demonstrate your righteousness by praying on the street corner? Let's go into the secret place of prayer and evaluate what happens there." The law doesn't change the heart. It never could.

I will pause here to point out that this is true not only of the Jewish or Old Testament law; it is also true of the laws of all religions. All laws, no matter how profound, ultimately lead to this kind of sterile, external conformity; a loveless, barren marriage. People sometimes compare religions and observe that they are very much alike. By this, they usually mean that their moral standards and requirements are often very similar. This is all well and good. But unless we can do something about the sin that indwells us, we cannot keep these laws and standards. They just stir up our passions, produce empty futility, create bondage and even at their best produce only a kind of external, hypocritical righteousness; the kind Jesus compared to "white-washed sepulchers" filled with decaying bodies.

But the good news that Paul is announcing to all who will listen and receive it with faith is that **we're free** from all of that.

Let's go back to Paul's analogy of marriage. This is the key to Paul's whole argument in verse 4: *"Likewise, my brothers, you also have died to the law through the body of Christ, that you may belong to another…"* There is the key. Justification by faith resulted not only in the end of the old marriage, but in the beginning of a new marriage to a new husband. We are now free to "belong to another." Who is this new husband? It is *"him who has been raised from the dead."* It is Jesus Christ.

Earlier metaphors that Paul used in chapter 6 stressed obedience and submission. The marriage metaphor he uses here captures the reality that ours is a very intimate and personal love relationship. We belong to Jesus Christ in the same way that a bride belongs to her husband. And it is a love relationship with a purpose, *"that we may bear fruit for God."* Contrast that to the old marriage; barren, futile, bearing fruit for death. *"Bearing fruit for God!"* What a wonderful description of the purpose of life; all of life. As our relationship with Jesus Christ grows, our lives will be transformed as we are sanctified and produce the fruit of righteousness as his life flows through us.

In this new spiritual marriage relationship, we are also set free from spiritual bondage as Paul tells us in verse 6: *"But now we are released from the law having died to that which held us captive, so that we serve in the new way of the Spirit, and not in the old way of the written code."*

"We have been released from the law." That is the new reality. We've been set free from the old husband. What does this mean? It means that the law's demands have been fulfilled for us by Christ. We are no longer required to strive to obey the law in order to earn our salvation or be accepted by God. **We're free!** It is not a freedom to run riot according to the pattern of the pagan in chapter 1. Rather it is a freedom to "serve in the new way of the Spirit."

Well, we have lots of ground yet to cover. As I said, this is the first of three chapters on Romans 7. Paul will continue to address the issue of the law and its role and purpose in the rest of the chapter.

I heard an illustration many years ago from one of my professors. It is a hypothetical story of a very unhappy woman, trapped in a loveless marriage to a harsh and demanding husband. The man treated her as a virtual slave. Every morning, before he left for work, he would make a list of all the household chores he wanted her to do while he was gone; wash the windows, do the laundry, wax the floor... The list would vary from day to day, but it was always long and exhausting. When he returned at the end of the day, he would take the list and go around the house to be sure that it had all been done to his satisfaction. If it wasn't, he would rant and rave and shout and sometimes even hit her.

Needless to say, she was absolutely miserable, living in fear and perpetually exhausted, hating every minute of every day. Then one day, her husband died. Time passed and she met another man. What a contrast! He was gentle, considerate, loving, and she soon fell deeply in love with him. They were married, and the marriage was very happy. It was hard to believe she was the same woman. She hated to see him leave in the morning, and she couldn't wait for him to return in the evening so they could be together.

One day as she was sorting through some old storage boxes while going about her chores, she ran across an old piece of paper. She recognized it as one of the lists her old husband used to leave, listing her required chores for the day. As she read it through she came to an amazing realization. That very day, she had already done everything on that list and more. And she had done it with a song in her heart and energy to spare, because she had done it freely, from her heart and out of love for her new husband.

We're free! We have been released from the law so that we may serve in the new way of the Spirit! The opening stanza of an old Philip Bliss hymn says it so well:

Free from the law, O happy condition!
Jesus hath bled, and there is remission.
Cursed by the law, and bruised by the fall,
Grace hath redeemed us, once for all.

14

WHAT'S THE PROBLEM?

Romans 7:7-13

In Romans 6 and 7, Paul has paused in his writing to deal with questions about the doctrine of justification by faith. In Romans 6, Paul has dealt with a question that might have been raised in reference to the godless, irreligious man Paul described in Romans 1: Does the doctrine of justification by faith encourage such a person to continue in a sinful lifestyle? Paul's answer: "No way!"

In Romans 7, Paul is dealing with a second question. What about the law? If we can be justified by faith, apart from observing the law, then what was the law's purpose? What was that all about? And what is our relationship to the law now as Christ's followers? In the first 6 verses of chapter 7, Paul told us that we are free from the law. We died to it, and like a woman whose husband has died, we are now free to enter into a new relationship; a new marriage to Christ. We are not under the law any longer.

But once again, Paul anticipates questions from his readers. Paul has made a couple rather inflammatory statements. In verse 4 he spoke of sinful passions being aroused by the law. And in verse 5 he spoke of the law as something which once bound us or held us in bondage. Paul can now see the hands going up once again. "Paul, are you saying that the law was the source of our problem? Are you telling us that the law was a bad thing?"

Look at the opening of verse 7: *"What then shall we say? That the law is sin?"* The wording is precise. He doesn't ask, "Is the law sinful?" He asks, "Is the law sin?" Are they equated in some way? Are they one and the same? Is the law the problem? Paul answers immediately: *"By no means! Certainly not! No way!"*

I have summarized Paul's message in these verses in three short, propositional statements. Here is the first one: **The law**

is not the problem. Is the law sin? No way! The law is not the problem. In fact, the law does exactly what it was intended to do. Paul goes on in these verses to describe **three things the law was intended to do**; three functions it was to fulfill.

The first thing he points out is that **the law reveals sin.** In the rest of verse 7, we read: *"Yet if it had not been for the law, I would not have known sin. For I would not have known what it is to covet if the law had not said, 'You shall not covet.'"*

Paul said something very similar a few chapters earlier, in Romans 3:20: *"...since through the law comes knowledge of sin."*

The law of God serves as a kind of moral "plumb line." A plumb line is a very simple device; just a string or cord with a heavy metal knob hanging on the end of it. Because of gravity and the weight of the knob, the string hangs straight down. So the carpenter or builder can hold the plumb line next to the wall or cupboard he is building, and he can tell whether it is straight or not. But it is important to understand that the plumb line itself does not make the wall straight or crooked. It only reveals whether it is straight or crooked. That is what the law does for us. It reveals God's holy and righteous standard. When we hold it next to our lives, we are made aware of our sin. We become conscious of how crooked we are. We discover that we are "out of plumb."

Let's look at verse 7 again. Why does Paul pick on this one commandment, the tenth one: *"Thou shalt not covet?"* The word used here for "covet" means either to strongly desire to possess something which belongs to someone else, or a strong desire for a forbidden, taboo or immoral action or object. I believe Paul chooses this one, because it is the commandment that takes the other commandments and exposes the inner motives that lead to their being broken. For example, the seventh commandment tells us "Do not commit adultery." But the tenth commandment tells us not to covet the neighbor's wife. The eighth commandment tells us not to steal. But the tenth commandment tells us not to covet "anything that belongs to your neighbor." The tenth commandment goes beyond the sinful action to the sinful intention, the sinful desire which gives rise to the sinful action.

It is a crookedness within us of which we might have remained ignorant without the law which says, "Thou shalt not covet." It is a plumb line that reveals the crookedness of our hearts as well as our actions.

But the law doesn't just reveal sin. The second thing Paul points out is that **the law stirs up sin.** Let's keep reading in verses 8-10: *"But sin, seizing an opportunity through the commandment, produced in me all kinds of covetousness. For apart from the law, sin lies dead. I was once alive apart from the law, but when the commandment came, sin came alive and I died. The very commandment that promised life proved to be death to me."*

We will look at this in detail in a moment. But for now I simply want to emphasize that one of the effects of the law is to stir up sin. Sin might be lying dead, not in an absolute sense, but relatively speaking. Then the law comes. And when our sinful heart hears those hated words, "Thou shalt not," we immediately rise up and demand, "Who says?"

During our early years living in Abu Dhabi, I used to enjoy taking long walks along the undeveloped beaches near the city. It was a great place to think and pray. One day as I was walking along the beach, I came upon a sea snake about a meter long, lying dead on the shore. I hadn't seen one before, and the markings were quite interesting, so I stood looking at it. Then I took a little piece of wood and tossed it at the snake. Suddenly the "dead" snake came alive, writhing wildly about as it thrashed itself back into the shallow water before swimming away! That's the effect that the law has on sin. Sin and sinful tendencies may lie dormant, undiagnosed and unidentified for long periods of time. Then the law comes and stirs them up, and our natural sinful nature comes flailing into life.

The third thing Paul points out is that **the law exposes sin in its true character.** Look down to verse 13: *"Did that which is good, then, bring death to me? By no means! It was sin, producing death in me through what is good, in order that sin might be shown to be sin, and through the commandment might become sinful beyond measure."*

Through the law, we become aware of the true character of sin;

its terrible rebellion, its awful grip on our lives, its invasiveness, and its final effects. Think of the law as a broom. Now imagine that you live in a house with a dirt floor. I don't mean a dirty floor. I mean a simple thatch house with a dirt floor. Now take your broom and try to sweep the floor. How long will it take before the floor is clean? The answer is never. It will never be clean. Because with every sweep of the broom you simply bring up more dirt. Now, here's my question. What is wrong with your broom? The answer is, there is nothing wrong with the broom. The problem lies in the nature of the dirt floor.

What Paul is telling us is that the law is not the problem. The law is doing what it was intended to do. Paul even goes on to make some very positive statements about the law in verse 12: *"So the law is holy, and the commandment is holy and righteous and good."*

There is nothing wrong with the law. So if the law is not the problem, what is? That brings us to the second of our three propositional statements: **Sin is the problem.** As we see the way Paul speaks of sin in this section as he compares sin and the law, we learn some very important truths about sin and about ourselves.

What the Bible teaches on this subject is in stark contrast to man's thinking and particularly contemporary thinking about man's nature and the nature of sin. In contemporary thinking, if sin is considered at all, it is an act; something external. Maybe we could describe it this way; sometimes good people do bad things. Those bad things could be called sins. But they are external acts, somehow separate from the basically good person who did them in a moment of weakness. And of course, those bad things are really only truly bad if they involve hurting someone else. That is modern man's concept of sin.

Paul paints a very different picture in these verses. First of all, he does not talk about "sins" at all, but about "sin." He uses a singular noun and he personifies sin as an evil entity or presence. In fact, we can discern five truths about sin from these verses.

The first is that **sin is an active, causative force.** We find this in verse 8: *"But sin, seizing an opportunity through the* *commandment, produced in me all kinds of covetousness."* Sin is depicted as active and as actually producing covetous desires in us. Sin is not just an act we commit in a moment of weakness. It is a force, a sinister power that actually produces evil desires and evil deeds. The language is quite interesting here. The phrase, *"seizing an opportunity through the commandment,"* is used to describe the starting point or base of operation for a military expedition or attack. The commandment is used almost like a Trojan horse to slip inside our defenses, and once within the walls, sin uses it as a base to launch an attack against us, stirring up sinful desires within us.

The second truth is that **sin is reactive and rebellious in nature.** Verses 8-9 states: *"But sin, seizing an opportunity through the commandment, produced in me all kinds of covetousness. For apart from the law, sin lies dead. I was once alive apart from the law, but when the commandment came, sin came alive and I died."*

Think with me. What was the first sin; the sin of Adam and Eve? It was a reaction to, and rebellion against, God's rule. All sin is ultimately rebellion. That is why the law stirs it up. The law is God's revealed will. It expresses what God wants. But sin reacts and rebels against what God wants. "I want to do what I want to do. I want to be God in my own life."

What is Paul telling us in verse 9 when he speaks about once being alive apart from the law? I believe Paul is speaking about his own perception and his experience, not actual reality. After all, Paul also wrote in Ephesians 2:1 that we were all *"dead in our trespasses and sins."* What he is saying here is that there was a time when he thought he was OK. He thought he was alive. All was well. Then the law came, or at least his own awareness of a particular commandment. As he considered this commandment, it was as though sin sprang to life. Once he saw it, it was everywhere. He could not overcome it. He could not stand up against it. He died, or at least, he realized he was dead. He realized how hopeless his condition was and how rebellious he was at heart.

The third truth is that **sin is deceitful.** In verse 11 we read: *"For sin, seizing an opportunity through the commandment, deceived me, and through it killed me."* How exactly does sin use the law to

113

deceive us? I am not sure I've figured it out, but here are a couple of suggestions. Sin deceives us by leading us to think that just having the law is enough to save us. You may recall the moral man in chapter 2 whose claim to righteousness was simply that "I have the law. I have high standards. I have high goals and aspirations," whereas the passage goes on to tell us that we will be judged, not by our aspirations but by our actual deeds. Romans 2:13 says, *"For it is not the hearers of the law who are righteous before God, but the doers of the law who will be justified."* Sin may also use the law to deceive us when we start thinking like the Pharisees and begin to see righteousness and law-keeping as a purely external thing, rather than as a matter of the heart as Jesus taught.

The fourth truth is that **sin produces death.** Verse 9, verse 10 and verse 11 each end with death. It is not the law that kills us. It is sin, as we are told in verse 13. But however we look at it, the end result is clear: death.

I just want to make one final point about sin. It is not found in this section, but in the next one. Looking forward to verses 17 and 20 we read: *"So now it is no longer I who do it, but it is sin that dwells within me."* And: *"Now if I do what I do not want, it is no longer I who do it, but sin that dwells within me."*

Here is the fifth and final truth: **Sin lives in us.** We will explore this further in the next chapter, but it is important to understand it here. Sin is not something out there; some act external to us. Sin actually lives in us.

When I was growing up in Tanzania, we lived in an area that was home to a number of types of snakes, most of them poisonous. It was not unusual to see them crossing the road or the path ahead of us. Normally it was not too traumatic. As long as we saw them first, it was easy enough to avoid them, or, if they posed a threat, to kill them. But there was always one particular cry we dreaded: "There is a snake in the house!" Suddenly, everything changed. The snake was no longer out there. It was in here and nowhere was safe. The snake could be under the sofa, in the closet, in a drawer, behind the curtain. In regard to sin, here is the bad news. The snake is in the house. It lives in us. This is our problem.

Let's summarize what we have discovered. **The law is not the problem.** That is proposition #1. **Sin is the problem.** That is proposition #2. But that brings us to one final proposition from this chapter. **The law is not the solution.** This is really where Paul has been headed throughout chapter 7 and where we will go in our next chapter. But let's just do a quick preview in our thinking. Knowing what we now know about the law and about sin, let me ask you a couple of questions.

Can the law conquer sin? Can we bring sin under control by making rules; by coming up with longer and longer lists of dos and don'ts? Can we change people through moral teaching and by educating people in ethics? Can the law produce a righteous life?

We should know the answer by now. No way! In fact, sin is so powerful and so deceitful that it actually uses the law as a staging ground to launch its attacks against us. So, what about the law? The law is not the problem, but neither is the law the solution. Paul will go on in the rest of chapter 7 to explore what happens when we treat the law as the solution and try to produce a righteous life in our own efforts.

But while the law is not the solution, it does have a role to play. Have you allowed the law to do its work in you? Have you used it as a plumb line to hold up alongside your life, to show you just how far short you fall of the righteous standards of God?

Jesus told a parable that powerfully illustrates what happens when the law is allowed to do its real work and what happens when sin uses the law to deceive us. It is the story of two men who went up to the temple to pray. One was a Pharisee. The other was a tax collector. In the temple, the Pharisee stood up and began to pray: "Lord, I thank you that I am not like other men – robbers, evildoers, adulterers - or even like this tax collector. I fast twice a week and give a tenth of all I get."

How did this man respond to the law? He became proud. Sin took the law, and deceived this man into self-righteousness, self-reliance and pride.

It was in the heart of the other man, the tax collector, that the law of God had done its true and intended work. This man stood at a distance. He didn't even dare look up to heaven, but beat his breast and said, "God, have mercy on me, a sinner."

Have you allowed the law of God to do its work in you? If you have, then you know that you are not a righteous person. You are not a good person. You are a sinner. Let the law do its convicting work. Then, if you have not done so already, let the law of God lead you to the foot of the cross. Let it lead you to echo the tax collector's prayer: "God be merciful to me, a sinner."

Jesus concluded that parable by saying, "This man (the tax collector) is the one who went home justified before God."

15

WHAT THE LAW COULD NOT DO
Romans 7:14-25

Please take the time to read the text in your Bible and keep it open.

Who is Paul describing in Romans 7:14-25? This is the urgent question which presses in as we read these verses. The obvious answer is that Paul is describing himself. The entire section is written in the first person, with first person pronouns and verb forms. Paul is writing about his own personal experience. The section is autobiographical. That much seems clear. But what part of his life is he describing? Is he describing his pre-conversion life as a Pharisee and student of the Law, or is he describing his on-going experience as a follower of Christ, even at the time of his writing, or some other time period in his spiritual journey?

It is interesting to note that church history is divided on the answer to this question. In the first three centuries of the church, the writers and church fathers almost universally took this section as a description of Paul's pre-conversion experience. However, since the Reformation, the Reformers and the Puritan writers and the majority of contemporary evangelical scholars have interpreted it as a description of Paul at the time of his writing, where he described his on-going struggle as a Christian against sin in his life.

Early in my ministry and the first few times I preached through Romans, I followed the path of the Reformers. After all, they have rarely steered me wrong. But when I prepared to preach it again later in my ministry I became increasingly uneasy with the idea that Paul was describing his Christian experience. The pieces didn't seem to fit. After considerable inner turmoil, and mental and spiritual wrestling with the text, I found myself increasingly leaning toward casting my vote with the church fathers of the early church. Let me try to explain my reasoning and my journey.

As we approach the question, we might make first appeal to the tense of the verbs which Paul uses. They are primarily present tense verbs throughout the section, which would lead us toward the conclusion that he is writing about his experience at the time of his writing. However, this is not fully determinative. The Greek language and grammar does allow, as does English, for something called the dramatic present, in which a story or experience in the past is told in the present tense for dramatic effect.

We must also acknowledge the difficulty in answering the question. Either way we answer it leaves us with some rather serious interpretive challenges. Let me explain. First, let us consider the position that this is Paul's present experience as a Christian. Look at some of the statements he makes about himself:

"I am of the flesh, <u>sold under sin</u>." (v. 14)

"For I have the desire to do what is right, but <u>not the ability to carry it out</u>." (v.18b)

"...but I see in my members another law waking war against the law of my mind and <u>making me captive to the law of sin</u> that dwells in my members." (v.23)

"Wretched man that I am! <u>Who will deliver me</u> from this body of death?" (v.24)

"...with my flesh <u>I serve the law of sin</u>." (v. 25) I would point out that this last statement is his conclusion to the section.

Why do these statements cause such problems? Well, if they indeed are meant to describe Paul's experience as a follower of Christ at the time of his writing then they must be reconciled with some other earlier statements Paul has made.

In Romans 6:6 we read: *"We know that our old self (man) was crucified with him in order that the body of sin might be brought to nothing <u>so that we would no longer be enslaved to sin</u>."*

Or consider this command in Romans 6:12: *"<u>Let not sin therefore reign</u> in your mortal body."*

Or this statement in Romans 6:14: *"For <u>sin will have no</u>*

dominion over you." And, "…_having been set free from sin_…" _(6:18)_ and "_But now that you have been set free from sin_…" _(6:22)_

We can even look ahead a few verses in Romans 8:2: "_For the law of the Spirit of life has set you free in Christ Jesus from the law of sin and death._

How can we reconcile such contradictory statements? If, in chapter 7, Paul is describing his present experience, is he not making a mockery of these declarations of freedom that he made in the previous chapter? Those who hold this position (and they are in the clear majority among evangelical scholars of the past 4 centuries) recognize the difficulty of the task. However, they still maintain that the passage is describing Paul's ongoing struggle against his own sin nature (the flesh), even as a Christian. They see it as a parallel passage to Paul's statement in Galatians 5:17, where Paul says, "_For the desires of the flesh are against the Spirit and the desires of the Spirit are against the flesh, for these are opposed to each other to keep you from doing the things you want to do._"

At first glance, this seems to fit. But I would add to the difficulties by also pointing to Galatians 5:16: "_But I say, walk by the Spirit and you will not gratify the desires of the flesh._" And also Galatians 5:24: "_And those who belong to Christ Jesus have crucified the flesh with its passions and desires._" Galatians certainly describes an ongoing struggle of the flesh against the Spirit, but the tone in Galatians 5 is very different from what is described in Romans 7. Yes, it is a struggle, but it is a struggle in which the Spirit leads us to victory, while Romans 7:23 describes a life of defeat in which Paul concludes in 7:23 that he is "_a captive to the law of sin that dwells in my members._" I might also bring in a passage from the Apostle John in 1 John 3:9, in which he states, "_No one born of God makes a practice of sinning, for God's seed abides in him and he cannot keep on sinning because he has been born of God._"

These contradictory statements are what made me increasingly uneasy with the position that Paul is describing his ongoing experience as a Christian and follower of Christ. What about the alternative interpretation: that Paul is describing his pre-conversion experience? Once again, we immediately encounter difficulties. Listen to some of these statements that Paul makes about himself in Romans 7.

"I _agree with the law_ that it is good." (7:16)
"For I _have the desire_ to do what is right." (7:18)
"When I _want to do right_..." (7:21)
"For I _delight in the law of God_, in my inner being;" (7:22)
"I _myself serve the law of God_ with my mind..." (7:25)

Here is the difficulty. Do these statements describe an unbeliever; a person who does not know Christ? Can we reconcile these statements with others Paul has made about a man in his pre-conversion state; as a man apart from Christ?

For example, _"as it is written: "None is righteous, no, not one; no one understands; no one seeks for God. All have turned aside; together they have become worthless; no one does good, not even one." (Romans 3:10-12)_

Or what about Paul's description, looking ahead to Romans 8:5-8? _"For those who live according to the flesh set their minds on the things of the flesh, but those who live according to the Spirit set their minds on the things of the Spirit. For to set the mind on the flesh is death, but to set the mind on the Spirit is life and peace. For the mind that is set on the flesh is hostile to God, for it does not submit to God's law; indeed, it cannot. Those who are in the flesh cannot please God."_

If this passage in Romans 7 is describing Paul in his unconverted state, how do we reconcile his statement that his mind and inner being delight in God's law with the statements that describe the sinful mind as being inherently hostile to God and his law?

This was my dilemma. There seemed to be contradictions either way I turned. Let me first tell you how I resolved the dilemma and interpreted this passage during the first half of my ministry. I concluded that Paul was describing his experience as a believer who attempted to keep the law. Do you remember the previous chapter and the question, "Is the law the solution?" We might phrase the question more specifically, "Is the law the solution to overcoming sin in my life? Will law-keeping lead me to sanctification?" In that context, this passage describes what happens when a believer attempts to deal with sin by relying on the law, on a list of do's and don'ts, on legalism. It is a believer who has been justified by grace, but now attempts to be sanctified by keeping the law. Such a person, (as Paul apparently was at some point in his Christian experience) soon discovers that he cannot keep the law by his own efforts, and therefore remains a slave to sin and the sin nature. What he needs to do is stop relying on the law and his own efforts, and begin relying on the Holy Spirit as the agent who is able to produce holiness in his life. He must "leave Romans 7 and move on into Romans 8," was the way I explained it.

In some respects, I still think that is a pretty good interpretation. I preached some good messages on that theme from these verses. They were not only good messages, but I believe they were doctrinally sound messages. But I have since come to believe that they were doctrinally sound messages preached from the wrong text. They were messages I should have preached from Galatians 5 instead of Romans 7.

What caused me to change my mind and cast my lot as an interpreter with the early church fathers rather than the Reformers? Let's go back to the idea that Paul is describing his pre-conversion experience. Let's look at some of those statements again; the ones that gave us trouble before.

"I agree with the law that it is good...For I have the desire to do what is right...When I want to do right...For I delight in the law of God, in my inner being...I myself serve the law of God with my mind..." (7:25)

Do these statements accurately describe the typical unbeliever? Clearly not. They certainly do not describe those Paul described in Romans 1, who have suppressed the knowledge of God available to them and live in open defiance of his standards. But then I asked another question. Are there any unbelievers and non-Christians whom this does describe? That caused me to ask another question: Who exactly was Paul targeting when he wrote this chapter?

Suddenly it clicked. Look back at Romans 7:1: *"Or do you not know, brothers – for I am speaking to those who know the law..."*

What is Paul's topic? The law. Who, among his readers, would have been particularly interested in this question? The Jews. So, how did a devout, but unconverted Jew regard the law?

To answer that question, let's look at Paul's own descriptions from earlier chapters. In Romans 2:17-20 Paul wrote: *"But if you call yourself a Jew and <u>rely on the law</u> and boast in God and <u>know his will and approve what is excellent, because you are instructed from the law;</u> and if you are sure that you yourself are a guide to the blind, a light to those who are in darkness, an instructor of the foolish, a teacher of children, <u>having in the law the embodiment of knowledge and truth…</u>"*

Look also at Romans 2:23: *"You who <u>boast in the law</u>…"* Or consider Romans 3:1-2: *"Then what advantage has the Jew? Or what is the value in circumcision? Much in every way. To begin with, the Jews were <u>entrusted with the oracles of God.</u>"*

What words do you think the Jews had in mind as being "the oracles of God?" The law of course! The Torah. The Jews had a very high view of the Old Testament Scriptures and of the Law of God. They memorized it. They wrote it on phylacteries to wear on their wrists and foreheads. They wrote it on their walls. Even today, one of the high points in the life of a boy growing up in the Jewish faith is his "Bar Mitzvah," when he is declared a "Son of the Law."

One of my favorite novelists is Chaim Potok. Mr. Potok set most of his novels in the context of the life of orthodox, "Hasidic" Jews in America in the 1900's. I enjoy his books because they are a window into a world and culture and community that I know very little about. One thing that impresses me about the stories is the descriptions of their great respect for the Torah and how carefully they handle the sacred scrolls as they take them out to read them as part of the Sabbath day worship. Truly it can be described as taking delight in the law of God. While the passages we considered do not describe all unbelievers, they do describe some; specifically, they describe those he was addressing in this chapter; the Jews, those who know the law. It is easy to imagine Paul, as a young Pharisee, singing every verse of Psalm 119 with its praise of God's Law and his commandments; verses like verse

97: *"Oh how I love your law! It is my meditation all the day,"* or verse 145: *"With my whole heart I cry; answer me, O Lord! I will keep your statutes."*

In Romans 7, I believe Paul is describing himself as a religious man; one who was relying on the law for his right standing with God. He is describing his own experience as one who grew up with the highest regard for the law; who believed that the law was the solution to his own sin problem. He tried to please God by keeping the law, but it didn't work and it can never work. Why not? Because, in Paul's words in verse 14: *"For we know that the law is spiritual, but I am of the flesh, sold under sin."* I like the way the NIV translates the verse: *"The law is spiritual but I am unspiritual, sold as a slave to sin."*

Thinking back to the previous chapter, "The law is not the problem." After all, the law is spiritual. The problem is in me. I am unspiritual. I am a slave to sin. But while the law is not the problem, nor is the law the solution. This is because the law cannot get to the root of the problem which is the sin that dwells in me. The harder I try to comply with the law, the more I am aware of my own sin. It was C.S. Lewis who wrote: "No man knows how bad he is until he has tried to be good." These verses in Romans are a description of Paul, the Pharisee, trying to be good enough to earn his righteous standing before God. And failing utterly.

What about the references to the unconverted mind in chapter 8 which is in rebellion against God? What about the references to the mind and the inner man in chapter 7 which wants to do good? Isn't this a contradiction? It certainly seemed so to me, until I realized that Paul, in fact, used two different Greek words for mind. In the verses in chapter 8, he consistently used a word that carries the idea of a way of thinking; a mind-set; a philosophy. In chapter 7, the word he uses for "mind" refers to the mind as the organ of thought, the intellect, the capacity to think. In chapter 7 we might paraphrase his words this way: "Intellectually, on an abstract thought level, with my mind, I admire the Law and I want to keep it. But on a practical level, the sin in me is too strong and holds me captive." As he says in

Romans 7:18b, *"I have the desire to do what is right, but not the ability to carry it out."*

So what is the conclusion of the matter? Well, you may or may not agree with my interpretation of this passage. If you choose to agree with Martin Luther, John Calvin, Matthew Henry, Martyn Lloyd Jones and countless others instead of me, I guess I can live with that! I recognize that I am swimming against the current of most evangelical scholarship. I do not do that lightly. I would only ask that you take the time to seriously consider my thought process in arriving at my conclusions.

You might ask, "Why does it matter?" It's a fair question. In many ways, I suppose it doesn't. No critical doctrine of the church is at stake. However, in one important way, I think it does matter. In my years in the church and interacting with Christians in countless Bible studies and discussions, this section of Romans 7 is quoted frequently. We read it, and everyone smiles in self-recognition. "I do what I don't want to do and I don't do what I want to do. That's me!" But as I analyze the application that is often taken from these verses, it seems like we are treating it almost as some kind of cop out and an excuse for continuing in our sin. "After all," we think, "If Paul struggled that way, even as an apostle and mature Christian, well, what hope is there for me? This is my reality. This is the normal Christian life, so why be so hard on myself? There is not much I can do about it. After all, it's the sin that dwells in me, not me that's doing it." It is revealing to me that I find Christians are much quicker to quote these verses in Romans 7 than we are to quote from Romans 6, where Paul has spelled out the path to spiritual victory and to increasing holiness when we *"reckon ourselves to be dead to sin and alive to God in Christ Jesus."*

It is not my intention in any way to minimize the struggles of growing in holiness and learning to walk in the power of the Spirit. However, it is a struggle that should, by the Spirit's power, be leading us on to victory, rather than one that leaves us "captive to the law of sin."

If you do find yourself agreeing with my interpretation, then we find that this final section of Romans 7 fits seamlessly with what Paul has been saying earlier in the chapter. The Jews among

Paul's readers would have been disturbed by his declaration in Romans 1-5 concerning justification by faith; that it is possible to be declared righteous before God apart from observing the law. In fact, Paul states it is the only way to be declared righteous in God's sight.

"If that is true, Paul, then what about the law?" In the first 6 verses, Paul uses legal reasoning to declare that by the death of Christ, and our death with Christ, we have been set free from the law.

"So, Paul, are you saying that the law was the problem?" In verses 7 to 13, Paul answers clearly. No, the law is not the problem. The law is holy and righteous and good. There is nothing wrong with the law. The problem is sin; specifically, the sin that dwells in me. The law is not the problem, but neither is the law the solution, because I lack the ability to keep the law. I believe this section of Romans 7 is a very effective, dramatized description of the inner struggle of a religious Jew who tries as hard as he can to earn his right standing with God by keeping the law and ends up in despair, crying out: *"What a wretched man I am! Who will rescue me from this body of death?"* It is a cry that echoes the tax collector in Jesus' parable: *"God, be merciful to me, a sinner."*

The law is not the problem. Sin is the problem. But neither is the law the solution. What, then, is the solution? Let's jump ahead into Romans 8:3 for the answer: *"For God has done what the law, weakened by the flesh, could not do..."* This is why Paul, in answer to his own question in Romans 7:24: *"Who will deliver me from this body of death?"* can also cry out in 7:25 the triumphant answer: *"Thanks be to God through Jesus Christ our Lord!"*

What about you? Have you been trying to please God with your own righteousness, by trying to keep the law, or live up to some stringent inner code? Are you weary of the struggle to satisfy God's requirements by your own efforts? Are you tired of failing, again and again and again, no matter how hard you try? There is another way. What the law could not do, God has done. He has provided a way to be right with him. It is the way of the cross. It is the way of justification by faith in Jesus Christ and his sufficient sacrifice.

I would point out that the Jews are not the only ones who have a high respect for law and for law keeping. Every religion has its own set of laws and standards; requirements not only for membership, but for earning "salvation" (however they might define that). Details of the law may vary, but the principle is very much the same. Right standing with God depends on obedience to a prescribed standard. Yet I believe that everyone who earnestly and honestly attempts to earn his or her salvation will run aground on the same rocks that Paul did; his or her inability to keep the law or to live up even to the standards he approved and took such delight in. For 25 years I lived among a people who had a very high regard for a law that they believe came from God. And they believe that their only hope for entering Paradise is by keeping that law. If you are in a close friendship with such a person and have the freedom to discuss spiritual things with him or her, let me suggest something. Type out this section of Romans 7:14-24 without the verse references and without anything to identify it as coming from the Bible; just a piece of prose describing someone's personal experience. Read it to your friend or give it to him/her to read, and ask him/her if it is an accurate description of his/her own inner struggle. See where the discussion goes from there. You might even get the chance to share what Paul says in Romans 8:3: *"For God has done what the law...could not do...by sending his own Son..."*

16

NOT GUILTY!

Romans 8:1-4

The makers of movies and television shows have always shown a great fascination with courtroom dramas. In those dramas, the whole structure of the story line and the building of drama and suspense throughout the show often comes to its peak when the jury returns from their deliberations. All the arguments are complete; all the evidence presented; all of it weighed and evaluated. Now the judge asks, "Has the jury reached a verdict?" The foreman responds: "Yes we have, your honor." "What say you?" says the judge. The foreman then says: "We, the jury, find the defendant…"

As the verdict is read, the camera frequently focuses on the face of the defendant. That is where the drama of the verdict will be played out. Will there be horror, anguish and tears? Or relief, joy and celebration? It all hinges on the words that come out of the foreman's mouth.

In the early chapters of the Book of Romans, the court of heaven has been in operation. Actions and motions have been made. Evidence has been presented. The jury has returned to the courtroom. The judge asks: "Have you reached a verdict?"

"We, the jury, find the defendant…NOT GUILTY!"

This is the verdict that Paul announces in the opening verse of Romans 8: *"There is therefore now no condemnation for those who are in Christ Jesus."* This is truly one of the most glorious sentences to be found in the Bible, in fact in all of human language and literature. Not guilty! There is no condemnation. None! Imagine the camera on the face of the defendant when that verdict is read. Now imagine that it is your face. You are the defendant. And this is the verdict of the high court of heaven. Not guilty! No condemnation. Let the prisoner go free.

This is the summary of the first 7 chapters of the Book of Romans. It is particularly a summary of the first 5 chapters of Romans and the glorious truth of the gospel; that we can be justified by faith apart from the Law and apart from works. Chapters 6 and 7 contain a rather lengthy detour as Paul addresses objections to this truth, but now Paul returns to his main line of thought. To demonstrate this, you only need to read from the end of Romans 5 directly to Romans 8 and you will find it a perfect sequitur. Romans 5 highlighted the distinction between what we inherited "in Adam" by our physical birth, with our inheritance as those who are "in Christ" by virtue of new birth. And here is the glorious conclusion: *There is therefore now no condemnation to those who are in Christ Jesus!*

Romans 8 is not only a perfect follow-on to Paul's argument in chapters 1-5; it is also a logical progression from his detour in chapter 6-7. Good detours work that way as the winding path rejoins the main road.

As we move into chapter 8, I want to raise an important question: **So, what's different?** Think back with me to the point or time in your life when you put your faith in Jesus Christ as Savior. Just for the sake of uniformity, let's imagine it happened on Sunday night. Now, imagine waking up Monday morning and asking yourself the question: "So, what's different?" What has changed? Most specifically, how have you changed? How are you different? What is the fundamental difference between you as a follower of Christ and the person you were before you became a follower of Christ? I want you to hold onto that question, but push it to the back burner of your mind for a moment.

I want to reintroduce and remind us of the definitions of a couple theological terms that will form an essential part of our vocabulary as we move forward. They are the words "justification" and "sanctification." They are both big words with big meanings and profound implications. But to simplify them and draw the contrast between them as clearly as possible, we have defined them this way. Justification means "declared righteous." Sanctification means "made righteous."

Justification is a legal declaration whereby the high court of heaven declares our standing and legal status as "righteous." It is a once and for all act of God that he performs when we place our faith in Jesus Christ and his death on the cross. God reckons our faith as righteousness and declares us "not guilty" before his court. It is the foundation for the glorious declaration of Romans 8:1: There is no condemnation. By faith we have been justified (declared righteous).

Sanctification, however, is a process whereby we are "made righteous," not legally, but in fact. Our actual behavior begins to change; our thoughts, attitudes, words and actions are transformed as we are molded increasingly into the men and women God desires us to be.

In Romans 1-5, Paul has spoken almost exclusively about our justification; how we can be declared righteous before God by faith. In Romans 8, Paul is moving into a discussion of our sanctification; how we become righteous. The question then comes. In Romans 8:1-4, is Paul speaking about our sanctification, or is he still describing our justification? I think he is doing both! While it is helpful in our minds to distinguish between justification and sanctification, the Bible does not draw a clear line between them. In the opening paragraph of the chapter, while Paul makes a careful transition from the one to the other, we see the one "bleeding into the other" in a way that makes them impossible to separate. It is this blending of the two aspects of our salvation that makes this passage of Scripture difficult to interpret.

Another confusing factor in the passage is Paul's use of the word "law" in verses 2-4. Let's examine this closely, as I believe it holds the key to understanding his logic.

"For the law of the Spirit of life has set you free in Christ Jesus from the law of sin and death. For God has done what the law, weakened by the flesh, could not do. By sending his own Son in the likeness of sinful flesh and for sin, he condemned sin in the flesh, in order that the righteous requirement of the law might be fulfilled in us, who walk not according to the flesh but according to the Spirit."

While Paul uses the same word in all four cases, Paul is actually referring to 3 different laws. There is the "law of sin and death" at the end of verse 2. There is the Mosaic law or the path to righteousness encoded in the Old Testament, (or what we might refer to as the Law with a capital L). This is the law referred to in verses 3 and 4. Finally, (and the first one mentioned in the text) there is the law of the Spirit.

Let's first consider the "law of sin and death." At one point in my study, I thought there were only two laws referred to in the passage, and that this was also a reference and therefore a description of the Law. While this might seem strange, I thought it is possible in light of what Paul said about the law in chapter 7; specifically, that the law stirs sin up and that sin takes advantage of the law to deceive us and kill us. At the end of the day, if we try to attain right standing with God by keeping the law, we end up condemned before God. We end up dead. Isn't this what he says in 7:9? "*...when the commandment came, sin came alive and I died.*" But now we have been set free from that law which killed us. When did this happen? It happened when Christ died on the cross, and cried out, "It is finished!" In what way were we set free from the Law? We were set free from the law as the means and path to justification (right standing with God; reference Romans 1-5 and especially Romans 7).

This makes good sense and it's even good theology. But then I looked back into Romans 7. There Paul makes reference to "another law," in verse 22-23: "*For I delight in the law of God in my inner being, but I see in my members <u>another law</u> waging war against the law of my mind and making me captive to the <u>law of sin</u> that dwells in my members.*" He continues to make a clear distinction in verse 25, where he declares, "*I myself serve the law of God with my mind, but <u>with my flesh I serve the law of sin.</u>*" With such clear references and contrasts between the law of God and the law of sin in the immediate context, it seems clear that his reference to "the law of sin and death" in 8:2 must be to this "other law" and not to God's law. If this is the case, in what sense and when were we "set free from the law of sin and death?"

Let's keep moving in the text and see if the picture will become clearer.

Verse 3 states: "*For God has done what the law, weakened by the flesh, could not do. By sending his own Son in the likeness of sinful flesh and for sin, he condemned sin in the flesh…"*

Here is where confusion can enter in. The word "law" in this verse is clearly referring to the Old Testament law. While the previous verse left us asking when it happened, this verse addresses an even more important question. Who set us free and how was it accomplished? The "who" is beyond doubt. There is one clearly identified subject to the sentence; only one noun in the nominative case. It is God. God did it. God is the subject, the acting agent, the only power great enough to set us free. Salvation is God's work from beginning to end. What the law (even God's Law) could not do… Why not? Because it was *"weakened by the flesh."* That is a good summary of Romans 7 and the description of Paul trying to keep the law. He couldn't do it! He was a slave to sin. He could not keep the law. There was nothing wrong with the law. The problem was in Paul. The problem is in us. Do you remember Paul's words in Romans 7:14? In the NIV it reads: *We know that the law is spiritual but I am unspiritual, sold as a slave to sin.* The ESV translates: *"For we know that the law is spiritual, but I am of the flesh…* It is the same word that is used here in verse 3: *"…what the Law could not do, weakened by the flesh…"* The problem is in you and in me. In the flesh, in our natural, unregenerate state, we cannot keep the law. The law is not the problem. But because of the weakness of our fleshly state, neither is it the solution. But what the law could not do, God has done.

That is the who. What about the how? How did he do it? That's what the rest of the verse tells us: *"by sending His own Son in the likeness of sinful flesh and for sin, he condemned sin in the flesh."*

We are working our way through one of those dense thickets of theological truth I referred to in my introduction! These are deep theological waters, so keep your thinking caps on! "God sent his own Son in the likeness of sinful flesh." The wording is very precise here. Jesus was God's own unique Son. We shall find a little later in Romans 8 that all believers are called "sons of God." But this identifies Jesus as the unique Son, his own Son. He sent him *"in the likeness of sinful flesh."* Jesus became the God-man. God in human flesh. It does not say that he was in "the likeness of flesh." That would mean he was not fully human, but only appeared human. As such he would not be one of us and could not have been a suitable mediator or sacrifice. On the other hand, if he had been exactly like us, he would have been a sinner. In which case, he would also not have been eligible to serve as a sacrifice for us. But God sent his own Son in the likeness of sinful flesh. Jesus was human or "flesh" in every sense except that he was without sin. The purpose of his coming is also clear. God sent him "for sin" or as the NIV translates, as "an offering for sin." As the sinless Son of God come in human flesh, he was the perfect and only suitable offering for sin.

By sending his own Son as an offering for sin, God accomplished something very significant. It is found in the concluding phrase of the verse and it is the primary, driving verb of the whole sentence. *"He condemned sin in the flesh."* What does this phrase mean? When you and I speak of condemning sin, it is usually the equivalent of identifying sinful behavior and saying it is bad. For example we might condemn lying, and cruelty, and immorality. Such behavior is bad. Such actions are wicked. We condemn sin, and in the process we condemn the people who practice such behaviors. But that cannot be what Paul is saying here. Condemning sin, in this sense, is the one thing that the Law does very well. It condemns sin as sin and pronounces it evil. Yet this is something that the verse tells us the Law could not do. It was something only God could do.

To understand what Paul is saying here, I believe we must expand our understanding of the word "condemn." Think of it as the response of the court to a guilty person. As such, it includes the determination of guilt, the declaration of guilt, the setting of the sentence and the carrying out of the sentence. All are included within and under the authority of the court. All are necessary in order to maintain justice. When God sent his own Son in the likeness of sinful flesh and as an offering for sin, *"he condemned sin in the flesh."* He determined the guilt of all of Adam's race, he declared us guilty, he set the sentence of death, and he carried out the sentence. He finished the matter then and there.

Paul says it this way in 2 Corinthians 5:21: *"He (God) made him to be sin who knew no sin."* And then God carried out the sentence of death on the cross. Isaiah 53:6 says it this way: *"All we like sheep have gone astray; we have turned—every one—to his own way; and the LORD has laid on him the iniquity of us all."* And when all our iniquity was laid on him, the sentence was carried out. Christ died. 1 Peter 3:18 says it this way: *"For Christ also suffered (died) once for sins, the righteous for the unrighteous, that he might bring us to God."* On the cross, Christ died for our sins, once and for all. The sentence was carried out. "Sin in the flesh" (our sin and our guilt) was determined, declared, and punished once for all time. And so, God *"condemned sin in the flesh,"* and by doing so, he set us free from the "law of sin and death" which had held us captive.

He did this, according to verse 4: *"in order that the righteous requirement of the law might be fulfilled in us."* We might ask: is Paul talking about our justification or our sanctification? I think he is talking about both!

Paul is still talking about our justification. The righteous requirements of the law have been met in us, not by our own righteous deeds, but by the fact that our sins were laid on Christ. He was the perfect sacrifice, and he paid the penalty for our sins. The righteous requirements of the law were fulfilled by the death of Christ for us. Not only that, but according to the rest of 2 Corinthians 5:21: *"For our sake, he made him to be sin who knew no sin, so that in him we might become the righteousness of God."* If we are in Christ, Christ's righteousness has now been laid on or attributed to us. The righteous requirements of the law have been fully met for us by Christ and his sacrifice and his righteousness has now been "reckoned" to us by faith.

We are back to where we began in verse 1: *"Therefore there is now no condemnation for those who are in Christ Jesus."* Why not? Because the righteous requirements of the law have been fully met for us and in us. Since the requirements of the law have been fulfilled, we have been set free from the Law as the means to our justification. We have been set free from ever again

133

needing to earn God's approval by our efforts to keep God's law because Christ kept the law and satisfied its demands for us. So in a very important sense, this verse looks back at our justification as described in the first 5 chapters of Romans.

But that's not all it does! One of the key outcomes of Christ's death on the cross and his resurrection was the sending of his Spirit to indwell us. This is what Paul will be discussing in the verses to follow. And it is by his power that we are able to fulfill the righteous requirements of the law. Not by legalistic law keeping (we are free from that!), but rather by walking in the new realm of the Spirit! This is where this section began, with reference to a third law: *"the law of the Spirit of life."*

Let me see if I can tie all this together. As I indicated above, I believe Paul is talking about three laws in these verses. First, there is the Law of God as represented in the Old Testament and the commandments. We might even call this *"the old way of the written code."* Second, there is "another law," a principle that sin dwells in us and holds us captive. This is the dilemma of the unregenerate man/woman, even one who "wants to do right." This law or principle not only holds us captive, but keeps us separate from God and will eventually lead to an eternal death. Third, there is *"the law of the Spirit of life"* referred to in verse 2.

So, from which of these "laws" have we been set free? We have been set free from the first two. We have been set free from trying to fulfill the requirements of God's Law by our own efforts, because God has fulfilled the righteous requirements of the Law for us by sending his Son to pay the price for our sins. But he does more. When we put our faith in the Son of God, he also sets us free from the tyranny of the flesh (the law of sin and death) which held us captive by placing his Spirit within us. In place of that law, we now live in a new realm and under a new "law" or jurisdiction; the realm of the Spirit. His law represents true freedom to become the people God intended us to be.

Understanding these 4 verses is crucial as they represent such a key hinge in Paul's thought as he moves in his discussion from justification to the topic of sanctification. He does so by introducing the key agent in our sanctification. He is the Holy

Spirit. In this verse, Paul is simply repeating his thought from Romans 7:6: *"But now we are released from the law, having died to that which held us captive, so that we serve in the new way of the Spirit and not in the old way of the written code."*

We were under the old way of the written code, the Law of God written on tablets of stone, on scrolls and on paper. We have been released from that law. But we have not been released to run riot into sin, but rather to serve in a new way, under a new law and a new authority. This new way is the way of the Spirit; the law of the Spirit of life. It is a law that he writes on our hearts. It is a new way because we are now empowered by the indwelling, life-giving Spirit of God to live as God intended us to live.

This is where Paul concludes verse 4. He identifies the recipients of the grace of God which he has been describing in the first 4 verses as those *"...who walk not according to the flesh, but according to the Spirit."* The Spirit of God is the key agent in producing sanctification and holy living in us. We will be discovering more about him in the rest of chapter 8, but let me just point out a few things very quickly. He is identified in several ways in these verses. First, he is simply called *"the Spirit."* Then in verse 9 he is called *"the Spirit of God."* Then in the second half of that verse he is called *"the Spirit of Christ."* And finally in verse 10 he is simply referred to as *"Christ."* In each of these references he is described as dwelling in the believer. In fact, in verse 9, Paul is so bold as to say, *"Anyone who does not have the Spirit of Christ, does not belong to him."*

In the introduction to this chapter, I asked the question: So what's different? If you believed in and trusted in Christ and were saved on a Sunday night, what would be different on Monday morning? I would now like to propose two answers to that question. The first one is that **you are in Christ.** All the glorious truths of justification that we have been talking about are yours because you have been baptized or placed into Christ Jesus and there is no condemnation. When you think of the doctrine of justification, think of that phrase: "I am in Christ."

But that is not all that is different. There is another reality; another dramatic, life-changing difference. **Christ is in you.** This is a glorious, liberating doctrine and life-changing reality. When you trusted in Christ, not only were you placed into Christ, but Christ, in the person of his Spirit, came to live in you. You became one of those who no longer walks in the realm of the flesh as a descendant of Adam. You became one of those who walks under the authority and influence of the life-giving, life-changing Spirit of God. It is a fundamental difference. You cannot and will not ever be the same again. When you think of the doctrine of sanctification, think of the phrase: "Christ is in me."

Neither doctrine is true without the other. Neither reality is complete without the other. Without justification, there can be no true sanctification. And where there is true justification, sanctification will follow, because one of the realities of our justification is that the Spirit of Christ takes up residence in the one who has been justified. If the Spirit of Christ is not in you, you are not in Christ. If you are in Christ, the Spirit of Christ is in you. This is Gospel reality: saving, life-changing, glorious reality. As Paul announced in Romans 1:16: *"For I am not ashamed of the gospel, for it is the power of God for salvation to everyone who believes…"* It is a salvation from the penalty of sin (because Christ paid that penalty on the cross), but it is also salvation from the tyranny of sin (because the Spirit of Christ now lives in me). And it all begins with believing (faith): *"Believe on the Lord Jesus Christ and you will be saved."*

17

WALKING ACCORDING TO THE SPIRIT
Romans 8:5-17

We have turned a significant corner in the development of Paul's thought. From the discussion of our justification (declared righteous) which dominated Paul's argument in the first 7 chapters, and concludes in the first 4 verses of Romans 8, he now pivots to a discussion of our sanctification (the process by which we are "made righteous" in our thoughts, words and actions). Remember that while these two great theological truths can be separated in our minds for the sake of understanding, they can never be truly separated in our lives.

As I explained in the conclusion to the previous chapter, justification is summarized by the wonderful truth that we are "in Christ." But there is another, equally wonderful reality; an equally dramatic difference. Not only are we **"in Christ"** but **"Christ is in us."** The Holy Spirit, also referred to as the Spirit of God, the Spirit of Christ and simply as Christ, now lives in us. It is from this remarkable truth and spiritual reality that our sanctification will grow and develop. This is *the law of the Spirit of life* referred to in verse 2. The Spirit of Christ is in the business of transforming lives from the inside out. This will be the primary theme of the rest of Romans 8 and in fact the rest of the book of Romans, (with the exception of another lengthy parenthesis or detour in chapters 9-11).

Let me just re-establish our ground here. I want to say it again so that no one misses it. One fundamental difference between the Christian and the non-Christian, the believer and the non-believer, the person who has been justified and the person who has not, is this. The Christian has the Spirit of Christ living inside him. I base this statement first on verse 4. At the conclusion of this summary of the believer's justification, Paul identifies those who are justified as those *"who walk not according to the flesh but according to the Spirit."*

This is not a reference to some elite brand of Christian. This is an identifying mark of everyone who has been truly justified by faith. They now walk in a new realm of life, a new kingdom, a new spiritual reality. It is the reality of all those who are indwelt by the Spirit of God. Consider verse 9: *"You, however, are not in the flesh but in the Spirit, if in fact the Spirit of God dwells in you. Anyone who does not have the Spirit of Christ does not belong to him."* That sounds pretty inclusive to me! In other words, everyone who belongs to Christ has the Spirit of Christ dwelling in him and therefore is no longer "in the flesh" in this sense.

This reality is also stated in verse 14: *"For all who are led by the Spirit of God are sons of God."* We can turn that around. Every son or daughter of God is being led by the Spirit of God. If you are not being led by the Spirit of God, then you are not a child of God. These are matters of essential definition. They are realities for everyone who has been truly born again and justified by faith. If we have been justified by faith in Christ, the Spirit of Christ lives in us and he is in the business of transforming lives.

So that brings us back to what it means to walk *"not according to the flesh but according to the Spirit,"* as described in verse 4. That is Paul's great topic in this section. What is different? What is new in this new realm of the Spirit in which all believers now live?

The first thing we are told is that we now have **a new mind-set.** In verse 5 we read: *"For those who live according to the flesh set their minds on the things of the flesh, but those who live according to the Spirit set their minds on the things of the Spirit."* I think the ESV translators miss something here by inserting the word "live" as it is not found in the original text. The NIV is more precise, simply translating the verb of being: *"For those who are according to the flesh set their minds on the things of the flesh, but those who are according to the Spirit, the things of the Spirit."* (verse 5) Paul is defining who we are, not some activity we engage in.

The original Greek word for mind or to "set the mind" which occurs in these verses is rather hard to translate. It is not the mind as the organ of thought, but rather the product of the mind; a way of thinking, a set of thoughts or ideas, a world view, a way of looking at life. Our way of looking at life when we were "according to the flesh" was to focus on the flesh; fleshly values, fleshly pleasure, fleshly solutions to life's problems. This doesn't mean sinful things necessarily but things that are fundamentally self-centered. Even man's religious efforts are essentially self-centered or "according to the flesh." But now that has changed. We have a new mind-set; a new way of looking at life based on the reality that the Spirit of Christ now lives in us. What matters to him now matters to us. His values are becoming our values.

Paul helps us understand how drastic this change is by contrasting the two mind sets in verses 6-8. *"For to set the mind on the flesh is death, but to set the mind on the Spirit is life and peace. For the mind that is set on the flesh is hostile to God, for it does not submit to God's law; indeed, it cannot. Those who are in the flesh cannot please God."*

Do you see how dramatic the contrast is? The mind-set that focuses on the flesh leads to death. It is hostile toward God. It refuses to submit to the law of God and couldn't do so even if it tried. I don't believe this is a contrast between different categories of Christ-followers. This is another description of the moral depravity of those who are outside of Christ. They cannot please God. But that is no longer true of us, as he goes on to say in verse 9: *"You, however, are not in the flesh but in the Spirit..."* As such, we now have a new mind-set that wants to please God and can please God. It is a mind-set that is full of life and peace. This is a dramatic difference that results from the new reality – that the Spirit of Christ now lives in us.

But we not only have a new mind-set, we also have **new obligations.** Look at verse 12: *"So then, brothers, we are debtors, not to the flesh, to live according to the flesh."* As we move into this new arena of life, our old obligation under which we lived according to the flesh, and which was based on fleshly values and principles – this old set of obligations, is now done away with. But the implication of what follows is that we have inherited a new set of obligations. We have been set free from the beat of the old drummer, not to walk in chaos or disorder, but to follow the cadence of the new drummer. In fact, it is not just a matter of owing nothing to the flesh. We are called to declare war on the old order. This is what Paul declares in verse 13: *"For if you live according to the flesh you will die, but if by the Spirit you put to death the deeds of the body, you will live."*

That is radical language to describe our battle against sin. "Put to death the deeds of the body." It brings to mind Paul's language in chapter 6, verses 11-12: *"So you also must consider yourself dead to sin and alive to God in Christ Jesus. Let not sin therefore reign in your mortal body to make you obey its passions."*

This is the language of our new reality and our new obligations. We have no obligation to the old order and its habits and patterns of thought, word and action. In fact, we are to declare war on them; kill them. It is a progressive present, describing ongoing, progressive action; over and over again, putting to death the deeds of the body because we now serve a new king. Why couldn't we do this before? Because we were powerless in our own strength. But look again at verse 13: *"But if by the Spirit you put to death the deeds of the body..."* He is the key agent in our sanctification. It is by his strength in us that we are able to gain victory and slay the deeds of the body.

Next we see that we have **a new navigating system**. We are *"led by the Spirit of God."* It is one of the indelible marks of the true child of God. They are led by the Spirit. Not just some elite brand of believers, but all of them. Look at verse 14 again: *"For all who are led by the Spirit of God, are sons of God."* What kind of leading is this that Paul is talking about? Often when we talk about the leading of God or the leading of the Spirit, we are talking about his leading in some important decision. Getting married. Choosing a career. Buying a house. Moving to a new job or new city. Certainly God does lead us in these important decisions as we seek his leading. But that is not the primary type of leading that Paul is talking about here. He is talking about moral leading with the Spirit of God as our moral compass and guide. In fact, we are told that one of the marks of the New Covenant is that the Law of God will be written on our hearts by the Spirit of God. He will lead us to do what is right. He will lead us in the battle against sin in our lives. He will show us right from wrong as well as give us the power to do what is right.

This is the Spirit's work and role within us, and every true child of God has the Spirit of God living inside him or her. Let me explain it this way. Do you know when I am most sure that I am a child of God? It is not when I stand in church and sing a beautiful praise song. It is not when I spend time in prayer and in the Word of God, or even when I get up to preach a sermon. No. The time I am most sure that I am a child of God is when I turn aside into sin. Why do I say that? Because when I sin, I experience a great turmoil in my soul. It is a turmoil in my spirit, stirred up by God's Spirit, leading me back to the right path. I wish I could say I always respond immediately. I don't. I resist at times. I may ignore the Spirit's leading. I may quench him. I may grieve him. But I do know this. I will have no true rest in my spirit until I listen and heed the Spirit's voice. That's how I know I am a child of God. I am led by the Spirit of God. Based on this Scripture, I think I can safely assume that if he works this way in my life, then he is working this way in the life of everyone who belongs to Christ.

What else is new in this new life as the Spirit-led people of God? The next truth is so rich in content and meaning that I can't decide what to call it. I first thought of calling it **new privilege.** Then I thought to call it **new relationship** or **new intimacy.** But then I thought it should be **new assurance.**

I will never forget an experience, a moment in time that is indelibly written in my memory. It happened not long after we moved to Abu Dhabi, our first experience in the Middle East. Our sons were attending the American Community School. I was there one afternoon, sitting by the softball field, waiting for a game to start. At that time the school employed a Yemeni man as a groundskeeper and maintenance man. He lived with his family in a small apartment on the campus. On this particular afternoon, he came striding across in front of the bleachers, intent on some errand. He was wearing the traditional Arab kandoura or robe.

But as he walked by, his little boy, about 3 years old, followed him out of their apartment. He was also wearing a kandoura, child-size but just like his father's. He was running to catch up, his little legs pumping. As he passed in front of me, he opened his little mouth and called out, "Abba! Abba!"

It was as though a jolt of spiritual and emotional electricity went through my body. I was familiar with this word, and had been reading these verses for as long as I could remember, but I'd never really "felt" them until that moment when I heard that word, used in a real life context from the mouth of a small child.

Look at Paul's words in verses 15-16: *"For you did not receive the spirit of slavery to fall back into fear, but you have received the Spirit of adoption as sons, by whom we cry, "Abba! Father!" The Spirit himself bears witness with our spirit that we are children of God..."*

Can you understand my dilemma in naming this new reality? **A new privilege!** We can call God, "Abba!" the title of endearment and yet respect reserved for the intimacy of the family circle. **A new relationship.** We have been adopted as sons and daughters of God. **A new intimacy** as we are now included in the family circle. **And a new assurance.** The indwelling Spirit of Christ himself testifies directly to us, Spirit to spirit, saying "You are one of God's children!" It is a deep assurance that wells up from deep within the soul; mystical yet real; emotional and yet based on theological evidence and proposition; a deep and abiding assurance that I am God's child.

Well there is still one more "new thing" and that is **a new hope** for the future and for eternity. We find this one in verse 17: *"and if children, then heirs—heirs of God and fellow heirs with Christ, provided we suffer with him in order that we may also be glorified with him."*

"Heirs of God and fellow heirs with Christ...Glorified with him!" This verse introduces the third great theological term that defines our salvation: justified (already accomplished by faith), sanctified (happening now by the power of God's Spirit within us) and in the future, "glorified with him." That is the Christian's hope. We will explore this further in the next chapter.

18

A WHOLE LOT OF GROANING

Romans 8:18-27

After reading the section of Scripture we'll be covering in the chapter, I'd like to suggest an exercise. (You'll probably need to be alone when you do this, or someone will think you need to go to the hospital!) Start by saying the word "groan" out loud. That was easy. Now say it again very slowly. "Grooooooooan!" Now put some volume and feeling into it. "GROOOOOOOOOAAN!"

We are going to talk about groaning in this chapter; groaning and its place in our world and in the Christian's life. The word "groan" occurs three times in the passage before us. And in each case, it has a different subject. There are actually three "groaners" identified in the text.

In verse 22, we are told that **the whole creation is groaning.** *"For we know that <u>the whole creation has been groaning together</u> in the pains of childbirth until now."*

In verse 23 we find that **the Christian is groaning.** *"And not only the creation, but <u>we ourselves, who have the firstfruits of the Spirit, groan inwardly</u> as we wait eagerly for adoption as sons, the redemption of our bodies."*

Finally, in verse 26 we see that **the Holy Spirit is groaning.** *"Likewise the Spirit helps us in our weakness. For we do not know what to pray for as we ought, but the Spirit himself intercedes for us <u>with groanings too deep for words.</u>"*

That's a whole lot of groaning going on! What is the cause of it all? And what kind of groaning is this? That's where I really want us to focus. We find in this passage that there are not only different "groaners" but there are also different kinds of groans. In fact, again we find three.

First there is **the groan of anguish.**

Now this is the kind of groaning that usually comes to our minds when we use the word. Groaning is a natural response to pain. You're walking down the hallway at night and you stub your toe: "GROAN!" You stand up too quickly from under the cupboard and bump your head; "GROAN!" You slam your finger in a door or hit your thumb with a hammer; "GROAN!"

As we consider the groan of anguish, we find that **the whole creation is groaning in anguish.** Why? Verse 20 tells us the answer. *"For the creation was subjected to futility, not willingly..."*

The word futility suggests emptiness, a lack of purpose or an inability to fulfill one's purpose. There is a phrase in the Book of Ecclesiastes that says, "Vanity of vanity, all is vanity." One translation renders that: "Meaningless, meaningless; everything is meaningless." That is a pretty good expression of futility.

How and when was the creation subjected to futility and meaninglessness? To answer that question we must go all the way back to Genesis 3:17-18 and the story of the Fall of Man.

"And to Adam he said, 'Because you have listened to the voice of your wife and have eaten of the tree of which I commanded you, "You shall not eat of it," cursed is the ground because of you; in pain you shall eat of it all the days of your life; thorns and thistles it shall bring forth for you..."'

God created man to rule over his creation. When man disobeyed and rebelled against God's command, it affected not only the human race, but also all of man's domain. As part of his judgment against man for his sin, God subjected the whole creation to futility. Nature and the creation as we see them and experience them today are not as God intended them to be.

In fact, Paul gives us a little more detail here. This frustration and the groan of anguish that accompanies it are related to death, dying and decay. In verse 21 we read: *"that the creation itself will be set free from its bondage to corruption."* Prior to Adam's sin, there was no death, no decay, nothing rotten. Nature, as we know it, is often cruel. Nature is described as being "red in tooth and claw" based on a food chain with different species preying on one another. Paul personifies the creation here and speaks of it as groaning in its bondage to this cycle of aging, dying, decaying. Ashes to ashes and dust to dust.

But creation is not the only thing that is groaning in anguish.

The believer also groans in anguish. Why? Because life is painful and full of suffering. Back in verse 18, Paul made reference to *"the suffering of the present age."* The Bible never promises that the Christian will have a life free of suffering and pain. This life and this present time are full of pain and suffering, and we are not immune. I am writing this chapter during the height of the coronavirus crisis. People are getting sick and many are dying. No one knows how bad it will get or when it will end. Maybe it will still be an ongoing reality when you read these words. We groan in anguish. This anguish is fundamentally related to that fact that we live in bodies that are mortal and subject to the same process of aging, illness and ultimately death that affects the whole creation. We face our own mortality and we grieve when people we love are snatched from us by death. These are real groans from real pain.

But I want to quickly highlight another note in the groaning that is described in this passage. The second kind of groaning described here is **a groan of anticipation.**

Have you ever been really, really thirsty? I recall a hike in an extinct volcano in Kenya. We set off from the cars without water for what we thought was a short hike to the peak. However, we were not aware that there was a very deep ravine between us and our destination. We ended up spending several hours laboring up and down large rocks before giving up and returning to the vehicles. By that time we were seriously dehydrated. I remember the last part of that hike being consumed with one thought and one thought only; "Water!" As I stumbled that last distance to the car, I could almost feel the cool water trickling down my throat and found myself groaning in anticipation for "cool, clear water."

Now, interestingly enough, the groan of anticipation is not in opposition to the groan of anguish. In fact, the very same groan often has both elements in it. The best example of this is the groaning of child birth. It is a groan of real pain, yet accompanied by anticipation and eagerness to welcome a new baby into the world. This is the analogy that Paul draws in verse 22: *"For we know that the whole creation has been groaning together*

145

in the pains of childbirth until now." There is anguish, but there is also anticipation; pain, but pain that is laced with hope.

The creation groans in anticipation. What exactly is the creation looking forward to? Look at verse 19: *"For the creation waits with eager longing for the revealing of the sons of God."*

Verse 21 goes on to tell us: *"that the creation itself will be set free from its bondage to corruption and obtain the freedom of the glory of the children of God."* When the sons of God are revealed and set free, the creation will be set free as well; set free from its futility, set free from its bondage to death and decay. The Scripture speaks of a time when the lion shall lie down with the lamb. All creation will be set free to fulfill God's initial purposes and designs. Creation can't wait! Creation is groaning in anticipation, even now, for that glorious day of liberation.

Not only does the creation groan in anticipation, but also **the believer groans in anticipation.** What are we anticipating? A number of different words or phrases tell us what we have to look forward to. The first word is **glory.** This word actually takes us back to the end of our passage from last week, in verse 17: *"and if children, then heirs—heirs of God and fellow heirs with Christ, provided we suffer with him in order that we may also be glorified with him."*

You may remember in the previous chapter that I said that one of the realities of those of us who are indwelt by the Spirit of God is that we have **a new hope.** I also told you that we'd come back to this topic. Well here we are. We have a new hope as those who have been adopted into the family of God. That is the reality that we shall share in his glory. We shall see, share and experience the glory of God. That is what we are promised in verse 18: *"For I consider that the sufferings of this present time are not worth comparing with the glory that is to be revealed to us."*

That glory is described as liberation or **freedom** in verse 21: *"that the creation itself will be set free from its bondage to corruption and obtain the freedom of the glory of the children of God."* When we experience the glory of God we shall be truly free. This is the wonderful truth of the third great doctrine of the Christian faith. We have talked about justification and sanctification. Now we are considering the truth of "glorification" when we shall share in the glory of Christ and be truly free.

Along with that freedom will come **new bodies.** *"And not only the creation, but we ourselves, who have the firstfruits of the Spirit, groan inwardly as we wait eagerly for adoption as sons, the redemption of our bodies."*

Now, you might be wondering at this point; haven't we already been adopted as sons and daughters of God? Why does Paul tell us here that we are waiting eagerly for our adoption? To understand this, we need to understand the Roman practice of adoption. In modern times, when we think of adoption, we usually think of adopting an infant or small child. A couple desires a child. A baby or small child needs a home and parents. Adoption meets both needs. It's about nurture, care and cuddly babies. In this practice, older children are often labeled, "hard to adopt."

The Roman practice was very different. It had more to do with the continuity of the family name, family honor and family inheritance. It was a practice of the upper classes. When a man had no heir to carry on the family name, he would begin to consider adoption. Only he would not necessarily think of adopting a child. After all, such a child might die. And who knows how such a child might turn out and whether he would be a worthy heir? So the man would often choose to adopt a young man of proven character and worth; someone who would prove able to carry the family honor as well as the family name. Such adopted sons were considered full sons in every regard.

While this practice of adoption had many legal and property implications, it was often a relationship accompanied by great personal affection and loyalty. It also took time to work out all the legal details. The relationship might be privately arranged and promises made and sealed. But when all of this was done and accomplished, there would come a great event in which the adoption was announced and celebrated publicly. There would be a great party. This was the adoption party, the official "adoption as sons." For various reasons the adoption might even be kept quiet until the great event was announced and celebrated.

We've been adopted. We already have the wonderful privilege of calling God, "Abba, Father!" But there is a step in the process that is yet to be completed; the adoption party; the celebration when the children of God are revealed openly before the watching universe. It is a party to which all creation will be invited. That celebration will be accompanied by the fact that we will receive new bodies, redeemed bodies; bodies that are no longer subject to pain and disease; to aging, death, and corruption.

Philippians 3:21 describes it this way, using the language of kingdom and citizenship rather than adoption: *"But our citizenship is in heaven, and from it we await a Savior, the Lord Jesus Christ, who will transform our lowly body to be like his glorious body, by the power that enables him even to subject all things to himself."*

What a glorious hope that is! No more pain. No more doctors, no more medicine, no more hospitals. (Some of you are going to have to find a new line of work!) No headaches, no sinus infections, no arthritis, no cancer, no heart disease, no Alzheimers and dementia, no aging. No Covid-19! Our bodies will be just like Jesus' own glorious resurrected and glorified body.

How do we know we will experience all of this? Well, we've already been given a down payment. That's what verse 23 tells us: *"And not only the creation, but we ourselves, who have the firstfruits of the Spirit, groan inwardly as we wait eagerly for adoption as sons, the redemption of our bodies."*

The Spirit of Christ who indwells us as believers is both a guarantee of our future resurrection as well as a foretaste of what is to come. That foretaste of God's glory is enough to set us groaning inwardly in eager anticipation of our adoption party and of our new bodies.

How does all of this affect our lives today? We live in a state of tension between the groan of anguish and the groan of anticipation. In this state, we need to do a couple things. First **we must do some calculating and comparing.** That is really where Paul began this paragraph in verse 18: *"For I consider that the sufferings of this present time are not worth comparing with the glory that will be revealed to us."*

I love that verse. There is no comparison! The darker and more painful this life becomes, the brighter this verse grows. The glory and joy of eternity is so much greater! Imagine how bright our life with Christ will be!

In addition to doing some comparing we are also called to **wait with endurance.** This is Paul's point in verses 24-25: *"For in this hope we were saved. Now hope that is seen is not hope. For who hopes for what he sees? But if we hope for what we do not see, we wait for it with patience."*

We live in a state of hope. In it, we are called to wait patiently and with endurance. What we have and experience now is not all that shall be. We live suspended between the "now" and the "not yet" of the Christian life. If we had it all now, we would not have to wait. But we don't have it all yet. This isn't all there is. There is more to come. Much more. Wait patiently.

That brings us to the third kind of groaning. It is one that we greatly need as we wait patiently, balanced between the groan of anguish and the groan of anticipation; the "now" and the "not yet" of the children of God. It is **the groan of assistance.**

In this interim time of waiting, we need help to cope with the suffering; help to endure the waiting. Good news! That help is at hand.

First of all, we are commanded to pray. We can pray and we must pray. But our prayer has limitations. That is what Paul tells us in the middle of verse 26: *"We do not know what to pray for as we ought."* We have been given a great privilege in prayer. We know that we can come to God and call on him as our "Abba! Father!" We can make our needs and requests know. But we often do not know exactly what to ask for. When that is the case, there is help as we are told in verses 26-27:

"Likewise the Spirit helps us in our weakness. For we do not know what to pray for as we ought, but the Spirit himself intercedes for us with groanings too deep for words. And he who searches hearts knows what is the mind of the Spirit, because the Spirit intercedes for the saints according to the will of God."

I love these verses! I love that phrase, *"the Spirit intercedes for us."* The root idea of intercession is to meet with someone;

149

usually someone with influence or authority or resources. And to meet with that person on behalf of someone else. The Spirit of God meets with the Father and the Spirit communicates on my behalf. The beauty of it is that in this process and by the Spirit's intercession, my heart and the will of God are brought into alignment. It often happens without words, but only a wordless groaning of the Spirit of God. It is this groan of the Spirit's assistance that will sustain us between the anguish and the anticipation of the Christian life.

These three kinds of groaning are actually a clear summary of the Christian experience. There is anguish in the Christian life, is there not? I have felt it. You have felt it. But this groan of anguish does not lead us to despair, because it is also a groan of anticipation – and oh, what we have to look forward to! What a glorious adoption party that's going to be! In the meantime, we do not despair because we have not been left alone; from alongside us and within us comes another groan – the groan of assistance as the Spirit of God intercedes for us according to the Father's will.

As Christians, we need not be afraid to groan. It is Biblical! There is no need to keep a stiff upper lip and pretend that all is well with the world. Go ahead and groan! But let it be a balanced groaning. A groaning that expresses the pain and suffering you are feeling and yet includes the hope and the anticipation for the glory that lies ahead.

19

GOD HAS A PLAN
Romans 8:28-30

If we were to take a survey of people's favorite Bible verses, I am sure that one of the verses that would appear near the top of the list would be one of the verses in this Scripture text. When I say the reference Romans 8:28, many people would be able to quote it. For me, it always comes back in the King James Version, because that's how I memorized it many years ago: *"And we know that all things work together for good to them that love God, to them that are called according to his purpose."*

But how many of us (without looking) can quote Romans 8:29, or know what Romans 8:30 says? We are going to cover just 3 verses in this chapter. We have already discovered one thing. In many of our minds, verse 28, the popular verse in this text, has become disassociated from the context. Yet it is absolutely essential that this verse be linked with verses 29-30 and that these three verses be linked to the larger context of which they are a part.

Let's look at the three verses together, this time from the ESV.

"And we know that for those who love God all things work together for good, for those who are called according to his purpose. For those whom he foreknew he also predestined to be conformed to the image of his Son, in order that he might be the firstborn among many brothers. And those whom he predestined he also called, and those whom he called he also justified, and those whom he justified he also glorified."

First, let's set the larger context. In the previous section, Paul has been talking about suffering. Do you remember all the groaning that was going on in that passage? Then we came to the reassurance of verse 26, that the Holy Spirit is praying for us. In our weakness, when we don't know what to pray for, the Holy

Spirit prays for us. Now the question is: what is the result of those prayers? What comfort can we take from them?

The answer is to be found in the 3 verses we are considering today. Verse 28 begins with the words: "And we know…" Because of the Spirit's intercession for us, even in our weakness, in our suffering and in all our groaning, we can know certain things. We can have certain assurances.

To understand those assurances and what they are based on, let me just highlight the logical flow and structure of the passage.

What do we know?

"And we know that for those who love God all things work together for good, for those who are called according to his purpose."

The heart of the passage is in the middle of the verse: *"…all things work together for good…"* The translations differ in how they render this phrase. But whether "all things work together for good" or whether "God works all things together for good," the essence is the same. God is clearly the active agent behind this assurance. But to whom does this assurance apply? To whom is this promise made?

Imagine walking down the street and finding a check for a million dollars. That is exciting, isn't it? But then you look at the name on the check: Daniel Smith. What good is that check to you? Here is someone's guarantee to pay one million dollars. But if it isn't made out to you, it won't do you any good at all.

So whose name is on this check, this guarantee that "all things work together for good?" To whom is this promise made? This group is identified in three ways. First we can go back a verse. This promise is made as an answer to the Holy Spirit's prayers in the previous verse. For whom does the Holy Spirit pray? According to verse 27 he *"intercedes for the saints in accordance with God's will."* Who are the saints? In some church traditions, this word has been used to refer to a special category of extra holy or spiritual people. But this is not the Biblical use of the term. In Romans 1:7, Paul wrote: *"To all those in Rome who are loved by God and called to be saints."* Paul uses the word "saints" to refer to all of those who name Christ as Savior and follow him by faith. They are the "set apart ones," set apart as God's special and holy people.

The second way to identify those to whom this assurance is given is found in the opening phrase of verse 28: *"for those who love God."* I believe that this phrase is used to identify every born-again child of God. Back in Romans 1:7 again, we see that Paul is writing to those who are *"loved by God."* In 1 John 4:19, John makes the connection that *"we love God because he first loved us."* As followers of Christ, we have experienced the love of God, and his love for us has produced in us a great love for God.

Finally, the verse concludes with another identifying characteristic of those to whom this assurance applies. It is *"for those who are called according to his purpose."* This promise is for those who are called and engaged in fulfilling God's purposes. We will flesh that out in a moment. But for now, I repeat that this is a definition that applies to every true, born-again follower of Jesus Christ. He had a purpose in saving you. He has a purpose for your life.

Let me stress what we have discovered so far. The promise of Romans 8:28 is not a promise of "common grace" that applies to all mankind. It is a very specific assurance to those who have been justified by faith; to those who are indwelt by the Spirit of God; to those who love God, and to those who have been called out of the general mass of humanity to fulfill God's special purpose. This is not a blind optimism of the human spirit that blithely declares, "everything will work out OK." It is a specific promise of God to specific people. The question each one of us must ask is whether we are in that group.

But assuming you are one of those people to whom Paul is referring, let's press forward with the logic of the passage. Verse 28 opens with the words, *"And we know…"* **How do we know?** On what do we base this assurance? Verse 29 begins with the word, *"For"* or *"Because."* That is why we must not separate verse 28 from verses 29-30. The promise of verse 28 depends on the spiritual realities described in the next 2 verses. Let me read them again.

"For **(because)** *those whom he foreknew he also predestined to be conformed to the image of his Son, in order that he might be the firstborn among many brothers. And those whom he predestined he*

also called, and those whom he called he also justified, and those whom he justified he also glorified."

These verses are packed with truth. We are swimming in deep theological waters. Whole libraries of books have been written in the effort to expound these verses. In these verses we come face to face with the mysteries of God's sovereignty and the paradox of how God's sovereignty interfaces with man's responsibility. In one short chapter, I am not about to untie this Gordian knot of theology even if I could. Rather than bog down in the details of what we do not understand in this passage, I want to simply make four assertions based on these verses; four bold statements of propositional, Biblical truth for us to take away and think about.

1. Salvation is God's work from beginning to end.

For me, this is the clearest "takeaway" from these verses. We tend to think about our salvation from our own, human perspective. We perceive the work of God as beginning in our lives when we heard the Gospel and responded to it by faith. But Paul turns back the clock into eternity past and God's foreknowledge and election. Listen to how Paul describes it in Ephesians 1:4-5: *"...even as he chose us in him before the foundation of the world, that we should be holy and blameless before him. In love he predestined us for adoption to himself as sons through Jesus Christ, according to the purpose of his will..."*

The beginning of our salvation is found "before the creation of the world" in the eternal sovereignty and purposes of God. It will be completed in eternity future. From beginning to end, it is God's work. God is the subject of every verb in these verses (Romans 8:29-30): *"He foreknew...he predestined...he called...he justified...he glorified."*

That brings us to the second bold assertion based on these Scriptures.

2. What God starts, he finishes.

There is no break in the activity of God. He never leaves a task unfinished. He leaves no abandoned projects; *those whom he foreknew he also predestined.* Not some of them; all of them. *Those whom he predestined he also called.* Not some of them; all of them. *And those whom he called he also justified.* Not some of them; all of them. *And those whom he justified he also glorified.* Not some of them; all of them. Here Paul is so certain of his ground that he speaks of the future as though it were already here. We know from earlier in chapter 8 that our final glorification as the sons and daughters of God is yet to come. We are called to "wait for it." Yet Paul speaks here as if it were already accomplished. What God starts, he finishes.

That leads us to the third bold assertion based on these verses.

3. God's purpose for his children is to make us like Christ.

Here we are zeroing in on the heart of this glorious passage of Scripture and the reassurances of this wonderful passage. To understand what God is doing, and to understand the "good" that he promises in verse 28, we must understand the eternal purpose of God. What does he want to do in your life and in mine? This is the heart of what Paul is proclaiming here: *"those whom he foreknew he also predestined to be conformed to the image of his Son, in order that he might be the firstborn among many brothers."*

God wants to conform us to the image of his Son. He wants to shape us and mold us until we bear the family resemblance. He wants a glorious spiritual family, in which all the adopted sons and daughters look and act like the honored elder brother, the firstborn Son of God, Jesus Christ.

A few years ago, I was invited to speak at a conference in Kenya for the Sudan branch of Wycliffe Bible Translators. In the 1970's and 80's, my oldest brother, Jon, pioneered the work of Wycliffe in Sudan. Throughout the week at the conference, I kept hearing the same thing over and over from those who had worked with him. "You look just like your brother, Jon." "You sound just like your brother, Jon." "You laugh just like your brother, Jon."

I wonder if people can say this about you and me. "You look like your elder brother, Jesus. You speak like your elder brother, Jesus. You act like your elder brother, Jesus. When I see you, I am reminded of Jesus."

Paul is harking back to what he told us earlier in verses 14-17. *"For all who are led by the Spirit of God are sons of God. For you did not receive the spirit of slavery to fall back into fear, but you have received the Spirit of adoption as sons, by whom we cry, "Abba! Father!" The Spirit himself bears witness with our spirit that we are children of God, and if children, then heirs—heirs of God and fellow heirs with Christ."*

We have been adopted into the family of God. Now we are called to bear the family resemblance. We are to be conformed to the image of Christ, our elder brother and "fellow heir." That is God's purpose. He is busy now transforming us into Christ's image in terms of character and behavior. And he will transform us physically in the future by giving us new bodies, just like Jesus' own resurrected body. What God starts, he finishes.

That brings us to the fourth bold assertion based on these verses.

4. God has a plan to fulfill his purpose and everything that happens to us fits into that plan.

Now we have finally come down to the essence of Romans 8:28 and its wonderful assurance. This is why it has been a favorite verse of believers down through the ages. Everything that happens to me; **all things** fit into God's plan and he is using them to fulfill his purpose of molding me into the image of Christ and making me a worthy son in the family of God.

Think of God as the sculptor and each individual child of God as an art project. God as the sculptor is carefully working together all the elements of our lives, all things, to carve into our character the image of Christ. In this wonderful verse, we are promised that there are no random or wasted strokes. This verse does not promise us that there will be no pain in our lives. But it does promise that there will be no unnecessary pain. God is sovereignly working "all things together for good" to fulfill his good plan and purpose.

God's plan for each one of us is different. He treats no two exactly alike, for we are not alike. We are each uniquely created, right down to the uniqueness of our fingerprints and personalities.

As the master craftsman, God knows exactly how to shape each one of us; what needs to be cut away; which tool will cut just deep enough but not too deep, and leave the right finish. There are no wasted strokes. **All things** work together for good.

This is the reassurance of Romans 8:28. God is at work in your life and mine. He has a plan, and everything that is happening to us fits into that plan. But remember, God is not finished yet. A workshop is often a messy place. There are shavings and chips and rough edges. Don't judge the craftsman by the neatness of his workshop; wait until you see the final product.

Let me ask. What are you facing in your life right now? Can you believe that God is sovereign over that circumstance or person or situation? Can you trust God to use that, as painful and hard as it may be, to shape and mold you into the image of Christ? Can you trust him not to cut too deep, or to strike the mallet too hard or to cut away too much? Can you trust him that there will be no wasted strokes; that God will do exactly what needs to be done to produce Christ's image in you? Can you trust him to finish the work that he has begun?

"And we know that for those who love God, all things work together for good, for those who are called according to his purpose." And that purpose is to shape us and transform us into the image of Christ.

20

YOU'RE SAFE!

Romans 8:31-39

The title to this chapter is, "You're safe!" When I preached on this passage to my congregation in Abu Dhabi, I introduced the international audience to the sign that umpires use in baseball to indicate that a runner has reached base safely. At strategic intervals during the sermon, I would give the sign, and the congregation would shout out **"Safe!"** It was a fun service, and no one fell asleep! You'd probably feel pretty foolish periodically shouting "Safe!" as you read this chapter, but I will inject the word in bold and capital letters from time to time to highlight the key concept in this final paragraph of Romans 8.

We live in a dangerous world. It is physically dangerous. Natural disasters, accidents, and disease can all strike without warning. I am writing this chapter at the height of the Covid19 pandemic in April, 2020. The world is a scary place right now! Then there is the threat of human violence and abuse against other human beings: school shootings, domestic violence, international conflicts, racist attacks. That is only talking about threats in the physical world; the ones we can see. There is another world that is invisible to the human eye, but is nonetheless very, very real. It is the spiritual world; a world of unseen but real spiritual powers and authorities; a world of demons and evil spirits, of curses and spells, of dark and occult powers. In a world like this, filled with known and unknown threats, visible and invisible dangers, where can we go to find safety and security? Where can we go and be truly safe?

To answer that question, we turn to Romans 8:31-39. As we do, let me once again set our context. Paul has been writing to tie together the great themes of Christian theology, and of God's great work of salvation. It is a work that is both past, present and future. When we speak of God's work in the past, we speak of **justification**; the great work of God whereby he declared us righteous in his sight based on Christ's sacrifice of atonement on the cross and our faith in Christ's work. When we speak of God's work in the present, we speak of **sanctification**; the great work of God as he works in our lives by His indwelling Spirit to conform us to the likeness of his Son. When we speak of God's work in the future, we speak of **glorification**; the great future work of God when he will give his children new bodies and we shall share in Christ's glory; the freedom of the glory of the children of God.

So, there are aspects of our salvation that are already accomplished. There are other aspects that are ongoing as we speak. And there are still others that are yet future. We are told to 'wait patiently" for them. One of the realities of this "now but not yet" existence in which we now live is that the now is not always pleasant. In fact, back in verse 18, Paul has described our "now" with the words "our present sufferings," and he even tells us that as God's children and heirs, we "share in Christ's sufferings."

How do we tie these different realities together? Let me use an illustration. Some years ago we were on vacation in South Africa visiting some former members of our church. While there, we were taken to a place called Oribi Gorge, near Durban. It is sometimes referred to as the Grand Canyon of South Africa. There is a dramatic suspension footbridge across a section of the Gorge. It is a rather long bridge. In the middle there is quite a bit of sway, or bounce, if you are brave enough to jump up and down. Think of our salvation as a suspension bridge. One end of it is firmly anchored in Christ's work on the cross. The other end of it is firmly fixed to the promise of future glory and an eternity with Christ. But you and I are currently in the middle of the bridge. It is swaying, the wind is blowing, and it's bouncing up and down. Just how safe are we?

The first consideration in answering that question is: Who built the bridge? Paul has already answered that question for us in the previous section. God built the bridge. In the previous chapter we learned that "salvation is God's work from beginning to end." Starting with his foreknowledge before the creation of the world and leading on to our glorification in eternity future, salvation is God's work. God built the bridge. Both the past and the future are securely anchored. The bridge is not going to fall.

But you and I are still in the middle of the bridge. It is swaying and bouncing. What if I fall off? What if someone or something comes along and knocks me off, or some evil force or presence blocks my way? What if some awful experience will cause me to lose my grip, or even make me give up and jump from the bridge? How safe am I? These are the kinds of questions that Paul answers in the final paragraph of Romans 8.

We know Paul is wrapping up this section of the letter by the way he begins verse 31: *"What then shall we say to these things?"* What conclusions can we draw? What applications can we make?

He then introduces this wonderful rhetorical question. If you haven't memorized it, I encourage you to do so. It is one of the most faith-building, faith-restoring questions in the Scripture: *"If God is for us, who can be against us?"*

The construction here is what is called a "first class condition." That means that the condition in the first part of the sentence is assumed to be true. We can translate it "Since God is for us, who can be against us?" We are…**SAFE!**

Now let me ask this. Do you think Paul is suggesting that the child of God has no enemies? Is he saying that we will experience no opposition? No. The Christian actually has many enemies. Satan for one. His name actually means "adversary" or enemy. The whole kingdom of darkness, over which Satan rules, stands in opposition to us. Not only his unseen, spiritual kingdom, but the present world system is also under his grip and influence. The entire value system and outlook of the unbelieving world is waging war against us. Even in our own flesh, our sin nature, we have a fierce enemy that will oppose the work of God in our lives. So when Paul asks, "Who can be against us?" what is he saying?

Another illustration may help. Many years ago, when I was in junior high (or middle school), around 12 or 13 years old, we used to play 7-a-side rugby in Physical Education class at the missionary school I attended in Kenya. That is the age when boys go through their growth spurt; only different boys go through their growth spurt at different times. There was one boy in the class whose nickname was "Harris." Harris hit his growth spurt before the rest of us. He shot up about 6 inches. He didn't just grow tall. He grew big and strong as well. On top of that, he'd always been a natural athlete. So he was tall, he was big, he was strong…and he was fast.

It didn't take the rest of us very long to realize something. No matter how we picked the teams for our rugby games, Harris' team always won! His team always won, because none of the rest of us could tackle him. Any time his team needed to score some more points, they just gave the ball to him and he would run across the goal line and score. The only way the rest of us had a chance to be on the winning side was by taking turns being on Harris' team. If Harris was on our side, it didn't matter who was on the other side. If Harris was for us, who could stand against us? The Bible translation, The Message actually translates verse 31 this way: *"So what do you think? With God on our side like this, how can we lose?"* "If God is for us, who can be against us?" We are…**SAFE!**

But some might ask: How do we know God is for us? How do we know God is on our side? How do we know he even cares? Paul goes on to add some additional logic in verse 32: *"He who did not spare his own Son, but gave him up for us all—how will he not also with him graciously give us all things?"*

Here Paul is going back to the truth of our justification. He is arguing from the greater to the lesser. If God went to all the pain and anguish of giving up his own Son, do you think he is now going to turn away from us, leave us alone, leave us to fend for ourselves? Think back to the bridge analogy again; after going to all the trouble of building the bridge across the great chasm of our sins, is he now going to let us fall because he doesn't care enough to take our hand and help us across? If he gave us his Son, is there anything he won't do for us?

Paul continues to ground our security in God's great work of justification in the following verses: *"Who shall bring any charge against God's elect? It is God who justifies. Who is to condemn? Christ*

Jesus is the one who died—more than that, who was raised—who is at the right hand of God who indeed is interceding for us."

Paul's is once again using legal language, and his logic is irrefutable. Paul is not suggesting that there is no one who would like to bring accusations against us in court. In fact, Satan is actually referred to in the Scripture as the "accuser of the brethren." He loves to bring accusations against us. "Did you see what Cam did? Did you hear what he said? Did you see what he failed to do?" Sadly, I give Satan far too much material to use and far too many accusations to bring – but notice the logic. Whose court is it? Who is seated on the bench? Who is the judge? God is. God is also the one who has justified me. If the Judge of all the universe has declared me righteous, what difference does it make who is bringing accusations against me? If God justifies us, we are…**SAFE!**

But that is not all. Not only is the Judge himself on our side. We have the most wonderful Defense Attorney in the world. If someone tries to condemn us, Christ, who died and rose again, is now seated at the right hand of God. Picture it this way: whenever an accusation is made, the Judge looks over at Jesus and Jesus simply shows his nail pierced hands and the spear mark in his side and says, "I paid for that one, too!" Oh yes, our bridge is firmly anchored. Our defense team is always at work. Nothing we can do or say will ever induce him to turn his back on us now. We are…**SAFE!**

But we are still in the middle of the bridge. Heaven and future glory still look a long way off. The bridge is still rocking and bouncing. Who knows what tomorrow may bring? Just how safe are we, really? To address this concern, Paul poses another rhetorical question in verse 35: *"Who shall separate us from the love of Christ?"*

The interrogative pronoun here can be translated "What?" as well as "Who?" We might expand the question this way, "Is there anyone or anything that can separate us from the love of Christ?" To "separate" is the verb form of the Greek word for "without." Thus it literally means "To cause to be without." Without what? The love of Christ. Is there anyone or anything that will stop Christ from loving us? Is there anyone or anything that can remove us and put us out of range of his love, and by implication, his loving care?

To explore the question, Paul then begins to list possibilities. In fact he lists seven of them in verse 35: *Shall tribulation, or distress, or persecution, or famine, or nakedness, or danger, or sword?"* All of these are painful experiences. They are part of the groaning of life that we saw earlier in chapter 8. I think it is important to make note of the fact that this was not simply a theoretical list for Paul. Consider a passage in 2 Corinthians in which Paul mentions things he has actually experienced.

In 2 Corinthians 6:4-5 we read: *"but as servants of God we commend ourselves in every way: by great endurance, in afflictions, hardships, calamities, beatings, imprisonments, riots, labors, sleepless nights, hunger..."* Paul has an even longer list in 2 Corinthians 11!

No, these were not theoretical things for Paul. They were part of his actual life experience! So coming back to Romans 8:35, we must notice carefully what Paul is saying and what he is not saying. He is not saying that as Christians we will be kept safe from all difficult experiences. He is not saying that the bridge will not rock and the wind will not cause the bridge to sway. He is not saying that we will be sheltered from the "present sufferings." He is saying that these experiences cannot separate us from the love of Christ. We can continue to rest in and experience the love of Christ in the most painful of earthly circumstances.

There is a wonderful example of this in Acts 16 in the life of Paul while he was in the town of Philippi. Let me read verses 22-24 to see what happened to them.

"The crowd joined in attacking them, and the magistrates tore the garments off them and gave orders to beat them with rods. And when they had inflicted many blows upon them, they threw them into prison, ordering the jailer to keep them safely. Having received this order, he put them into the inner prison and fastened their feet in the stocks."

That's pretty brutal, isn't it? But while all this was going on, what was happening in Paul's heart? What was he experiencing on the inside? Look at verse 25: *"About midnight Paul and Silas were praying and singing hymns to God, and the prisoners were listening to them."* What were Paul and his companion Silas doing? They were praying and singing hymns to God. A hymn is a song of praise. They weren't singing the blues! They were singing praise to God. They were experiencing and basking in the love of God in the most dire of human circumstances.

As Christians, the Bible does not promise that we will be spared the painfulness of life. In fact it says just the opposite. Let's look at Romans 8:36: *"As it is written: 'For your sake we are being killed all the day long; we are considered as sheep to be slaughtered.'"* This is actually a prophecy that the followers of Christ will be persecuted and considered as "sheep to be slaughtered." Here Paul is taking us back to what he said in verse 17: *"We are heirs — heirs of God and fellow heirs with Christ, provided we suffer with him."* If they hated our elder brother, Jesus, how will the world treat us as his followers? There have been times and places in church history when this has been all too real; when Christians were thrown to lions in the coliseum; hung on crosses and set on fire to provide light for Roman celebrations. Even in our day, there are places in the world where to name the name of Christ is to put one's very life at stake. Many are still suffering and dying. No, Paul is not saying that as Christians we will never suffer. What he is saying is that there is no experience of present, earthly suffering that can separate us from the love of Christ.

In fact he goes on to a ringing statement in verse 37: *"No, in all these things we are more than conquerors through him who loved us."* "More than conquerors!" We not only overcome. We do so with strength and resources to spare. We win a resounding victory.

During the Reformation in England, there were two church leaders and preachers named Ridley and Latimer who were condemned to death for their strong adherence to the doctrine of justification by faith. They were tied to the stake on top of stacks of wood and the wood was set on fire. As the flames leaped higher and higher, one was heard to say to the other: "Be of good cheer. We shall light such a candle of God's grace in England that it shall never go out." More than conquerors through him who loved us!

Paul concludes with a final, ringing statement of confidence. You're not really supposed to answer a rhetorical question. But that is exactly what Paul does here. "Is there anyone or anything that can separate us from the love of Christ?" Here is his answer:

"For I am sure that neither death nor life, nor angels nor rulers, nor things present nor things to come, nor powers, nor height nor depth, nor anything else in all creation, will be able to separate us from the love of God in Christ Jesus our Lord." (Romans 8: 38-39)

It is an absolutely inclusive list, covering all logical possibilities.

Neither death nor life. What is death for the believer? It is the gateway into the presence of God. What is life? Continued opportunity to serve him.

Neither angels nor rulers (demons). Angels won't – they've been sent to minister to us. Demons can't, because "greater is he that is in us than he that is in the world."

Nor things present nor things to come. Nothing we are facing now, nor anything we might face in the future.

Neither height nor depth. This could refer either to spatial distances, or to the rankings of spiritual powers.

Finally, lest he may have left anything out, he adds, *"Nor anything else in all creation."* God, the Creator, is on our side. No created thing (which includes everything else) is able to separate us from his love.

Safety, security, a feeling of being safe is one of the fundamental needs we have as human beings. The need for safety and security is one that is in-born and recognized even by the very young. The tiniest baby has a way of sensing if he/she is safe. A baby often equates his security with the presence of his mother. If mother is near, the baby feels safe. As a result, a baby may go through a stage when he experiences what is called "separation anxiety." He is only happy in his mother's arms. If the mother leaves him, even for a few minutes, the baby will feel anxious and begin to fuss and cry.

The message of Romans 8:31-39 is clear and simple. As Christ's followers, we never need to suffer from separation anxiety. There is absolutely nothing in all creation that can separate us from the love of God that is in Christ Jesus our Lord. This was the promise Jesus gave his disciples. Do you remember the scene? Following the resurrection, Jesus was about to ascend into heaven. Before he left, he gathered his disciples together. He commissioned them, giving them a very large task: "Go, and make disciples of all nations." Do you remember the last thing he said to them in Matthew 28:20? *"And behold, I am with you always, to the end of the age."* No matter how much the bridge may rock and bounce, no matter how hard the wind may blow, no matter how many rocks are thrown at us, we are never alone. Jesus is with us. His love surrounds us. We are absolutely and eternally…**SAFE!**

21

QUESTIONS, QUESTIONS, QUESTIONS
Romans 9:1-29

In this chapter, we are entering one of the most difficult and controversial sections in Paul's letter to the Romans and possibly in all of Scripture. Books have been written on it. Debates have raged and continue to rage whenever it is discussed. Everyone has questions, but final and definitive answers often seem in short supply.

Structurally, Romans 9, 10 and 11 represent another detour in the larger outline of the book of Romans. It is another parenthesis in Paul's logic. (We saw the first two in Romans 6 and 7.) To demonstrate this fact, I would again invite you to read directly from the end of Romans 8 into the opening verses of chapter 12. In doing so, you will not find anything missing in the flow of Paul's thought or logic.

The issue that Paul discusses in these 3 chapters is Israel; the Jews, God's chosen people. How does the gospel of justification by faith fit with the Old Testament and God's plan and promises made to the descendants of Abraham? As such, this text is a very important passage as a kind of hinge between the Old and New Testament and how the two narratives fit together.

The reason the passage is so difficult and controversial is that it brings us face to face with one of the most puzzling and baffling paradoxes of Scripture and of the universe itself. That is the interface and interaction between the absolute sovereignty of God and the responsibility and accountability we have as human beings for our own choices and actions. While Romans 9-11 deals with these issues, I will confess that it often seems to raise as many questions as it answers, and it always stirs up fierce debates. In approaching these difficult and controversial matters, do not expect me to succeed where others have failed. I will not attempt to answer all the questions that may arise, and I doubt I will satisfy you with the answers I do give.

Here is my approach. During my years living in Abu Dhabi, we lived on the edge of one of the largest deserts in the world. One popular activity for many was called "dune bashing." It required a sturdy 4-wheel drive vehicle and considerable skill to drive across the desert and up and over the endless dunes without getting stuck. I lacked the 4-wheel drive vehicle, but I was often a passenger as we explored the edges of the desert. The key to driving through loose sand is to keep up one's speed. If the driver slows down or stops or allows his wheels to begin spinning, the vehicle bogs down, and it is soon time to get out the shovels and start digging out. I am going to approach this section the same way. If we go slow or stop or allow our wheels to start spinning, we are certainly going to bog down and get stuck. If we keep up our speed, maybe we'll have a chance of getting through!

Let's begin by introducing Paul's topic. He describes it in verse 3 as: *"For I could wish that I myself were accursed and cut off from Christ for the sake of my brothers, my kinsmen according to the flesh. They are Israelites, and to them belong the adoption, the glory, the covenants, the giving of the law, the worship, and the promises. To them belong the patriarchs, and from their race, according to the flesh, is the Christ, who is God over all, blessed forever. Amen."*

This is not only a good description of the Israelites, but it is a masterful summary of the whole Old Testament. As I read these verses, I find myself standing again at the foot of Mt. Sinai as the glory of God descended on the mountain with the peal of trumpets, the rolling of thunder and the flashing of lightning as God came down to seal his special covenant relationship with Israel and to adopt them as his own special people. I see Moses descending from the mountain with the tablets of stone on which God had inscribed the Ten Commandments with his own finger. I am reminded of the detailed beauty of the earthly tabernacle, the place of worship, with all the careful regulations of worship and sacrifice. I am reminded of God's promises to Abraham, Isaac and Jacob of a seed, a descendant through whom God would bless the entire world. I am even carried into the New Testament and particularly the story of Jesus' entry into Jerusalem as the people cried out "Hosanna to the Son of David!"

What a glorious inheritance! Yet Paul acknowledges that his own heart is now filled with unceasing sorrow for his people. So Paul asks a question; an awful, unthinkable question. Has God's word failed? Was God simply another politician, making promises he could not fulfill?

To this implied and painful question, Paul answers clearly in verse 6 and the first part of verse 7: *"But it is not as though the word of God has failed. For not all who are descended from Israel belong to Israel, and not all are children of Abraham because they are his offspring,"*

Paul addresses the question squarely and shows that a careful reading of the Old Testament reveals that God never promised salvation to everyone who was physically descended from Abraham. He first goes to the story of Abraham and his two sons: Ishmael and Isaac. They were both physically descended from Abraham, but God's promise was clearly made to Isaac. Let's pick up the reading again in the second half of verse 7: *"but 'Through Isaac shall your offspring be named.' This means that it is not the children of the flesh who are the children of God, but the children of the promise are counted as offspring. For this is what the promise said: 'About this time next year I will return, and Sarah shall have a son.'"*

If that example were not enough, he goes on to the next generation; to the sons of Isaac: *"And not only so, but also when Rebekah had conceived children by one man, our forefather Isaac, though they were not yet born and had done nothing either good or bad—in order that God's purpose of election might continue, not because of works but because of him who calls— she was told, 'The older will serve the younger.' As it is written, 'Jacob I loved, but Esau I hated.'"*

We need to be clear what Paul is saying here. He is simply reinforcing his basic point. God's word has not failed because God's promises never extended to every physical descendant of Abraham. He is citing the Old Testament and Jewish history to make that point. Although both Isaac and Ishmael were physical

169

sons of Abraham, Isaac played a different role in God's unfolding plan than Ishmael. Although both Jacob and Esau were not only physical sons of Isaac, but actually twins, yet Jacob was blessed in a way that Esau was not. One was preferred over the other, and contrary to human expectation, it was not the older, but the younger who was blessed.

Let me just make a brief comment on verse 13: *"Jacob I loved, but Esau I hated."* This verse should not be taken to apply to the two individuals involved, but to the two nations or races that descended from them. Paul is continuing to make his argument that not all physical descendants of Abraham were included in God's plan. The verse is a quotation from the Old Testament book of Malachi. In that book, God is seeking to demonstrate his love for the nation of Israel and he does so by comparing the history of the two nations. *"'I have loved you,' says the Lord. But you say, 'How have you loved us?' 'Is not Esau Jacob's brother?' declares the Lord. 'Yet I have loved Jacob but Esau I have hated. I have laid waste his hill country and left his heritage to jackals of the desert.'"* (Malachi 1:2-3) In other words, God is saying is saying to Israel, if you doubt my love for you as a nation, compare your history with the history of Esau's descendants. Esau and Jacob were brothers, yet their history and the history of their descendants followed very different paths. Clearly, not all of Abraham's descendants were included in the promise.

If physical descent is not enough, what was the distinguishing factor? It is here that our human reasoning and sensibilities are in for a shock. If we were writing this account, we would be quick to cite a human element – one was good and the other was bad; one worked hard and the other did not; one was more righteous than the other. Yet Paul says no such thing. In fact he contradicts our reasoning. The blessing of God and the transmission of the Messianic line was based on three things, according to Paul. It was based on **God's promise**, it was founded in **God's election**, and it was transmitted by **God's call.** Not only that, but the promise and the election were delivered, declared and established before the children involved were even born. The promise was delivered to Abraham before

Sarah conceived. The pronouncement concerning Jacob and Esau was made while they were still in the womb. It was not based on works but on the sovereignty of God.

Now, let's pause here a moment to recap. Paul is addressing the question: Has God's word failed? Has the plan of God for the descendants of Abraham failed because the nation as a whole has rejected Jesus as Messiah and turned away from him? In very broad terms, Paul's answer is, "No. God's word has not failed because God never said that every physical descendant of Abraham would inherit the spiritual promises of Abraham." And he has supported that answer with quotations and examples from the Old Testament and the history of Abraham's descendants. Before we go on, let's not miss the primary point Paul is making in this opening section. **God's Word has not failed.** God's Word never fails. As Isaiah declares in Isaiah 40:8: *"The grass withers, the flower fades, but the word of our God will stand forever."*

But now, Paul recognizes that in answering one question and addressing one difficulty, he has in fact raised another question in the minds of his readers. Here it is: **Is God unjust?** This is the question Paul takes up in verse 14: *"What shall we say then? Is there injustice on God's part?"*

This is the question that springs immediately to our minds in light of what he has just said about Jacob and Esau. Paul's answer is immediate and emphatic: *"By no means!"* There is no injustice on God's part. The Scripture makes this declaration clearly in passages like Deuteronomy 32:3-4: *"I will proclaim the name of the Lord. O praise the greatness of our God! He is the Rock, his ways are perfect and <u>all his ways are just</u>. A faithful God who does no wrong, <u>upright and just is he</u>." (from the NIV)*

The Scripture declares the justice of God. God is never unjust. But what, exactly, is justice? The word is related to the word "righteous." As we saw earlier in Romans, righteous means to be right according to some rule or legal standard. When we talk about the justice of God we are saying that he always judges people according to this standard of righteousness. By declaring God's justice, we know that God will never condemn the innocent. He will never punish anyone who does not deserve to be punished. He will treat everyone as well as they deserve to be treated by the law.

Let's go back to see how this is described earlier in Romans. In Romans 2:6-7, we find: *"He will render to each one according to his works: to those who by patience in well-doing seek for glory and honor and immortality, he will give eternal life;"*

This is the positive side of God's justice. He will not condemn or judge the innocent or the righteous. He will give them eternal life. But there is another side to God's justice. Romans 2:8 tells us: *"but for those who are self-seeking and do not obey the truth, but obey unrighteousness, there will be wrath and fury. There will be tribulation and distress for every human being who does evil."* That is the other side of God's justice. He will judge the wicked; those who have not lived up to his commandments and his righteousness.

God is never unjust; but here we must walk a careful line in following Paul's reasoning. Let's continue reading in Romans 9:15: *"For he says to Moses, 'I will have mercy on whom I have mercy, and I will have compassion on whom I have compassion.' So then it depends not on human will or exertion, but on God, who has mercy. For the Scripture says to Pharaoh, 'For this very purpose I have raised you up, that I might show my power in you, and that my name might be proclaimed in all the earth.' So then he has mercy on whomever he wills, and he hardens whomever he wills."*

Listen carefully to the balance of God's truth: **God is never unjust, but he is sovereign in his bestowal of mercy.** To understand this truth, we must hear this and hear it clearly. **God owes justice to everyone. God owes mercy to no one.** Mercy, by its very definition, cannot be demanded as a right or an obligation. Mercy means suspending judgment and not giving someone the punishment they deserve. Therefore it cannot be demanded, because in asking for mercy, we are admitting that we deserve judgment. It is essential that we understand this.

People who have heard Christian teaching about the mercy of God sometimes get this wrong. In the muddled thinking of our day, many have come to presume that the mercy of God is something that is ours by right; something we can demand. I remember reading an account of a famous atheist. He spent his life railing against the existence of God. On his deathbed, apparently he began to have second thoughts. He was heard to mutter the words; "God will forgive. It's his job!"

It is essential to Paul's argument here to understand that God does not owe mercy to anyone. He does not owe it to the Jews. He does not owe it to the Gentiles. He does not owe it to you because you are an American, or a Briton, or a South African or an Arab. He doesn't owe it to you because you come from a Christian family or because you go to church or because you are religious. God owes justice to all. He owes mercy to no one. **God is never unjust, but he is sovereign in his bestowal of mercy.**

I am not going to try to explain this or even defend it. I am simply going to proclaim it, for the Scripture proclaims it. God says: " *'I will have mercy on whom I have mercy, and I will have compassion on whom I have compassion.' So then it depends not on human will or exertion, but on God, who has mercy.*"

A question burns in our minds at this point. Paul does not shy away from it. He raises it himself in verse 19: *"You will say to me then, 'Why does he still find fault? For who can resist his will?'"*

Paul's answer to that question is blunt and simple – but maybe not very satisfying. Look at verses 20-21: *"But who are you, O man, to answer back to God? Will what is molded say to its molder, 'Why have you made me like this?' Has the potter no right over the clay, to make out of the same lump one vessel for honorable use and another for dishonorable use?"*

Ultimately, Paul says, we don't have the right to ask that question. God is sovereign in his bestowal of mercy. He is the potter. We are the clay. But let us be careful to understand the nuances of what Paul is saying here. Let me flesh it out with Paul's words in verses 22-23: *"What if God, desiring to show his wrath and to make known his power, has endured with much patience vessels of wrath prepared for destruction, in order to make known the riches of his glory for vessels of mercy, which he has prepared beforehand for glory..."*

Let me point out some distinctions in the original vocabulary here. In verse 22, we see the words "vessels of wrath prepared for destruction" and in verse 23 we see the phrase "vessels of mercy, which he has prepared beforehand for glory." I want to point out that the word "prepared" in verse 22 is a completely different word from the one translated "prepared" in verse 23. They are also different in grammatical form. The word "prepared" in verse 22 is passive in form. There is no stated actor, and the word meaning is that of something that is fitted and appropriate for a particular use and function. We are not told how it arrived at that state; only that it is in a state of being fit for destruction. In verse 23, however, the word is active. God is the subject of the verb, and he is seen as actively preparing or making vessels ready for glory.

So let us be careful to see what Paul is not saying as well as what he is saying. It is easy to go astray.

Paul is NOT saying that all people are inherently neutral objects; clay that is neither good nor bad. Then God comes along and chooses some of this neutral clay; from it he takes some and prepares vessels for destruction, and from it he takes some and prepares vessels for glory.

What Paul DOES say (if we keep all of Romans in mind) is that the clay is not neutral. We are all, by nature, vessels fitted and deserving of destruction. But God, in his sovereignty, has chosen some who were fit for destruction, and he prepared them for glory in order to display his grace and his mercy. He is sovereign. He is the potter. He has the right to do that. God is sovereign in his granting of mercy.

Let me put it another way. In eternity, there will be no one who experiences God's judgment who does not fully deserve it. That is the guarantee of God's justice. On the other hand, Heaven will be populated by people like you and me who deserve God's judgment, but instead have experienced his mercy. God is sovereign in his bestowal of that mercy. In Paul's eyes, the marvel of this doctrine is not that many are lost, but that any are saved. The emphasis of Paul's understanding of God's elective grace is not that some are left out, but the wonder that any are included. And what's more, that those who are included are both Gentiles and Jews as he goes on to record in the remaining verses in the text:

even us whom he has called, not from the Jews only but also from the Gentiles? As indeed he says in Hosea, "Those who were not my people I will call 'my people,' and her who was not beloved I will call 'beloved.'" "And in the very place where it was said to them, 'You are not my people,' there they will be called 'sons of the living God.' And Isaiah cries out concerning Israel: "Though the number of the sons of Israel be as the sand of the sea, only a remnant of them will be saved, for the Lord will carry out his sentence upon the earth fully and without delay." And as Isaiah predicted, "If the Lord of hosts had not left us offspring, we would have been like Sodom and become like Gomorrah."

Here Paul has gone back to where he began the chapter: Has God's Word failed? Once again, he uses Old Testament Scripture to demonstrate that the inclusion of Gentiles in salvation and the fact that only a Jewish remnant would be saved were clearly prophesied in Scripture. All who are included in the plan of God are vessels of his mercy and are included because God himself has called them. God is sovereign in his bestowal of mercy.

Does this truth, then, make all men simply pawns in the hands of a capricious God? Not at all. Here is where the paradox of God's truth lies. Paul will follow this declaration of God's sovereignty in the work of salvation with Romans 10 in which he will emphasize man's responsibility and a ringing and universal offer of God's mercy to anyone who calls on the name of the Lord.

To put it simplistically, Romans 9 looks at salvation and the lostness of man from God's viewpoint. Chapter 10 will look at it from man's viewpoint. To our finite view, these two seem ultimately to contradict one another. Yet God consistently presents both views side by side. The renowned preacher Charles Spurgeon was once asked how he reconciled the doctrine of God's sovereignty with man's responsibility. He responded, "I never try to reconcile friends."

Well, that's enough to think about and meditate on for one chapter. Let me just remind you of the main points of truth that have been clearly proclaimed in this text.

God's Word has not failed. God's Word never fails. His truth stands and will stand for all eternity.

God is not unjust. While we may not always understand or even agree with the way God runs his universe, we have this clear proclamation. God is not, and never can be, unjust. As Abraham declared with his rhetorical question, *"Shall not the Judge of all the earth do right?" (Genesis 18:25b)*

God is sovereign in his bestowal of mercy. God owes justice to all, but he does not owe mercy. It is his to give as, when, and to whom he chooses to give it.

So there we will leave it. Have I answered all your questions? I recognize that I have not. Have I said things that made you feel uncomfortable? I probably have.

I could hide behind the fact that we are not finished, and we are not. I hope you will continue reading. But I am all too aware that when we have finished our study, I will still not have answered all your questions and you will still probably feel a certain degree of puzzlement, uncertainty and even discomfort.

The reality is that we are face to face with mystery in these chapters, for in fact we are face to face with God. Our human tendency is to crave a God whom we understand and who marches to our beat; who fulfills our expectations and obeys our rules. We view the world through a man-centered portal. But the universe is not man-centered. It is God centered. For too long as human beings we have tried to create God in our image and make him answerable to us. But such a God is not the true God. He is an idol of our own making. The true God refuses to be confined in a box. He refuses to conform to our expectations or even to answer all our questions. By his own grace and will he has chosen to reveal himself to us. But in his revelation, he does not feel any obligation to explain himself, nor does he seek our approval. The ultimate reality is this. He is God. We are not. He does not answer to us. It is we who answer to him.

As the mysterious God of the universe, he reveals to us this marvelous truth. He is even now calling out for himself a people; *"Those who were not my people I will call 'my people' and her who was not beloved I will call 'beloved.' And in the very place where it* was said to them, 'You are not my people,' there they will be called 'sons and daughters of the living God.'" (Romans 9:25-26) He is even now preparing us as "vessels of his mercy" in order to "make known the riches of his glory." All we need to do to be included among God's vessels of mercy is to heed the voice of his calling and respond by faith. For this same God, who declares his sovereignty in election and who declares that he chose us before the foundation of the world, is the same God who has given us the gospel and declares that this gospel is "the power of God for salvation to everyone who believes."

And so I conclude this chapter the same way I concluded so many of these chapters with this simple question: Do you believe?

22

WHERE ISRAEL WENT WRONG
Romans 9:30-10:13

In this chapter we find ourselves "knee deep" in a very challenging, confusing, controversial, and yet vitally important passage of Scripture. In the previous chapter, I said that Romans chapters 9-11 are a parenthesis or detour in Paul's main line of logic in this letter. However, it is a detour that allows him to shed light on some very critical questions. They are questions to which we must have answers if we are to properly understand the relationship between the Old Testament and the New Testament; between the old covenant and the new covenant; between law and grace. At the heart of this passage is the question of the Jews; Israel, God's chosen people.

Paul began this passage in Romans 9:2-3 by saying: *"I have great sorrow and unceasing anguish in my heart... for the sake of my brothers, my kinsmen according to the flesh... the Israelites.."*

Clearly, all is not well with the Israelites. The question Paul is wrestling with is: Why not? What went wrong?

In the first 29 verses of chapter 9, Paul raises the question of whether God is at fault. Has God failed? Paul answers with a vigorous defense of the character of God. No, God's word has not failed. No, God is not unjust. However, God is sovereign in his bestowal of mercy. If God now chooses to grant his mercy to Gentiles instead of Jews, that is his right as Creator and Ruler over the universe.

God is not at fault. He has been and continues to be true to his Word, his character and ultimately to his plan. God has not failed. But we may ask, "Then what went wrong? Who did fail?" The answer to that question is, "Israel failed." Which brings us to the critical question we are considering in this chapter: How did Israel fail? Where did Israel go wrong?

Before we move forward, let me say that this is not simply an academic question. It is not a question with only historical significance. It is a question that is vital to every one of us today, because Israel's failure is a very common one. It is a failure that countless multitudes have made both before and since Paul wrote these words. It is a failure that is particularly common to religious people; people who go, not only to synagogues, but to churches, temples and mosques. It is a failure, an error that some of you who read these words may be making.

So where did the Jews go wrong? They went wrong by choosing the wrong road to salvation. There are two roads described in this passage; a wrong road and a right road. Before I go on, I must clarify something about these two roads we will be talking about. We are not talking about the road of sin vs. the road of good deeds. We are not contrasting a life of disobedience with a life of obedience. We are not talking about a road of rebellion which clearly leads away from God as opposed to a road that leads to God. Both of the roads we shall be discussing are roads that people take because they believe that they will lead to salvation and to right standing with God. Both of these roads carry sign posts that seem to point toward heaven. But one of these roads is a wrong road. It is a dead end. It will not take us to heaven. The other road is the right road. It will lead us to God and to eternal life.

In saying this, I realize that I have already contradicted one of the most sacred and popular beliefs of our modern and relativistic age; that is the belief that all roads lead us to the top of the same mountain. It is the belief that there is no wrong road. As long as we are sincere and we are doing our best, it doesn't matter which road we take, we will get there in the end. That is what many people in the world today believe. But it is not what the Bible says. It is not what Paul tells us in these verses. There is a wrong road and there is a right road. Israel took the wrong road. That is where they went wrong.

What road did Israel take? Israel chose **the road of DIY righteousness.** You may ask what I mean by the acronym DIY. It stands for Do It Yourself. I have borrowed it from the commercial world where it is used to describe a certain kind of hardware store or the section of the hardware store for people who like to think of themselves as handy men or handy women who do their own repairs and home improvement projects, rather than call a qualified plumber, carpenter or painter. But it also serves as a good description of the road Israel chose – the road of DIY righteousness. Let's look at how this road is described in the passage before us.

First of all, we find that it is a road that is characterized by **deliberate effort.** We might refer to this as the sweat factor. We find in both verse 31 and verse 32 of Romans 9 that the Jews *pursued* something. One lexicon I looked at rendered the idea of pursuing this way: "to do something with intense effort and with definite purpose or goal." You don't pursue something by accident. You have to make a deliberate choice and then you have to put effort and actions to your decision. But the key is this; this is human effort or self-effort. That is why I am calling this the road of DIY righteousness.

The second description of the road that they have chosen is that the right standing with God that they are pursuing is **based on keeping the law of God**. In verse 31 we read that *"Israel... pursued a law that would lead to righteousness."* In other words, they believed that their right standing with God was based on their own ability to conform to the law of God.

The third characteristic of this road is the belief that right standing with God is **based on works.** In verse 32, we find the words, *"as if it were based on works."* So it is a road that they believe leads to right standing with God based on human performance.

There is another mark of this road and those that travel it. It is a road that is **marked by a zeal for God.** Does that surprise you? Yet it is clear in Paul's words in Romans 10:2: *"For I bear them witness that they have a zeal for God..."* I looked up that word "zeal" in my Greek lexicon. It means "a deep and earnest concern or devotion." Those are strong words. Paul testifies to his Jewish brothers that they have a "deep and earnest concern and devotion for God."

We might ask, "Isn't that a good thing?" Well, yes, it can be.

But there is another more vital question. Is it enough? Many people say it is. The Bible says it is not. Listen and listen carefully. According to the words of Scripture itself: **Sincerity alone is not enough. Zeal alone will not save us.** Paul goes on to complete his thought in the rest of that verse: *but not according to knowledge.* They have zeal. It is even described as a "zeal for God," but their zeal is not based on a true understanding. Sincerity and zeal are not enough.

It reminds me of the old joke of the airline pilot who came over the PA system to announce: "I have bad news and good news. The bad news is that our navigation system has malfunctioned and we are lost. The good news is that we are making excellent time." That is the problem with zeal without knowledge. It is a case of traveling rapidly down a road which ultimately leads in the wrong direction.

Finally, in Romans 10:3, Paul adds one more marker on this road. It is one that summarizes and encapsulates all the others. This road is **based on establishing our own (DIY) righteousness.** Verse 3 of chapter 10 reads, in part: *"For, being ignorant of the righteousness of God, and seeking to establish their own..."* This is why I have called this road the **road of DIY righteousness.** It is the road that says, "I will base my standing with God on my own righteousness; my own choice and diligent effort, my own works and performance in keeping the commands of God, my own sincerity and zeal for God." This was the road that Israel as a whole, the majority of the Jews, chose to travel.

Before we leave our consideration of this road, let's look at where the road ends up. As we consider Paul's words, we find that he does not tell us where the road ends up so much as tell us where the road will not take us.

First of all, we know that the outcome is not a happy one. We know that because back in Romans 9:2 he spoke of the "great sorrow and unceasing anguish" that he had in his heart for his fellow Jews. He also says in Romans 10:1 that his heart's desire and his prayer for them is that they might be saved. So the road they have chosen has not led them to salvation.

He spells this out even more clearly in Romans 9:31: *"but*

that Israel who pursued a law that would lead to righteousness did not succeed... " Remember what Paul said in Romans 3:20? *"For by works of the law no human being will be justified in his sight."* He expounded on that in Romans 8:3: *"For God has done what the law, weakened by the flesh could not do."* The problem with the law is that we cannot keep it. The problem with the road of DIY righteousness is that we are not righteous. In our own efforts we do not and we cannot measure up. We fall short of the glory of God. We are sinners; every one of us.

Now, here is the sad reality of the Jewish race as Paul reflects on it. In their passionate pursuit of their own righteousness they missed their one and only true hope. This is what he tells us in Romans 10:3: *"For, being ignorant of the righteousness of God, and seeking to establish their own, they did not submit to God's righteousness."* What tragic words! God offered them a way out, but in their ignorance and in their pride, they rejected it. They refused to take the road to a right standing with God that was offered to them. They refused to submit to God's way and God's plan. They refused to accept his offer of the righteousness that is by faith.

At the end of Romans 9, Paul describes this as "stumbling." He quotes the Old Testament prophet Isaiah as he writes in verses 32-33: *"They have stumbled over the stumbling stone, as it is written, 'Behold, I am laying in Zion a stone of stumbling, and a rock of offense; and whoever believes in him will not be put to shame.'"*

Paul is left with a great ache in his heart, praying for the salvation of his fellow Jews; praying that, before it is too late, they will open their blinded eyes to see that there is another road available to them. This is the road that will lead to right standing with God. This is the road that will lead to salvation.

This is **the road of faith righteousness** that Paul has been describing from the very opening words of this letter. It is **a road that recognizes that right standing with God is not something that can be pursued by human effort, but rather a gift to be received.** This is the contrast that Paul laid down in the opening verse of this section, Romans 9:30: *"What shall we say, then? That*

Gentiles who did not pursue righteousness have attained it, that is a righteousness that is by faith..." The word translated "attained" means to receive something and make it one's own. The Gentiles whom Paul is referring to are the Gentile believers whom God is calling to be his people. They were not seeking or pursuing God, but God pursued them. He called them. When they heard the call, they answered it and received the gift of right standing with God.

The key to this road and to this righteousness is that **it is a gift that must be received by faith**. This is what Paul has been hammering home to us since the first chapter. The theme of faith echoes loudly once again in this text. Let's read the section through again. Watch for the repetition of faith and belief in Paul's words. (Remember that "faith," "believe," and "belief," are the same in the Greek language.)

"What shall we say, then? That Gentiles who did not pursue righteousness have attained it, that is, a righteousness that is <u>by faith</u>; but that Israel who pursued a law that would lead to righteousness did not succeed in reaching that law. Why? Because they did not pursue it <u>by faith</u>, but as if it were based on works. They have stumbled over the stumbling stone, as it is written, 'Behold, I am laying in Zion a stone of stumbling, and a rock of offense; and <u>whoever believes</u> in him will not be put to shame.' Brothers, my heart's desire and prayer to God for them is that they may be saved. For I bear them witness that they have a zeal for God, but not according to knowledge. For, being ignorant of the righteousness of God, and seeking to establish their own, they did not submit to God's righteousness. For Christ is the end of the law for righteousness <u>to everyone who believes</u>." (Romans 9:30-10:4)

So, if this righteousness with God is something that we did not pursue, but which we must receive, and if receiving and submitting to God's righteousness is something we must do by faith or by belief, I think we can all agree that it is important to know how to do that. That is where Paul turns in this very last verse we just read. This faith is first and foremost belief in a person. It is noteworthy that Paul does not first refer to him by name, but rather (in this Jewish context) by title: "Christ,"

"Messiah," the promised anointed Redeemer whom God had promised to send. *"Christ is the end of the law for righteousness to everyone who believes."* We no longer rely on the law for our righteousness. We rely on Christ, the Messiah.

The next few verses use a rather interesting way of expounding the Gospel. Let's pick up the reading in verse 5:

"For Moses writes about the righteousness that is based on the law, that the person who does the commandments shall live by them. But the righteousness based on faith says, 'Do not say in your heart, "Who will ascend into heaven?" (that is, to bring Christ down) or "Who will descend into the abyss?"' (that is, to bring Christ up from the dead). But what does it say? 'The word is near you, in your mouth and in your heart' (that is, the word of faith that we proclaim); because, if you confess with your mouth that Jesus is Lord and believe in your heart that God raised him from the dead, you will be saved. For with the heart one believes and is justified, and with the mouth one confesses and is saved. For the Scripture says, 'Everyone who believes in him will not be put to shame.' For there is no distinction between Jew and Greek; for the same Lord is Lord of all, bestowing his riches on all who call on him. [13] For 'everyone who calls on the name of the Lord will be saved.'"

In this section, Paul is both expounding on the essential facts of the gospel which we must believe in order to be saved and at the same time showing how inadequate our own DIY righteousness is. First of all, in verse 5, he quotes Moses to point out that it is only by actually keeping all the commandments that one can establish DIY righteousness and find true life – and as Scripture and our own experience teaches us, not one of us is able to do that. In the next few verses he uses Old Testament quotes to ask two rhetorical questions: *"'Who will ascend into heaven?' (that is, to bring Christ down) or 'Who will descend into the abyss?' (that is, to bring Christ up from the dead)."*

Here Paul cites three fundamental facts of the Gospel message; three absolutely non-negotiable realities of Biblical truth. They are the incarnation, the crucifixion and the resurrection of the Messiah. The Christ, the Messiah, came down – he descended from heaven. He died and descended into the abyss. He came back from the dead. These are the central, historical facts of the Gospel. And Paul asks us – "Did you accomplish that? Were you able, with your DIY righteousness, to go up into heaven and bring Christ down? Were you, by human effort, able to go down into the abyss to bring Christ back from the dead?" How puny our own attempts at righteousness are when compared to the mighty acts of God in salvation.

So if the great work necessary for salvation has already been accomplished by God himself and his Christ, what is left for us to do? Look at verses 8-10: *"But what does it say? 'The word is near you, in your mouth and in your heart' (that is, the word of faith that we proclaim); because, if you confess with your mouth that Jesus is Lord and believe in your heart that God raised him from the dead, you will be saved. For with the heart one believes and is justified, and with the mouth one confesses and is saved."*

We must pay close attention now! This is crucial to our understanding of where the Jews went wrong and where we must get it right if we want to be right with God. So far in this text Paul has consistently used the title: Christ. Remember, devout Jews believed in the Christ. They believed in a coming Messiah. But now, in verse 9, Paul introduces a human name. He introduces the name Jesus. You have to believe that Jesus, from the line of David, son of Mary, born in Bethlehem, raised in Nazareth; this Jesus is Lord. He is Messiah. He is the One who descended from heaven. You have to confess that and you have to believe that he died and that God raised him from the dead. This was where the Jews stumbled. They believed in a Messiah, a coming Christ. They just didn't believe that Jesus was that Messiah. They stumbled and they fell over the stumbling stone, and continued to try to satisfy God with their own DIY righteousness. They chose the wrong path.

But the right path is right here, nearby. Anyone can take it. It involves just two things: your heart and your mouth. It is interesting to note that in verse 9, Paul puts the mouth first and then the heart, while in verse 10 he puts the heart first and then the mouth. I believe he does that to illustrate that the order is not important, but that both must be involved. We must believe in our hearts that Jesus is

Lord. Jesus is Messiah. He came down from heaven. He died for our sins. He rose from the dead. Then we must confess it.

What is the significance of this confession? To confess means to agree; to say the same thing. We must acknowledge verbally and aloud what we believe in our hearts. Paul is telling us that it is impossible to truly believe in your heart without acknowledging that belief verbally. It may not be in a dramatic fashion in front of a church full of people, but it seems to me that we should at least confess our faith to the significant people in our lives. One very powerful way to make this confession is by being baptized. During 40 years of pastoral ministry I had the privilege to perform countless baptisms in an interesting variety of venues; from frigid Alaskan lakes with the salmon swimming around my legs, to muddy canals in India, with a water buffalo swimming past. Regardless of the setting, I always asked the same question: "Do you believe that Jesus is the Christ and have you trusted in him as your Savior from sin?" When they answered, "Yes, I do!" they were confessing with their mouths.

"For with the heart one believes and is justified, and with the mouth one confesses and is saved."

When we believe and confess we are justified. We are saved. We receive and make our own the righteousness that comes from God and is by faith. We embark on the right road, the road of faith righteousness; the road that leads to eternal life.

Paul goes on to once again make clear that this road, this road of faith righteousness is open to all in verses 11-13: *"For the Scripture says, 'Everyone who believes in him will not be put to shame.' For there is no distinction between Jew and Greek; for the same Lord is Lord of all, bestowing his riches on all who call on him. For 'everyone who calls on the name of the Lord will be saved.'"*

There are two roads. There is a wrong road and there is a right road. There is the road of DIY righteousness and there is the road of faith righteousness. One of these roads will lead to eternal life. The other will not. So I conclude with this question. Which road are you on?

23

AN ENQUIRY INTO THE OBLIGATIONS OF CHRISTIANS...

Romans 10:14-21

The title I have chosen for this chapter is **An Enquiry Into the Obligations of Christians...**

I don't usually make a habit of borrowing other people's titles, but I have done so in this case. Well, actually I have only borrowed part of the title. The author was William Carey. The full title of his tract was: **An Enquiry into the obligations of Christians to use means for the conversion of the heathens in which the religious state of the different nations of the world, the success of former undertakings and the practicability of further undertakings are considered.**

How is that for a title that just rolls off the tongue! Yet his little booklet became a Christian classic and served a vital role in launching the modern mission movement. William Carey was born in 1761 He was a shoemaker by profession, but God got hold of his heart and, practicing what he preached, he spent his life in India proclaiming the good news of Jesus Christ.

In that booklet, right after the title and before the "Introduction" is a quotation taken from the Book of Romans chapter 10 beginning in verse 12 (I am not sure what Bible translation he used. I am quoting from the ESV):

"For there is no distinction between Jew and Greek; for the same Lord is Lord of all, bestowing his riches on all who call on him. For 'everyone who calls on the name of the Lord will be saved.' How then will they call on him in whom they have not believed? And how are they to believe in him of whom they have never heard? And how are they to hear without someone preaching? And how are they to preach unless they are sent?"

This quotation bridges the passage where we finished the previous chapter, as well as introducing the text we are considering in this chapter. The previous passage concluded with the ringing, open invitation to salvation to Jew and non-Jew alike; to everyone who will believe and call on the name of the Lord Jesus for salvation. With that invitation comes the promise that *"everyone who calls on the name of the Lord will be saved."*

In this chapter we are going to consider the sacred obligation that we incur when we accept that offer of salvation. This is **an enquiry into the obligations of Christians...**Chief among those obligations is the responsibility we have to pass the message of Christ on to others.

This passion for sharing the message of Christ permeated the life and writings of Paul. We could go through passage after passage in his writings and find numerous examples. I am limiting myself simply to his epistle to the Romans. This passion was rooted in his deep compassion for the lost.

There is a passage we looked at back in chapter 9 that haunts me. It is Romans 9:1-3: *"I am speaking the truth in Christ—I am not lying; my conscience bears me witness in the Holy Spirit— that I have great sorrow and unceasing anguish in my heart. For I could wish that I myself were accursed and cut off from Christ for the sake of my brothers, my kinsmen according to the flesh."*

I read that and I ask myself the question: Do I have that? Do I carry *"great sorrow and unceasing anguish in my heart"* for the lost people all around me? Paul says that he is not exaggerating. He is not lying. He even calls on the Holy Spirit to be his witness. "Great sorrow and unceasing anguish!" Why, Paul? "Because my fellow countrymen, my kinsmen, my race, my people are lost!" Leave aside the technicalities of Bible interpretation for a moment and hear and feel the raw human emotion! Do you share that? Do I share that?

Verse 3 is almost beyond belief: *"For I could wish that I myself were accursed and cut off from Christ for the sake of my brothers, my kinsmen according to the flesh."*

Hear what Paul is saying. He uses a rare grammatical form here that protects him from outright heresy. It is rendered "I could wish." He doesn't quite say that he does wish it. He says, so to speak, "I am this close!" The potential is there. My concern for my brothers is so great that if I could exchange my salvation for theirs (and I know I can't), I am right on the point of being willing to make that exchange and take their place in Hell if that would lead to their salvation.

Can I say that? Do I have that same passionate concern for the lost that I would be willing to give up my own salvation for them? And if that is too much to ask, if that is too high a bar, what am I willing to give up so that others can hear the Gospel of Jesus Christ and come to salvation?

A quote from William Carey's little booklet speaks powerfully to this point: "Some attempts are still making, but they are inconsiderable in comparison of what might be done if the whole body of Christians entered heartily into the spirit of the divine command on this subject. Some think little about it, others are unacquainted with the state of the world, and others love their wealth better than the souls of their fellow-creatures." Tell me! Does that pinch just a little?

Paul's passion for the lost found a practical expression in the form of prayer. We find this in Romans 10:1: *"Brothers, my heart's desire and prayer to God for them is that they may be saved."* Paul carried this burden with him into his prayer life – and he regularly and passionately prayed for the lost. In his case he carried a special prayer burden for the Jews. I believe that God does give particular prayer burdens to us. We may not all be equally burdened for every one or every people group, race or nation. However, I believe we should all carry a burden of prayer for the lost. If you don't have that, ask God to give it to you. It may be certain individuals among your family or friends. It may be a wider category of people, or an entire people group. When my parents were in Bible College in California in the 1930's, their college was organized into "prayer bands" to pray for particular regions of the world. They both went to the prayer band for Africa. In fact, that is where they met. They ended up spending almost 45 years in Africa, sharing the gospel. It began with a prayer burden. Who are we praying for?

This passion for the lost found expression in his prayers. But it didn't stop there. When Paul compares the eternal destiny of the lost with the incredible spiritual riches offered in Christ and in his gospel, it prompts him to ask a series of rhetorical questions which lead to a clear picture of our obligation as Christians.

"How then will they call on him in whom they have not believed? And how are they to believe in him of whom they have never heard? And how are they to hear without someone preaching? And how are they to preach unless they are sent? As it is written, 'How beautiful are the feet of those who preach the good news!'"

It is a perfectly logical sequence, is it not? In order to experience the riches that are in Christ, people must call on him. In order to call on him, they have to believe in him. In order to believe in him, they have to hear about him. And how will they hear about him? Someone has to tell them! And that is our job. That is our obligation as those who have received the riches of Jesus Christ and been justified by faith.

The word "preaching" here is not limited to something that happens in a church building, and it does not require a pulpit and a microphone. It means to serve as a herald; someone who makes an official message known by proclaiming it. It can be done before multitudes or it can be done one to one. It is a task for every follower of Christ.

There is one final link in this chain of responsibility. Not everyone lives within reach or sound of a gospel-preaching community or people. They live on the other side of some kind of barrier of geographical, cultural or linguistic distance. They will not be reached in the natural course of everyday life. Someone must go to them. That requires "sending." This is where William Carey focused his famous work. At that time, England had many churches. Anyone in England who so desired could find a church where the gospel was proclaimed. William Carey did not disparage the work or the gospel preaching of these churches. He did write to declare that it was not enough. There were many peoples and places in the world where there was no gospel witness. It was time to be deliberate and intentional to send people to those places and to those people, because, as followers of Christ, our obligation is ultimately to the whole world.

William Carey was not content simply to call for prayer. Listen to another quote from his book: "We must not be contented however with prayer, without exerting ourselves in the use of means for the obtaining of those things we pray for." I know Paul would have said a hearty "Amen" to William Carey's writings.

Paul makes no attempt to sugar coat the difficulty of the task. He makes it clear that there are many who will not believe even when they hear the message. This is what he tells us in verse 16: *"But they have not all obeyed the gospel. For Isaiah says, 'Lord, who has believed what he has heard from us?'"*

When I was in university, I was active with a campus ministry that trained me to share my faith. I have always been grateful for that training. But there was one statement that they used repeatedly that I struggled with. It went something like this: "Most people want to accept Christ. They just don't know how." The implication was that the only thing people lacked was information. Just tell them and "most" will follow Christ. Frankly, that was never my experience. Most people I talked with about Christ did not choose to follow him. Paul tells us that we should be prepared for this. He quotes from the heart of Isaiah 53, that great prophecy of the coming Messiah. The quote is almost a despairing one. It is almost as if Isaiah asks, "Will there be any who believe my message?" Paul goes on in the passage to quote several more passages about the refusal, particularly of the Jews, to respond to God's offer of mercy. No, not all will obey the Gospel when they hear it. However, that does not relieve us of our responsibility to tell them. While not everyone who hears will believe, one thing is for sure. If there is no proclamation, there is no hearing and without hearing there will be no faith. This is Paul's point in Romans 10:17: *"So faith comes from hearing, and hearing through the word of Christ."* We have an obligation to pass the message on – whether or not the recipients respond.

That same campus ministry taught us something else, and this I have held on to over the years. It was a definition for successful witnessing. "Successful witnessing is sharing the good news of Jesus Christ in the power of the Holy Spirit, <u>and leaving the results to God.</u>" Results are God's domain. Our responsibility and obligation is to share the good news.

As I conclude this chapter, let me level with you. As a

preacher, I always knew that there were a couple of topics I could preach on that would inevitably leave my hearers feeling defeated and guilty. One of those topics is prayer. We all know or feel that we don't pray often enough, hard enough or long enough. A few good quotes about famous Christians who spent 4 hours a day in prayer before breakfast leave us all feeling inferior and guilty. Another of those topics is witnessing. Most of us are intimidated by the topic and feel guilty that we are not doing enough. I'll be honest with you. I don't particularly like preaching (or writing) on these topics, because they leave me feeling guilty too!

I don't want to send you away with another load of guilt and inferiority. Let's break it down into bite size pieces. First of all, start with prayer. It doesn't have to be 4 hours of prayer before breakfast! Just simple, sentence prayers asking God to give you a burden and a passion for a particular individual or individuals, or even a particular category of people or a people group. Don't try to manufacture the burden. Ask God to give the burden to you. Then make those individuals or that group a regular part of your intercessory praying.

Then arm yourself. Many people are afraid to share their faith because they are not sure what to say. Sometimes a good tool can take some of the fear out of that. I encourage you to find such a tool or tools. It might be a book, a tract, a link to a website; anything that presents the Gospel clearly and powerfully.

Now put the two together. As you are praying to God to give you a burden and passion for the lost, ask God if there is anyone to whom he wants you to give this tool. Don't rush it. Let God show you who to give it to and when to give it. Then when they have had the opportunity to read or watch it, you can ask what they thought of it. Then continue to follow the Holy Spirit's leading from there. Remember, results are God's domain. Our obligation is simply to share the good news and leave the results to God!

"How then will they call on him in whom they have not believed? And how are they to believe in him of whom they have never heard? And how are they to hear..." unless someone (like you or me) tells them?

24

BUT WHAT ABOUT ISRAEL?

Romans 11

We are continuing to navigate our way through the complexities of this section of Scripture. Three controversial and potentially divisive issues are raised in chapter 11. The first issue is a repeat of one we saw earlier in chapter 9: the doctrine of God's election. The second issue is that of the future of Israel. Is there a future in God's plan for Israel as a people, or did God officially write the nation off in 70 AD with the destruction of Jerusalem, and transfer all of his promises to the church as the new Israel, the new people of God? The third issue is that of the eternal security of the believer. Is it possible to lose one's salvation once one has put his or her faith in Jesus Christ and has been justified?

Any one of these three issues can raise a firestorm of debate among sincere, Bible-believing Christians. Here we are faced with all three. What makes it even more difficult is that, while the chapter raises all three issues, it does not fully answer any of them. There are clues, evidence and hints to add fuel to the debates, but to fully answer any of these questions would require a much broader survey of the Scriptures than falls within the scope of this book.

I recognize, therefore, that if you have come looking for definitive answers to any of these questions, I am going to leave you disappointed. We will examine the text. I will comment on the clues and the light that I believe this chapter sheds on these debates. However, I fear we will still be left with some ambiguity and possibly some areas in which we may simply need to agree to disagree. Finally, though, I hope to conclude by looking at some clear and positive commands and statements of Scripture that we can all obey and upon which we can all agree, whether or not all of our questions are answered, and whether or not we agree on every detail of the interpretation of this difficult and complex text.

Let me once again set the immediate context. After the great sweeping offer of salvation to "all who call on the name of the Lord," and the obligation of Christians to spread that message to the whole world, Paul concluded chapter 10 with several Old Testament quotations. These quotations highlighted God's intention to now reveal himself to the Gentiles (those who had not sought after God) as well as the prophet's prediction in describing the stubborn refusal of the Jewish people to follow God by faith.

Now Paul continues, using one of his favorite literary devices by anticipating a question in the minds of his readers, asking it, and then answering it. Let's look at the first 10 verses together.

"I ask, then, has God rejected his people? By no means! For I myself am an Israelite, a descendant of Abraham, a member of the tribe of Benjamin. God has not rejected his people whom he foreknew. Do you not know what the Scripture says of Elijah, how he appeals to God against Israel? 'Lord, they have killed your prophets, they have demolished your altars, and I alone am left, and they seek my life.' But what is God's reply to him? 'I have kept for myself seven thousand men who have not bowed the knee to Baal.' So too at the present time there is a remnant, chosen by grace. But if it is by grace, it is no longer on the basis of works; otherwise grace would no longer be grace.

"What then? Israel failed to obtain what it was seeking. The elect obtained it, but the rest were hardened, as it is written, 'God gave them a spirit of stupor, eyes that would not see and ears that would not hear, down to this very day.' And David says, 'Let their table become a snare and a trap, a stumbling block and a retribution for them; let their eyes be darkened so that they cannot see, and bend their backs forever.'"

The first question Paul anticipates in this section is this: **Has God rejected Israel totally?** His answer is clear and strong. "No way!" The repudiation of Israel as a people is not total. There was still a Jewish remnant who were saved by grace. Paul's first proof of that reality is himself. "Here I am," Paul says. "I am follower of Jesus, the Messiah, saved by grace through faith. Yet I am still a Jew, an Israelite, a physical descendant of Abraham and a member of the tribe of Benjamin."

The doctrine of the faithful remnant is a prominent theme of the Old Testament Scriptures. Paul cites the well-known story of the prophet Elijah. In deep discouragement, Elijah poured out his complaint to God that he was the only true "God-follower" left in Israel, and they were trying to kill him. God responded by telling him that there were in fact 7000 faithful worshipers of God left in Israel. Paul now points out that the same is true in his own day in verse 5: *So too at the present time there is a remnant, chosen by grace.*

In spite of the unbelief of the majority of Jews, a faithful, believing remnant remained. They are the elect, the chosen, and they have been chosen and saved by grace, not on the basis of their own works. God was exercising his sovereign right to "Have mercy on whom he would have mercy." The early church in the Book of Acts was made up entirely of the remnant of believing Jews. However, gradually as the Book of Acts and the early history of the church unfolded, God opened up his kingdom to the Gentiles. As believing Gentiles began to flood into the community of those who were called "God's people" the percentage of Jews rapidly declined. But they were still there; people who were physically descended from Abraham who also shared the faith of Abraham.

There remains such a remnant today. When I was a small child on the mission field in East Africa, a young single man joined my parents at our mission station. His name was Jerry. He was a Jew, raised in New York City, but he was also a follower of Jesus and had followed the call of God to preach the gospel in Africa. He spent his entire career there, preaching and teaching in Bible Schools. Jerry followed a common path, blending with the mainstream of Christianity, with little to distinguish him as a Jew. Others have chosen a different path, gathering together in Messianic congregations, preserving their Jewish traditions and forms of worship, yet faithfully giving allegiance to Jesus as the Messiah and Redeemer.

Has God rejected his people totally? No. There is still a remnant of believing Jews today. Yet, sadly, the great majority have turned away and remained in their unbelief. They are the *"rest who were hardened"* (verse 7), but even this hardening was a fulfillment of prophecy as Paul points out by quoting several Old Testament texts in the rest of the paragraph.

That is the present reality; a believing remnant with the rest hardened in their unbelief. But what about the future? The second question Paul asks is: **Has God rejected his people permanently?** Let's look at the next section (Romans 11:11-32):

"So I ask, did they stumble in order that they might fall? By no means! Rather through their trespass salvation has come to the Gentiles, so as to make Israel jealous. Now if their trespass means riches for the world, and if their failure means riches for the Gentiles, how much more will their full inclusion mean!

"Now I am speaking to you Gentiles. Inasmuch then as I am an apostle to the Gentiles, I magnify my ministry in order somehow to make my fellow Jews jealous, and thus save some of them. For if their rejection means the reconciliation of the world, what will their acceptance mean but life from the dead? If the dough offered as firstfruits is holy, so is the whole lump, and if the root is holy, so are the branches.

"But if some of the branches were broken off, and you, although a wild olive shoot, were grafted in among the others and now share in the nourishing root of the olive tree, do not be arrogant toward the branches. If you are, remember it is not you who support the root, but the root that supports you. Then you will say, 'Branches were broken off so that I might be grafted in.' That is true. They were broken off because of their unbelief, but you stand fast through faith. So do not become proud, but fear. For if God did not spare the natural branches, neither will he spare you. Note then the kindness and the severity of God: severity toward those who have fallen, but God's kindness to you, provided you continue in his kindness. Otherwise you too will be cut off. And even they, if they do not continue in their unbelief, will be grafted in, for God has the power to graft them in again. For if you were cut from what is by nature a wild olive tree, and grafted, contrary to nature, into a cultivated olive tree, how much more will these, the natural branches, be grafted back into their own olive tree.

"Lest you be wise in your own sight, I want you to understand this mystery, brothers: a partial hardening has come upon Israel, until the fullness of the Gentiles has come in. And in this way all Israel will be saved, as it is written, 'The Deliverer will come from Zion, he will banish ungodliness from Jacob;'... 'and this will be my covenant with them when I take away their sins.'

"As regards the gospel, they are enemies of God for your sake. But as regards election, they are beloved for the sake of their forefathers. For the gifts and the calling of God are irrevocable. For just as you were at one time disobedient to God but now have received mercy because of their disobedience, so they too have now been disobedient in order that by the mercy shown to you they also may now receive mercy. For God has consigned all to disobedience, that he may have mercy on all."

Now we are face to face with the difficult questions of doctrine and interpretation that I referred to in my introduction. Let's face them head on. First of all, let's face the doctrine of divine election and the sovereignty of God. I will not say a great deal about this. We faced it before in Romans 9. What I would highlight here is the clear teaching that God is the sovereign and active agent in salvation and in his plan for the history of the world. He is the sovereign one who is breaking off branches and grafting them into the tree in his garden. He is sovereign in showing his mercy as well as in displaying his severity and judgment. This is once again viewing the work of salvation from God's perspective. It makes us uncomfortable because we are used to looking at salvation and life from a man centered perspective. But the world and the universe are not man-centered. They are God-centered. He is carrying out his plan in history and in eternity. Now if we had only this chapter to go on, we might conclude that this makes us, as human beings, simply pawns in his hands. Yet sandwiched between the declaration of God's election and sovereignty in chapter 9 and this chapter and the parable of the olive tree, we have Romans 10 and the offer of God's salvation to any and all who will believe and call on the name of the Lord. The clear implication is that Israel's fall from favor came because of their persistent refusal to respond to God's multiple offers of grace, love and mercy. They therefore bear the responsibility for that rejection as Paul makes clear in 10:21: *"All day long I have held out my hands to a disobedient and contrary people."* We have trouble reconciling those two realities (God's sovereignty and man's responsibility) in our finite minds. Yet Scripture repeatedly places them side by side and declares them both to be true.

This brings us to the question I raised earlier; that of the future of Israel. **Is God's rejection of Israel permanent?** As Paul poses the question in verse 11: *"So I ask, did they stumble in order that they might fall?"* I think we are accurate in capturing Paul's thought by adding the word "permanently" to that question. Is this a temporary stumble or a permanent fall from which there will be no recovery? I recognize that there is a diversity of opinions on this subject. Whatever position we hold, we must wrestle with and interpret the following statements from the text.

First of all, Paul answers his own question with another strong denial. "By no means!" What exactly is Paul denying? Then we must interpret verse 12: *"Now if their trespass means riches for the world, and if their failure means riches for the Gentiles, how much more will their full inclusion mean!"* What does he mean by the phrase "their full inclusion?" Next there is the parable of the olive tree and the prophecy of the "grafting back in of the natural branches." Certainly this can be accounted for by the salvation of individual Jews during this age; a repetition of the earlier teaching on the believing remnant. But what is the correct interpretation of verses 25-27?

"Lest you be wise in your own sight, I want you to understand this mystery, brothers: a partial hardening has come upon Israel, until the fullness of the Gentiles has come in. And in this way all Israel will be saved, as it is written, 'The Deliverer will come from Zion, he will banish ungodliness from Jacob'; 'and this will be my covenant with them when I take away their sins.'"

What is this mystery and when will this prophecy be fulfilled? What is the "fullness of the Gentiles" and what does the reference to "all Israel" being saved mean in verse 26? And what does Paul mean when he says in verse 29: *"For the gifts and the calling of God are irrevocable."*

Personally, I cannot read these verses without believing that God has a future in mind for the Jews; the physical descendants of Abraham, Isaac and Jacob. Of course, how we answer this question has great implications for what we believe about God's plans for the end of the age. Such a discussion is once again beyond the scope of this book, even if I were wise enough to unravel such mysteries. I simply invite you to study these Scriptures and form your own opinion. **Is God's rejection of Israel total?** I think most would agree and answer that question in the negative, based on the first 10 verses of the chapter. **Is God's rejection of Israel permanent?** I leave that one to you to answer in the light of these Scriptures.

The third difficult question that faces us in this text is the question of the eternal security of the believer. If believers are secure and saved once and for all by faith in Christ, then what is Paul saying when he warns us in verse 19-22: *"Then you will say, 'Branches were broken off so that I might be grafted in.' That is true. They were broken off because of their unbelief, but you stand fast through faith. So do not become proud, but fear. For if God did not spare the natural branches, neither will he spare you. Note then the kindness and the severity of God: severity toward those who have fallen, but God's kindness to you, provided you continue in his kindness. Otherwise you too will be cut off."*

This is possibly the most difficult question of all. To answer it correctly, we must keep the metaphor in mind and recognize that we are dealing with categories and not individuals. The contrast here is between the Gentile church and the Jewish race. The Jewish race turned away in unbelief and as a whole those natural branches were broken off. In their place, the (largely) Gentile church, made up of Gentile believers (and a believing Jewish remnant), was grafted into the tree. Paul is warning those within that group not to become arrogant and to take to themselves a sense of entitlement and of superiority to the Jews. We were not grafted in because we were better or more worthy. We were grafted in by faith and by the kindness of God. The true believer recognizes that and "stands fast" through faith. The church organization, denomination, or member that lacks true faith and thinks they are entitled to the grace of God simply because they call themselves the church or wear the name "Christian" are as sure to be cut off as the Jews who believed that they were entitled to their place in the kingdom just because they were physical descendants of Abraham.

As I said, these are difficult questions that have engaged Bible scholars and theologians for hundreds of years. I am sure there is a diversity of opinions among those who may read this chapter. As and when we engage in these discussions, let us hold and express those differences with Christian charity and mutual respect.

I want to conclude by turning from the puzzling aspects of this chapter to some points of command and application which are crystal clear and upon which, I hope, we can all agree.

First of all, let us hold on to the truth of our salvation with **humble gratitude.** Twice in verse 18, the original text has the word for arrogance or boasting and warns against it: *"Do not be arrogant toward the branches. If you are (arrogant) remember…"* Verse 20 reads *"So do not become proud…"* using a phrase that speaks of having an exalted mind or high self-opinion. As those who have been the recipients of God's grace and mercy, we have nothing to be proud of or to boast about. We were lost sinners with no claim on God's love or attention whatsoever – only a fearful expectation of his judgment. But now we have been saved by grace through faith. The overwhelming response of our hearts should be one of humility and gratitude for God's mercy.

This humility and gratitude should flow in two directions. **The first recipient of our gratitude is God himself.** Clearly from this text and the rest of the Book of Romans, God is the author of our salvation. Salvation is his work from beginning to end. This is God's kindness we are enjoying. This should not lead to a sense of arrogance or entitlement. We were not grafted into the tree because we were righteous. We were grafted in because of God's grace and kindness and we remain by faith – a gift which itself comes from God and not from our own efforts.

But in this passage, Paul also points in a second direction toward which our humility and gratitude should flow. It should **flow toward the Jews!** They are the original people of God. They are the people to whom God chose to reveal himself and through whom God worked to reveal his glory to the world – both in the history of the Jewish race and ultimately by sending his Son as a physical descendant of Abraham. We owe this race a great debt. As Paul says in verse 18, *"Do not be arrogant toward the branches. If you are, remember that it is not you who support the root but the root that supports you."* God's work of redemption and his plan for the ages was rooted in eternity, but ultimately grew in earthly soil into a Jewish tree. The heroes of our faith in the Old Testament are all Jewish heroes; Abraham, Moses, David and the prophets were all Jews. Jesus was a Jew! We should be deeply grateful for that spiritual heritage of faith and the revelation of God. The nation's fall from its privileged place should cause us deep sorrow and concern, not arrogance. One of the most unsightly blemishes on the history of the church of Jesus Christ is the history of anti-Semitism that has marked some chapters and eras in the life of the church. I believe a careful reading of Paul's words here in Romans 11 would have prevented that terrible error. Do not be arrogant toward them. Be humbly grateful.

The second application I find growing out of this chapter is an invitation to **an expectant hope for the future.** As I acknowledged earlier, the theological discipline of eschatology, or the study of the end times, is one that is fraught with a wide diversity of opinions. I have no interest in opening, let alone resolving that debate here. I would just highlight some rather cryptic references Paul makes to something yet future – something exciting; something to look forward to.

"Now if their trespass means riches for the world, and if their failure means riches for the Gentiles, how much more will their full inclusion mean!" (verse 12)

"Lest you be wise in your own sight, I want you to understand this mystery, brothers: a partial hardening has come upon Israel, until the fullness of the Gentiles has come in. And in this way all Israel will be saved…" (verse 25-26)

Something is coming and it is going to be wonderful. We are now in a temporary state. It is a mystery. Gentiles (non-Jews) are pouring into the kingdom. Israel is in a state of partial hardening.

But when this chapter is complete, there will be another chapter, a conclusion, a wrapping up, a completing of the divine story of redemption. We may disagree on what we think that will look like or how it will play out on the earthly stage. But can we all agree that it is something to look forward to? When the people of God, Jew and Gentile alike, the *"fullness of the Gentiles"* and *"all Israel"* have been cleansed of their sins and are united in faith around the throne of the Messiah singing the praise of the eternal God of heaven and earth, "what a day of rejoicing that will be!"

That leads to one final application from this chapter. I believe it is actually the conclusion, not only of this chapter, but of the entire first 11 chapters of Romans. It is a call to **exalted worship of the God of our salvation.** There are some texts of Scripture which require no commentary. In fact, any words of explanation only seem to detract from the power of the divinely inspired words of praise. The concluding verses of Romans 11 contain such a text. So as a conclusion to this chapter let's simply read the sacred text and allow our hearts to respond in worship:

"Oh, the depth of the riches and wisdom and knowledge of God! How unsearchable are his judgments and how inscrutable his ways! For who has known the mind of the Lord, or who has been his counselor? Or who has given a gift to him that he might be repaid? For from him and through him and to him are all things. To him be glory forever."

Amen and amen!

25

HOW SHALL WE THEN LIVE?

Romans 12:1-2

In this chapter we are embarking on the final leg of our journey as we enter the last major section in the Book of Romans. In the 1970's, a well-known Christian thinker/writer/speaker by the name of Francis Schaeffer wrote a book and produced a video series with the title: **How Shall We Then Live?** I have borrowed that title for this chapter. Actually, it makes an excellent title for the entire last section of Romans (Romans 12-16).

I remember many years ago sitting in an adult Sunday School class that was studying Romans. When we reached chapter 12, the teacher heaved a great sigh of relief and said something to the effect of: "I am so glad that we have finished with all the theoretical and theological sections of Romans and we are finally in the practical section."

I think I understand what he was feeling, but I still believe there is something drastically wrong with his thinking. We may refer to Romans 12-16 as the practical section of Romans, but let me tell you what is utterly impractical. That is any attempt we may make to apply and live by the teachings of Romans 12-16 that is not firmly and squarely built upon the teaching and theological truths of the first 11 chapters. These "practical" sections of the Book of Romans are only practical if they are grounded in the theological realities of our justification by faith and the presence of the indwelling Spirit of God.

This brings us again to the title for this sermon. **How shall we then live?** Since these things are true, what difference should it make in the way we live? That is the question that Paul will be addressing in these final chapters in Romans. Romans 12:1-2 is a key "hinge" section of the letter.

"I appeal to you therefore, brothers, by the mercies of God, to

present your bodies as a living sacrifice, holy and acceptable to God, which is your spiritual worship. Do not be conformed to this world, but be transformed by the renewal of your mind, that by testing you may discern what is the will of God, what is good and acceptable and perfect."

These verses begin with an appeal, but the appeal is based on the inferential word, "therefore." Paul is drawing conclusions. They are based not only on the verses or chapter that immediately precede this verse, but on the entire first 11 chapters. They are conclusions based on the gospel message that he has been expounding and the truth that there is available to us "a righteousness from God that is by faith."

"I appeal to you therefore brothers, by the mercies of God..."

We immediately learn something important here. In the remainder of Romans, Paul is speaking specifically to believers; to members of God's family. He refers to them as "brothers." While Paul sometimes refers to his fellow Jews as "brothers" or even a general audience, in this case he is clearly addressing his fellow believers, his spiritual brothers and sisters; those who have experienced the "mercies of God."

In fact, he makes this the basis for his appeal: *"by the mercies of God."* The first 11 chapters of Romans have been filled with the mercies of God, haven't they? Grace, redemption, Christ's blood shed as the sacrifice of atonement, Christ dying for us while we were still sinners, saving us from the wrath of God. The gospel is all about mercy. So now he addresses us in this way: as those who have believed the gospel and received this mercy from God, what should our response be? **How shall we then live?**

What is his appeal? *"To present..."* If we have kept our mind engaged, this appeal should raise some echoes. All the way back in Romans 6, we came across a nest of commands or imperatives. They are the only commands to be found in the whole first 11 chapters. It begins with the command to *"consider yourselves dead to sin and alive to God in Christ Jesus."* That command to mental calculation or reckoning is followed by the command to *"present yourselves to God as those who have been brought from death to life, and your members to God as instruments of righteousness."*

(Romans 6:11-13) In Romans 12:1, Paul is picking up on a seed he planted in Romans 6 with the intention of now fleshing it out in fuller detail. While the word "present" is not grammatically in the imperative form, it takes on an imperative force from the strength of Paul's "appeal."

In both these references, Paul is using the language of sacrifice. There were many sacrifices and offerings called for in the Old Testament; sacrifices of atonement, sin offerings, fellowship offerings, thank offerings… "Come to the temple and offer your sacrifices," was the call to the people of God.

What kind of sacrifice is Paul calling for here? What are we to present and to lay on the altar? *"Your bodies."* We might ask, "Why our bodies?" Think about it this way. Our bodies are the only means we have of expressing ourselves; of acting in the world. When Paul calls on us to offer our bodies, it is his way of saying, "Offer God everything. Offer yourselves, in totality, to God."

As Christians we are fond of dedicating buildings to God. "This building was dedicated to the glory of God on such and such a date," the plaque might read. We sometimes even talk like that. We tell our children, "Don't run! Don't make noise! This is God's house!" The thing about dedicated buildings, though, is that you can leave them. You can go outside and run and make noise. But when is the last time you went anywhere without your body? If your body is dedicated to God, all of life is dedicated to God.

Other things we like to dedicate to God are special days. "This is a holy day!" we sometimes say. The implication is that this day belongs to God in a way that other days don't. But you and I don't have different bodies for Sunday than we have for the rest of the week. When we offer our bodies to God, it means every day of the week belongs to him.

Paul continues. We are to offer our bodies *"as a living sacrifice."* We don't have to offer blood sacrifices anymore. Jesus shed his blood for us once and for all. Now we are called on to offer ourselves as living sacrifices, and our lives to serve God. When I was young, I was intrigued by stories of Christian martyrs; followers of Christ who died for their faith. I used to wonder if my faith was strong enough. If I was faced with that ultimate question, would I have the courage to die for Christ? That question remains unanswered. But every day, God (and life itself) asks me a different question. Will I live for Christ?

There is another adjective we need to consider here. What kind of sacrifice are we to offer? It is to be *"holy."* What does that mean? For many people, holiness conjures up certain images accompanied by organ music, stained glass windows and white robes, or at the very least, a backward collar. If you ask the average young person if he wants to live a "holy life," he/she will probably look at you cross-eyed.

The word "holy" can actually be understood in much more practical terms. The basic term or concept means to set something apart for a particular use. As an illustration, let me introduce you to one of my most "holy" possessions. It is my toothbrush. Does that sound strange? Let me ask you. What do I use my toothbrush for? That's right – for brushing my teeth. What else do I use my toothbrush for? That's right – nothing else! (At least as long as I'm using it as a toothbrush.) Let me ask a second question. Whose teeth do I brush with it? I must confess that I am very selfish with my toothbrush. My wife and I share many things, but I do not share my toothbrush with her. If you ask to borrow my toothbrush, I will say, "No!" I will not share my toothbrush with you! My toothbrush is holy! It is mine and mine alone and it has one and only one use! That is what it means to be holy – set apart for a particular purpose and use. That is the kind of sacrifice Paul is calling for here. To give our bodies (and our members) to God for his specific purpose – to serve him and him alone.

The next adjective only adds to this concept: *"acceptable to God."* I prefer the translation "pleasing to God" here. That's our calling. To live a life that is pleasing to God. Paul describes his life-goal this way in 2 Corinthians 5:9: *"So whether we are at home (in the body) or away we make it our aim to please him."* In other words, as long as I live, as long as am here in this body, my goal is to please God. That is what it means to be a living sacrifice.

Paul concludes with this phrase: *"which is your spiritual*

worship." There has been a great emphasis in recent years in churches on the subject of worship. Much of the discussion has focused around music and musical forms and what music is worshipful and what is not, and what is the "worship" like in our churches. Here Paul cuts through all of that. Without discounting music or its importance, Paul tells us clearly that the most sincere and authentic act of worship is this: to offer yourself wholly, body and soul to God for his service. True worship involves offering our whole lives to God.

This is the response that Paul calls for. This is the "therefore"; the conclusion to the first 11 chapters of Romans. This is the answer to the question: **How shall we then live?** He will go on to expand on the specifics of that call in the rest of the letter, but the basic response is clear and fundamental. Christ offered himself for us as a sacrifice of atonement. Now, as recipients of that mercy, we are to offer ourselves to God for his service.

I want to come back one more time to this word, "present." What kind of act of presentation is this? As I have told you before, there are different tenses in Greek that describe different kinds of action. There is a tense which describes action that is progressive, ongoing, repeated, and continuous. There is also a tense that describes action that takes place decisively, clearly at a point in time. Which tense do you think Paul uses for this verb?

Does it surprise you that he uses the tense for decisive, point in time action? Lest we think this is an error or an oversight on his part, if we go back to Romans 6:13 where Paul told us to "offer yourselves to God," we will find that he also uses the same point-in-time tense there as well. I want to review some of what I said in that chapter on Romans 6. I believe Paul is calling for a commitment; a deliberate, life-altering decision in which we clearly and without ambiguity say to God: "Here I am. I belong to you. I will do whatever you ask. I will go where you want me to go. I will do what you want me to do. I will be what you want me to be."

When we discussed Romans 6, I compared this decision to someone joining the army or armed services of his country. One day he is a civilian, free to come and go as he chooses. Then he stands in front of an officer to be enlisted as a soldier. He takes an oath. Suddenly everything changes. He must now salute every officer. He must obey commands. He must please his commander. In Romans 12:1, Paul is repeating his earlier call for us to enlist and take the oath of service to our new commander in chief; to offer ourselves in service to him.

Maybe another illustration will help us understand how this call relates to all of life's decisions. I spent 7 years in Alaska. Alaska is a very large state with very few roads. Many of its communities are only accessible by small airplane. Hence there are many such aircraft coming and going. Imagine a small airplane taking off from an airstrip. It takes off into the wind to get maximum lift. After getting into the air, the pilot may circle the airstrip to get his bearings. But then he does something very important. He fixes on his destination. Whether he is flying visual or flying by instruments, he sets his eyes or his instruments on the direction he wants to go, and he begins his journey. That initial setting of his objective is crucial if he is to reach his destination safely and on time. Now, admittedly, things can happen during the journey. He may get distracted by something he sees on the ground and fly down to take a closer look. He may develop mechanical difficulties. Strong winds may blow him off course. But when he realizes he has drifted he can lift his eyes once again, or reset his instruments on his original goal or destination and resume the journey.

But here's the tragedy. There are many Christians who are still circling the airstrip. They have never made that original decision of fixing on their destination, on the essential direction of their lives. They are still zigging and zagging around the countryside, without direction or purpose. It is this decision that Paul is calling for in Romans 12:1. It is the issue of life direction and purpose. It is the issue of sovereignty over life's decisions.

"I appeal to you therefore brothers, by the mercies of God, (in view of all that God has done for us through the gospel), to present your bodies as a living sacrifice..."

Have you ever made that commitment? Have you ever presented yourselves to the Lord in submission and obedience, to serve him in whatever way he chooses to use you? Maybe you made that commitment at some time in the past, but the distractions of life and the strong winds of adversity have blown you far off course. It is never too late to renew your commitment and climb back on the altar!

Let's keep moving into verse 2. It is a powerful verse that contains a wonderful description of both the process of sanctification, as well as its goal or promised result. The process of sanctification is described in two commands; a negative one and a positive one.

First the negative command: *"Do not be conformed to this world."* We can actually strengthen this translation a bit. The grammatical form of the original text expresses the idea of stopping an action or behavior that is currently going on. It is a "cease and desist" order. We could accurately translate it: *"Stop being conformed to this world."* Or, as the NIV translates it, *"Do not conform any longer..."* This assumes the reality of the old life; the person we were before we came to Christ, or the person we would be if we had never trusted Christ. We belonged to the world. "The world" in this context is used to describe the practices and standards of those without God; the whole system of secular values, standards, ethics and patterns of interpersonal behavior. That is how we used to live. But now that we have been justified, now that we are indwelt by the Spirit of God, now that we have presented our bodies to God as a living sacrifice, that must stop. There is to be a radical change. We must stop being conformed to this world. We must stop letting the world be our standard. We must stop allowing society and "everybody's doing it" set our agenda. We can't go on being like everyone else.

Putting it positively, we are told: *"but be transformed..."* This is an interesting word. It is used to describe a change from the inside out. The Greek word used is *metamorpheo*. It is a word that has come over into English as the word "metamorphosis" which we use to describe one of the most dramatic changes in nature. A caterpillar spins itself into a chrysalis and emerges a few weeks later as a beautiful butterfly. It is changed from the inside out so that the outer appearance now matches the inner reality of its essential "butterfly nature."

This is a beautiful metaphor for the truth of sanctification. We are now children of God. That is our new and essential inner identity and nature. Sanctification is a change that occurs so that our outside, visible behavior now matches the inner reality. It is becoming on the outside what we already are on the inside. This is a present imperative, which means this is a continuous, ongoing process. It is not a once for all transaction like justification, but a process that will take a life time. We are called to present our bodies to God, lay ourselves on the altar and then be progressively transformed into the men and women God wants us to be.

How does this transformation take place? Paul is quick to address this question: *"by the renewal of your mind."* The process of sanctification begins in the mind. Before we act in new ways, we must begin to think in new ways. Here, Paul is actually picking up on something he said earlier in Romans chapter 6. Let me elaborate here with a slight detour. In the entire first 11 chapters of Romans, there are almost no imperative verbs; there are almost no commands given to us as followers of Christ. Romans 1-11 is about what God has done for us. God is the active agent in our justification. But there is one exception. That is the little cluster of commands found in Romans 6. The very first one is found in Romans 6:11, but let me remind you of the context.

In Romans 6, Paul is addressing the question of whether the doctrine of justification by faith encourages people to continue in a life of sin. To address that question, Paul calls us back to the realities of our justification and certain things we now know: we know that we are now united with Christ. He died for sin and we died with him so that we are now dead to sin. He rose from the dead and we rose with him, so we now share in the power of that new, resurrected life. This is our new spiritual reality.

Now comes this command in verse 11: *"So you also must consider yourselves dead to sin and alive to God in Christ Jesus."* Where does that reckoning occur? It occurs in our minds. We must deliberately remember, calculate and reckon our new spiritual identity. We are dead to sin and we are alive to God.

We must allow the Spirit of God to renew our minds with the new spiritual realities of our new identity as the children of God. We must allow the doctrinal and theological truths of Romans 1-11 to shape our thinking and our self-perception. Then we are to live out that new reality by the Spirit's help and transforming power. *"Be transformed by the renewing of your mind."* One great way to do that is by memorizing Scripture – especially powerful doctrinal passages like Romans 6 and Romans 8.

If I can venture into the world of IT for a metaphor – we have been operating off an old, defective operating system or software program. We need a new operating system. As we allow the truths of the gospel to reprogram our minds to reflect our new identity in Christ, our entire lives will be transformed. This is the process of sanctification; transformation from the inside out.

Let's finish the verse: *"...that by testing you may discern what is the will of God, what is good and acceptable and perfect."*

The will of God is an intriguing subject. Many sermons have been preached and many books have been written on what the will of God is and how we can know the will of God. Simply put, God's will is that which God desires or that which God wants. When we ask, "What is God's will?" we are asking, "What does God want me to do in this particular situation?" Fundamental to the whole issue of Christian living and sanctification, then, is the relationship between my will and God's will. Which one will reign and rule and direct the path of my life? The importance of this question is illustrated in the life of Jesus himself. Look at how Jesus described his own commitment to the will of his Father.

In John 4:34 Jesus said, *"My food is to do the will of him who sent me and to accomplish his work."* In John 6:38, Jesus states it again, *"For I have come down from heaven, not to do my own will but the will of him who sent me."* In the Garden of Gethsemane, Jesus wrestled in prayer with his Father before he went to the cross. His prayer concluded with these words of submission: *"Nevertheless, not my will but yours be done."*

So let us be clear; when God asks us to live according to his will, he is not asking anything of us that Christ himself did not fulfill. But just what is the will of God for us? When we think of God's will, we often think of the big decisions of life: where to live, what job to take, whether to marry and whom to marry, and so on. These are the times when we become concerned about knowing the will of God. I certainly do not wish to diminish the significance of those decisions or of seeking God's will in those decisions. But when we turn to the Scripture, this is not the emphasis we find.

Let's consider some Scriptures together. Ephesians 3:17-21: *"Therefore do not be foolish, but <u>understand what the will of the Lord is</u>.... be filled with the Spirit, addressing one another in psalms and hymns and spiritual songs, singing and making melody to the Lord with your heart, giving thanks always and for everything to God the Father in the name of our Lord Jesus Christ, submitting to one another out of reverence for Christ."*

I Thessalonians 4:3 tells us: *"For <u>this is the will of God, your sanctification</u>: that you abstain from sexual immorality; that each one of you know how to control his own body in holiness and honor, not in the passion of lust like the Gentiles who do not know God; that no one transgress and wrong his brother in this matter, because the Lord is an avenger in all these things, as we told you beforehand and solemnly warned you. For God has not called us for impurity, but in holiness."*

Are we beginning to get the picture? Let's try 1 Peter 2:15-17: *"For <u>this is the will of God</u>, that by doing good you should put to silence the ignorance of foolish people. Live as people who are free, not using your freedom as a cover-up for evil, but living as servants of God. Honor everyone. Love the brotherhood. Fear God. Honor the emperor."*

Peter summarizes it this way in 1 Peter 4:2: *"so as to live for the rest of the time in the flesh no longer for human passions but <u>for the will of God</u>."*

I like this quote I jotted in my journal many years ago. I cannot remember the source, so my apologies to the author: "In Scripture, God's will is presented, not as something cleverly concealed which we are to discover, but as something clearly revealed which we are to obey."

This is the answer to the question: **How shall we then live?** We are called to life the same way Jesus did: "Not my will but yours be done."

We might still ask: But what about those big decisions of life? How can I know God's will in those times? While that is not the subject of this chapter I can tell you this. If you are living in obedience to the known and revealed will of God and fulfilling his will in all the many moral and ethical choices you make day after day, you won't have to worry about missing God's will in the big decisions. On the other hand, if you are not living according to the will of God in the daily choices, you will be out of the will of God no matter where you are. After all, what is the point in asking God to lead you to the right college if you are not prepared to be the right person in college? What is the point in asking God to lead you to the right woman to be your wife if you are not ready to fulfill God's will by being a godly man who will make a good husband? What is the point in asking God to lead you to choose the right career or job if you are not prepared to honor God in your vocation?

Theologians sometimes use the phrase "progressive sanctification." That's what Paul is describing in these verse. As we pursue the will of God in all areas of life, we will grow in our ability to discern the will of God. *"...that by testing you may discern what is the will of God, what is good and acceptable and perfect."* God's will for us is made up of that which is good, acceptable and perfect. As we do those things, we will not only test God's will, but grow in our ability to discern these "good, acceptable and perfect" things and thus continue in the process of our progressive sanctification; of being progressively transformed into Christ's image. And as we grow in our discernment and fulfillment of God's will for our lives, I believe we will be filled with a deep and abiding sense of fulfillment and satisfaction. After all, by fulfilling God's will we are fulfilling the very purpose for which God created us.

People all over the world are seeking for fulfillment in life. They are looking for life that is significant and meaningful. But they are seeking for it outside the will of God. They are making up their own recipes for fulfillment, but the results never satisfy. Isn't that what Adam and Eve did? They tried to find their fulfillment and to become "like God" by doing what God told them not to do! The sons and daughters of Adam and Eve continue to rush down that same path of disappointment and disillusionment. But now, as the children of God, we have been set upon a different path – a life lived according the will of God. As we follow his path, we will discover life as God intended us to know it. The only source of true and lasting fulfillment and joy is to be found within the will of God as he transforms us from the inside out.

Let's come back to the call Paul makes in verse 1. Present your bodies as a living sacrifice! Put yourself on the altar of submission and obedience to God and to his will. Why do we hesitate to answer that call? Why is that a scary thing to do? I think we hesitate, because we are afraid that we will miss out on the best life has to offer. We'll miss out on all the fun. We're afraid our lives will become boring, drab, and dreary. That's what the devil wants us to think. But the reality is just the opposite. Jesus told us that he came so that we could have life and have it abundantly. He told us that when we lose our life for his sake that is when we actually find it.

How shall we than live? There is a simple answer to that question: *live for the rest of your time here on earth no longer for human passions but for the will of God.*

26

JUST DO IT!

Romans 12:3-8

What does living "the rest of our lives for the will of God" look like? This is the question that Paul will address in the closing section of this letter. It is intriguing to see where Paul starts.

In the very next paragraph he stresses the importance of Christian service or ministry within the church. We have been called to serve, and such service begins at home within the family of faith. Paul also points out that we have not only been called to serve, but we have also each been uniquely equipped to serve. Romans 12:3-8 is one of four key passages in the New Testament that are devoted to the subject of spiritual gifts. (The others are found in 1 Corinthians 12-14, Ephesians 4 and 1 Peter 4.)

Before we begin this discussion, I am going to digress a little bit to trace my own journey in regard to this topic. I attended seminary in the 1970's. It was an era in the life of many churches in North America when Christians were discovering the doctrine of spiritual gifts. It was the hot new topic. Everyone was talking about it. Everyone was teaching and preaching about it. There were seminars on it and workshops on it to help us discover our spiritual gifts. There were spiritual gift inventories and questionnaires and page after page of notebooks filled with definitions of the different spiritual gifts. There was always a happy buzz at these seminars. We all like gifts. It was like Christmas, as we opened our packages and compared our gifts. "What did you get?" we asked each other. But I have a confession to make. Over time, as I diligently attended the seminars and took notes and filled my own notebooks, I found myself getting more and more confused. The definitions and the descriptions never quite seemed to line up. I filled in the questionnaires and added up my scores. From one seminar, I came away with the conclusion that I had the gift of prophecy. Another seminar told me that I had the gift of a pastor/teacher. Still another led me to the conclusion that I had the gift of teaching. Still another led me to the conclusion that I had the gift of exhortation. Now it would be one thing if I concluded that I was so multi-gifted. But that wasn't what was happening. These seminars and diagnostic inventories were just hanging different labels on the same basic gifts or skill set.

I was also troubled by several things that I saw happening. The first was a preoccupation with what seemed like a game called, "Name that gift." Most of the seminars took the position that there was only a limited number of spiritual gifts. By comparing the different passages (none of which are identical) and making a list of the gifts mentioned, it was possible to come up with a list of 17 or 18 or 21 (also based on one's interpretation). The conclusion was that every believer had one or more of those particular gifts. We were told that it was very important to decide which one we had. All the energy went into the labeling and the defining of each gift – yet the definitions frequently varied from seminar to seminar and from teacher to teacher.

The second thing that troubled me was that I was finding more and more people who didn't feel like they fit in any of the categories. They did not resonate with any of the gift definitions on offer. Too many people felt like they were being left out. They were actually demotivated by the whole subject – some even concluding that somehow God had left them out when he distributed the gifts.

A third confusing aspect of the discussion was the inability to ever answer definitively the distinction between spiritual gifts and talents. If it wasn't on the "list" the conclusion was that it must be a talent and not a gift. Of course, if we had the talent before we trusted in Christ, clearly it must be a talent and not a gift, so we were required to keep looking for our gift. Sadly, that seemed to leave many very talented people demotivated in their service for Christ.

The fourth troubling outcome of these seminars was the

emergence of what we might call the "ungiftedness doctrine." It became a tendency for people to use their gifts as an excuse for not serving. When asked to serve in various necessary capacities in the church, too often the response was, "Oh, that's not my gift."

Why was it all so confusing? So I began to dig a little deeper. Where were all these definitions and paragraph after paragraph of descriptions coming from? Where were the dogmatic assertions (such as the conclusion that the Biblical lists were exhaustive) originating from? As I searched the Scripture, I became more and more convinced that much of the material was essentially man-made. The Scriptural data was actually very sparse. In many cases, it came down to a single word or phrase in a list, with no definition or description attached. The spiritual gift gurus were then taking those single words or phrases and extrapolating to come up with long paragraphs of definitions and distinctions which simply cannot be supported by the Biblical evidence. What we ended up with had closer resemblance to many secular personality and temperament profiles than anything that could be found in the Scripture. Now, I don't deny that such profiles can be useful. But the gurus seemed to be claiming Biblical authority for what was simply applied common sense. Sometimes it almost seemed that even the common sense was lacking.

As I continued to study, I concluded that we were taking something that was rather simple and making it far too complicated. To make a long story short, I became a minimalist in my approach to the subject of spiritual gifts. By now I may have upset you, but bear with me. Let me apply this approach to the passage in front of us. I think it is a good example of the Bible's simple message on this subject. In this passage, Paul lays out two essential realities of life in the church and then applies them.

Fact #1: We are one.

Fact #2: We are different.

This is fundamental to what Paul and the Bible teach on this subject of spiritual gifts and the use of them. It is at the heart of this text. In verse 4, Paul says: *"For as in one body we have many members, and the members do not all have the same function, so we, though many, are one body in Christ, and individually members one of another. Having gifts that differ..."*

Do you see it? We are one and we are different. To drive these two realities home, Paul uses the analogy of the human body; one body with many members, and the members do not all have the same function. We are one and yet we are different. We all belong to the same body. We belong to one another. Yet we have different gifts and different functions within the body. This is the essential truth we need to keep in mind.

The first thing this foundational truth should do is **safeguard us against the sin of pride**. This is actually how Paul opens this paragraph in verse 3: *"For by the grace given to me I say to everyone among you not to think of himself more highly than he ought to think, but to think with sober judgment, each according to the measure of faith that God has assigned."*

Proper thinking about spiritual gifts will not lead to pride. We will not have an exalted opinion of ourselves. Instead we will have a realistic assessment of ourselves and our gifts. We will recognize first that any abilities or strengths we have to contribute to the body of Christ are ultimately gifts of God's grace. Even the measure of faith we have to exercise these gifts is given to us by God. A gift is just that; a gift. It is something we have been given, not something we have earned or deserve. God is the distributor of the gifts. There is no pride involved in receiving a gift.

Next, recognize the interdependence of the members of the body. No one has all the gifts. We all need one another. We have different gifts and different functions, but all are necessary. We are one and we are different and each member needs the other members. In the parallel passage in 1 Corinthians, Paul even engages in some humor as he depicts a human body in which different members are described as engaging in a dialogue. The eye says to the hand, "I don't need you!" The head says to the feet, "You're not necessary!" We can see the nonsense of that reasoning in the human body. Now apply the same reasoning to the church. We are one and yet we are different. Each function is important to the health of the whole. There is no call for pride or any sense of superiority. There should be no competition or comparing in this matter of spiritual gifts or abilities. A proper understanding of spiritual gifts and the functioning of the church will not lead to pride or competition. Think and think clearly. Have sober, realistic judgment in these matters.

Paul does not simply tell us how to think about the matter. He also exhorts us to action. Note what he says in verse 6: *"Having gifts that differ according to the grace given to us, let us use them: if prophecy, in proportion to our faith; if service, in our serving; the one who teaches, in his teaching; the one who exhorts, in his exhortation..."*

This is where the spiritual gifts seminars tend to spring into action with their definitions and descriptions; what is prophecy? What does serving refer to? What is teaching and how is it different from exhortation? When we do that, I think we're trying to become far too specific. Paul is actually using rather general, non-specific categories and words here. He is not concerned with detailed distinctions and definitions. This is a call to action. Paul is simply telling us, "Whatever your gift is, get on with it." Whatever special grace God has given us for ministry, "let us use them." Exercise them. It is a call to action and a call to service. Let me introduce you to what I like to call the Nike philosophy of spiritual gifts. **Just do it!** Get in the game. Start serving. The church needs you. The Body of Christ needs you. Don't worry about labels or titles or positions. Find a place to serve and start serving. Just do it!

There is one more point that Paul makes in this text. Whatever we do for the Lord and for his church, it is important to **do it well.** This is service for God. This is the will of God we are doing. This is the Body of Christ we are serving. **Do it well.** This point is made in the second part of verse 8: *"the one who contributes, in generosity; the one who leads, with zeal; the one who does acts of mercy, with cheerfulness."*

I think what Paul is doing is taking each of these three gifts or areas of service and defining what excellence looks like in the exercise of that gift. The one whose special gift is giving, should give generously. The one who exercises leadership should do so, not haphazardly, but with genuine effort and zeal. The one who does acts of mercy should do so, not reluctantly or begrudgingly but with genuine cheerfulness. If it is worth doing, it is worth doing well. It is worth doing with excellence. I believe that is true not only in these three domains, but in all the domains of service for Christ and for his church.

So that's it. That's my minimalist approach to the subject of spiritual gifts of service within the church. It is built on two fundamental realities. We are one and we are different. From those two realities come these three applications.

There is **no place for pride** or competition. There should be no ranking of the gifts or areas of service. There should be no superiority or inferiority feelings. We are one. God made us one. We are different. God made us different and gave us different gifts. It is all a result of his grace and there is no pride attached to grace. The second application is very simple: **Just do it!** Get on with it. Start serving. The third application is also simple. **Do it well.** Serve with excellence.

At this point, you might be waving your hand at me and saying, "But I still don't know what I should do. I don't know where to start. I don't know what my gift or area of service is." That's fair. Let me depart from the text here and leave you with some common sense advice. This isn't God speaking, or even the Apostle Paul. It's just me, based on my 40 years of experience in the church. So, take it with a grain of salt and feel free to disregard it. I won't be offended!

First of all, start by praying and asking God to show you how and where he wants you to serve. Put yourself on the altar again in this specific arena. "God, here I am, reporting for duty. Show me what you want me to do." Then, if you don't get a specific answer or leading from the Lord, start experimenting. That may not sound very spiritual, but I think it's good advice. Someone has wisely said, "You can't steer a parked car." Start moving. Do something. As you do, keep praying. God will show you. He will confirm your abilities and strengths in different areas of service. Just keep emphasizing those areas and God will lead you into the different ministries he wants you to be involved in. But you've got to get off the sidelines and get into the game.

How will you know when you've found your area or areas of service; your special niche? Again, this is common sense reasoning, not Biblical doctrine, but I think it works. First, you will find that when you serve in your area of giftedness, you will gain a sense of joy and fulfillment. You will enjoy it. Secondly, you will quite quickly gain a sense of confidence and competence. Thirdly, others will affirm you and confirm your ability and competence as your skills develop. When that happens, remember to give the glory to the Giver of the gifts.

At the end of the day, you may or may not agree with my approach to spiritual gifts. That's OK. But one fact remains crystal clear. On this, I believe, we can all agree. The life of a follower of Christ is a life of service. We have been called to serve Christ and to do his will. And we have been called and equipped to serve one another in the Body of Christ. It's time to stop thinking about it, talking about it and theorizing about it. It's time to **just do it!**

27

A CALL TO ARMS!

Romans 12:9-21

There is a battle raging. We engage in that battle every day of our lives. Not one of us is immune. It is a battle that consumes, invades and pervades every arena and sphere of life and every hour of the day. What makes it more confusing is the fact that, as followers of Christ, we are both combatants in the struggle and the battlefield itself. The question is not whether we are experiencing the battle. The only question is: which side is winning?

The battle is between evil and good; between wrong and right; between being conformed to the world and its standards and being transformed by God's Spirit from the inside out. Paul describes that battle in the passage before us - (Romans 12:9-21). We might describe this passage as a call to arms. It is definitely a motivating call to victory in the battle. But the weapons and strategies called for in the struggle surely make this the strangest army that ever marched.

Paul first describes the identifying mark of the soldiers in Christ's army. The ESV Bible translates the opening phrase, *"Let love be genuine."* It is a legitimate effort to make this into a command, but the original text simply has the definite article, followed by the noun and adjective. There is no verb. "The love, genuine." This is our supreme calling. This is the color of our uniform, the symbol on our flag. This is the most powerful of all our weapons. Love. Not just any kind of love, but real love. Sincere love. Love without hypocrisy. Love without masks. Love without pretending.

Having described our identifying mark, Paul now describes the nature and arena of the battle; the two opposing forces that wage war in the world and in our hearts. He then calls us to

instead to find a reaction that is good, noble and honorable in the sight of all who are watching. Truly, this is upside down living.

We're not done yet. Listen to the rest of the section: *"If possible, so far as it depends on you, live peaceably with all. Beloved, never avenge yourselves, but leave it to the wrath of God, for it is written, 'Vengeance is mine, I will repay, says the Lord.' To the contrary, 'if your enemy is hungry, feed him; if he is thirsty, give him something to drink; for by so doing you will heap burning coals on his head.'"* (Romans 12:18-20)

This is surely the strangest strategy for an army that has ever been laid out! It is as though a commanding officer is addressing his troops before a great battle, and this is what he says: "We are entering a great and fierce battle against vicious troops. I want you to represent me courageously and honorably in this battle. And above all, no matter what happens in the battle I want you to live by this one cardinal rule: **Never fight back!**"

Does that sound reasonable to you? Does that make sense? Yet this is what we are being commanded to do. This is how we are told to respond to evil when it smacks us in the face. Don't curse. Don't return evil for evil. Don't take your own vengeance. Instead of cursing, bless your enemy. Instead of returning evil, respond nobly and honorably to him. Instead of seeking his harm, feed him when he's hungry and give him drink when he is thirsty. It is upside down and backwards. It makes no sense. What kind of army is this we've joined? What kind of strategy is this for waging war? Yet we are told that this is the path to victory. That is the concluding verse in the section: *"Do not be overcome by evil but overcome evil with good."*

This is the verse that finally brought it all into focus for me. There is a battle going on. It is a battle between good and evil. As a follower of Christ, I am enlisted in the army of those who desire good to triumph. And so I go forth to do good. The first thing that happens is someone pokes a stick in my eye. They do something evil or harmful to me. Instinctively, I grab a stick and poke him back. Poking a stick in someone's eye is an inherently evil act. So now I have done something evil or harmful to him. But wait a minute. I was on the way to do good! Instead I have now done something evil. His evil has overcome my good. Evil has triumphed. By doing evil to me, he has caused me to do evil. That is what happens whenever we return evil for evil, and curse those who persecute us. Instead of abhorring evil, we are now doing evil. As long as we continue with this strategy of returning evil for evil, we give evil the upper hand. We allow evil people to bring us down to their level. They are setting the agenda.

So what is the alternative? Do good. Do what is honorable. Bless instead of curse. Return good for evil and kindness for harm. But someone will say, "But then evil will win. Wrongs will go unpunished. Injustice will reign." No, Paul says, you are forgetting that God is on his throne. He is the ultimate judge. He will punish the wicked in due time. That is his job, not our job. *("Vengeance is mine, I will repay, says the Lord.")* Our task? Sincere love. Abhorring evil. Clinging to what is good. This is how good will triumph over evil. To emphasize his point, Paul quotes a passage from the Book of Proverbs chapter 25: 21-22: *"if your enemy is hungry, feed him; if he is thirsty, give him something to drink; for by so doing you will heap burning coals on his head."*

What does it mean to heap burning coals on someone's head? This is an ancient Hebrew idiom and, unfortunately, we cannot be certain of its meaning as it has been lost in history. However, I did read one suggestion that I like. It is the suggestion that burning coals on the head is a description of someone blushing in embarrassment. Just as burning coals glow red, so does the face of an embarrassed person. So when we heap burning coals on someone's head, we are embarrassing them. This is what we do when we return good for their evil rather than retaliating. The person who has done evil is embarrassed. Evil loses. We triumph, and we do it by doing good rather than doing evil. Even if the evil person does not admit their embarrassment, and even if our good behavior is mocked, we have another promise we can keep in our hearts. It is found back in that passage in Proverbs, a concluding phrase that Paul doesn't even include here. It reads, *"and the Lord will reward you."* As soldiers in the Lord's army, that should be promise enough.

Before I conclude, I want to make an additional set of

applications from this passage. So far we have looked at two areas. The first is how we treat our fellow soldiers; our brothers and sisters in the family of God. The second is how we respond to our enemies: people who do harmful things to us. In the passage, it appears that Paul's primary application of this second teaching is to people outside the kingdom of God, our enemies. But here is my question; what happens when our friends become our enemies? What happens when the harm we experience comes from our brothers and sisters in Christ – the very people we are looking to for support and comfort? What happens when the "enemy" who is inflicting harm is a spouse, or a parent, or a son or daughter, or a brother or sister; a fellow missionary or member of the church staff; a member of our church or our small group – even though they are, themselves, followers of Christ? Now the battle grows especially difficult and intense, but the answer is still to be found in this text. The basic reaction called for is still the same: *"Do not return evil for evil but give thought to what is honorable...Do not be overcome by evil but overcome evil with good...Bless and curse not."*

Our marriages, our homes, our families, and our churches are a great testing ground for the principles that Paul is laying out here. Retaliation, tit for tat, insult for insult; such response patterns will devastate a marriage and mar the serenity and harmony of any family and every church. Every family and church is vulnerable. We are all too human and too quick to take offense and fire back with our own sarcastic and hurtful comments. When we do, evil wins. Good loses. We have been overcome by evil. That is not the pattern God has laid out for us. Whether in our spiritual family or in our human families, as followers of Christ, our calling is clear. Whatever its source, do not be overcome by evil, but overcome evil with good.

The battle is raging. It will continue to rage every day of our lives. Good versus evil. As those who have been justified by faith, we have been enlisted in God's army on the side of all that is good; all that conforms to his good, acceptable and perfect will. Genuine love is our identifying characteristic as we abhor evil and hold fast to what is good.

This kind of living is not natural. It is, in fact, supernatural. We cannot live this way by our own will-power and strength. We can live this way only as we rely upon the indwelling Spirit of God to lead us and give us strength.

As we rely upon God's Spirit and engage in the struggle, we have another resource. We can keep our spiritual eyes firmly fixed on our supreme and perfect model. There is another way to read this entire passage. We can read it as a description of the life of Jesus himself, our Commander in Chief. His love, his abhorrence of sin, his pursuit of all that was right and holy, his zeal of spirit, his persistence in prayer, his humility, his empathy, his befriending of the needy and outcasts of society, and above all, his response to his enemies. Truly, as Peter tells us in 1 Peter 2:21-23, he left us *"an example, so that you might follow in his steps. He committed no sin, neither was deceit found in his mouth. When he was reviled, he did not revile in return; when he suffered, he did not threaten, but continued entrusting himself to him who judges justly."* As they nailed him to the cross, he prayed, *"Father, forgive them..."*

And when he died, good triumphed over evil. Let us follow in his steps.

28

LESSONS IN CITIZENSHIP
Romans 13:1-7

The Book of Romans is a letter, written in the first century to believers in the city of Rome. At the time of Paul's writing, Rome was near the pinnacle of its power, with an empire that extended through most of Europe and the area surrounding the Mediterranean. It was one of the most powerful military and political empires in history. Paul's readers lived in the capital, the very heart and center of that empire, surrounded by politics, politicians, government buildings and government officials; the trappings of human government and governmental power and authority were everywhere.

In Romans chapter 6, Paul drew on that background and imagery to present a powerful word picture when he told his readers that they were now subjects of a new king, a new ruler, a new emperor. They were no longer to allow sin to reign over them, but they were to present themselves in allegiance to God as their new ruler. "Let not sin reign!" Paul said. "Sin shall no longer have dominion over you."

But now a different question arises. Yes, spiritually we are subjects of God, owing our ultimate obedience and allegiance to him. But what now is our relationship to earthly kings, governments and rulers? Since we are now under God's rule and subjects of his kingdom, are we free to ignore earthly governments? How do we reconcile these two kingdoms and authorities?

This is the subject Paul takes up in Romans 13:1-7. What is the believer's relationship to earthly government and political power structures? As I have meditated on this passage, I believe we can summarize Paul's teaching on the subject rather simply: **A good heavenly citizen makes a good earthly citizen.**

In this passage, Paul first of all lays down certain theological propositions: a theology of government, if you will. He then fleshes that out into certain practical applications and instructions. In laying out his theology of government, Paul makes two points:

First, **all government authorities are established and ordained by God.**

In Romans 13:1 we read: *"Let every person be subject to the governing authorities. For there is no authority except from God, and those that exist have been instituted by God."*

That is a powerful statement. "No authority except from God." Every authority that exists "has been instituted by God."

Verse 2 contains more of the same: *"Therefore whoever resists the authorities resists what God has appointed..."*

All government authorities have been established and ordained by God. I believe this has two elements or implications to it. First of all, the institution of human government is God's idea. We can actually trace this all the way back to the Book of Genesis and the covenant God made with Noah when he emerged from the ark. Prior to the Flood, man's evil ran unrestrained. This is what led to God's judgment. When Noah and his sons stood upon the earth, even though it had been "washed clean" in one sense, God knew that evil still resided in the hearts of men. So he issued this instruction:

"From his fellow man I will require a reckoning for the life of man... Whoever sheds the blood of man, by man shall his blood be shed..." (partial quote from Genesis 9:5-6)

God gave man the authority to restrain human evil and to demand an accounting and a reckoning. Theologians have long identified this as the initial institution of human government with this most basic of tasks – the protection of human life and the punishment of those who violate its sanctity. Government – humans governing other humans – is God's idea.

But I believe there is more for us to consider here. The second clear declaration is this: Not only is human government (in the abstract) God's idea, but **the people in authority have been placed there by God.**

This is implied in Paul's words here: *"For there is no authority except from God, and those that exist have been instituted by God."*

It is not just the offices of government that have been instituted by God, but the actual officers themselves hold their position and authority by God's appointment. Other Scriptures also bear this out.

Daniel 2:20-21: *"Daniel answered and said: Blessed be the name of God forever and ever, to whom belong wisdom and might. He changes times and seasons; he removes kings and sets up kings…"*

Daniel 4:17: *"The sentence is by the decree of the watchers, the decision by the word of the holy ones, to the end that the living may know that the Most High rules the kingdom of men and gives it to whom he will and sets over it the lowliest of men."* This word was spoken to Nebuchadnezzar in a dream just before God removed him from his throne because of his pride and arrogance.

Jesus himself referred to this truth of God's authority over human government when he spoke with Pilate at his own trial in John 19:10-11: *"So Pilate said to him, 'You will not speak to me? Do you not know that I have authority to release you and authority to crucify you' Jesus answered him, 'You would have no authority over me at all unless it had been given you from above.'"*

This matter of God's authority and sovereignty over human government and governors is clearly proclaimed in Scripture. Now, this does not mean that all leaders are godly, or righteous, or that they acknowledge God's authority. Many have not and do not. But it does mean that every leader has his place of authority by divine permission and by divine appointment. God sets them up and removes them as and when he chooses.

This reality leads us on to the third clear teaching of this passage: **Government officials are God's servants.** Lest we miss this point, Paul actually states it 3 times in plain language. He does it twice in verse 4: *"for he is God's servant for your good. But if you do wrong, be afraid, for he does not bear the sword in vain. For he is the servant of God, an avenger who carries out God's wrath on the wrongdoer."*

He repeats this in verse 6: *"For because of this you also pay taxes, for the authorities are ministers of God, attending to this very thing."* In this verse, Paul actually uses a different word for servant or minister, a more specific word for a servant with a special task or assignment. What is their specific assignment? As God's servants, this passage tells us that government authorities have three functions.

First, **they are there for our good, the good of the citizens, and they should reward good behavior with praise.** This is the gist of verses 3-4: *"For rulers are not a terror to good conduct, but to bad. Would you have no fear of the one who is in authority? Then do what is good, and you will receive his approval, for he is God's servant for your good."* So rulers and authorities are there for the good of the citizens and to approve and reward good behavior.

Secondly **they are in place to punish bad behavior** as the rest of verse 4 states: *"But if you do wrong, be afraid, for he does not bear the sword in vain. For he is the servant of God, an avenger who carries out God's wrath on the wrongdoer."* By the way, this should be kept in the context of Romans 12:19 where we are told not to take our own vengeance but leave room for the wrath of God. How does God exact his vengeance on the wrong doer? One way is in eternity and by divine, eternal judgment, but another way, according to this verse, is through the appropriate penalties assigned by governmental authority. This is God's vengeance in action.

The third way in which human authorities are servants of God is by their **full time dedication to governing.** This is the point behind verse 6: *"For because of this you also pay taxes, for the authorities are ministers of God, attending to this very thing."* We are told to pay our taxes, because the authorities are God's servants, carrying out a necessary task on his behalf and ours. It is a task to which they are to be dedicated and diligent. It is interesting that the word used here for "attending to this very thing" is the same word that describes how we as believers should be attending to prayer in Romans 12:12.

Now this is dramatic stuff! This is theology with significant applications. It first of all has implications for every believer who may find himself or herself in a position of authority or governance over others. This is God's work! There is nothing "secular" about such roles. People in government and in places of authority over others are servants of God; Christians doubly so! Govern well. Lead well. Reward good behavior. Punish bad behavior when necessary. And be dedicated to the specific task and role to which you've been assigned.

We know that the early church included believers with significant roles in government. In Philippians, Paul extends greetings "especially from those who belong to Caesar's household." In this very letter to the Romans that Paul wrote while staying in Corinth, Paul mentions a man named Erastus, the city treasurer. (Romans 16:23). (Note: There is an actual stone in the ruins of Corinth with an inscription containing the name of Erastus, a city treasurer.)

But while the church no doubt contained people in positions of authority and government, of course the vast majority were people who were under such authority; whose lives were influenced daily by the governing decisions of others. Those of us in this category must also take this theology of government and use it to shape our daily actions and behaviors. This is where Paul focuses most of his instructions.

Let me summarize these instructions with some quick bullet points.

1. We must all submit to the governing authorities.

This is clear in the very opening words of the paragraph: *"Let every person be subject to the governing authorities."* (verse 1). That is pretty inclusive. "Every person." Literally, "Every soul." "To be subject" is a word taken from a military context. It means literally "to line up under" or to "fall in line."

2. When we rebel against government authority we are rebelling against God's authority.

This is not just an implication to be drawn. It is stated in clear black and white in verse 2: *"Therefore whoever resists the authorities resists what God has appointed..."* Both of these words for "resist" have the idea of standing up against or lining up against... We are not just falling out of line, we are taking a stand of defiance against God's rule. These are strong words!

3. If we do what is right and good, we need not fear the

governing authorities.

This is what Paul states in verses 3-4: *"For rulers are not a terror to good conduct, but to bad. Would you have no fear of the one who is in authority? Then do what is good, and you will receive his approval, for he is God's servant for your good."*

4. If we defy government and do wrong, we have legitimate cause for fear.

Paul also makes this point clearly in this passage. First in verse 2: *"Therefore whoever resists the authorities resists what God has appointed, and <u>those who resist will incur judgment.</u>"*

It is not clear in this verse whether Paul is referring to God's judgment or to the judgment of the governing authorities. Both are true, and both are a cause for fear as he points out in verse 4. *"But if you do wrong, be afraid, for he does not bear the sword in vain. For he is the servant of God, an avenger who carries out God's wrath on the wrongdoer."*

5. As believers, we should submit to governing authorities, not only out of fear, but as a matter of conscience.

Verse 5 is very clear: *"Therefore one must be in subjection, not only to avoid God's wrath but also for the sake of conscience."*

In other words, as Christ's followers, the bar is set even higher. We have a higher reason for obedience and submission. We should do it because it is the right thing to do. That means we will obey the laws whether anyone is watching or not.

6. We should fulfill all of our governmental obligations appropriately.

This is Paul's final conclusion to the matter in verses 6-7: *"For because of this you also pay taxes, for the authorities are ministers of God, attending to this very thing. Pay to all what is owed to them: taxes to whom taxes are owed, revenue to whom revenue is owed, respect to whom respect is owed, honor to whom honor is owed."*

I don't think anyone particularly likes paying taxes, or customs charges, or government fees. But our instructions are pretty clear, are they not? This is part of our earthly duty as a heavenly citizen.

A good heavenly citizen makes a good earthly citizen.

I would like to add one more bullet point to our obligations – one that is not found here in Romans but is found in Paul's writings in 1 Timothy 2:1-2.

7. Pray for those in authority.

1 Timothy 2:1-2 reads: *"First of all, then, I urge that supplications, prayers, intercessions, and thanksgivings be made for all people, for kings and all who are in high positions, that we may lead a peaceful and quiet life, godly and dignified in every way. This is good, and it is pleasing in the sight of God our Savior."*

This is also an important responsibility we have as good citizens, and it is one that joins our heavenly and our earthly responsibilities.

So, we need to start with a strong theology of government. Then we need to allow our theology of government to shape and form our attitudes and actions as we relate to the layers and levels of governmental authority, both within our home countries and within our temporary adopted country if we live in other countries. We must start with a renewed mind, a new way of thinking, and allow that new thinking to transform our actions and attitudes as we recognize that a good heavenly citizen makes a good earthly citizen.

Before we conclude this chapter and discussion of this important topic, let's step away from the text for a moment. I think the logic and rationale of the passage is fairly straightforward. I think we can all understand it and even embrace it, as long as we live in a peaceful country that has righteous laws and wise and good leaders. But what if that is not the case? What happens when a nation's leaders are corrupt, godless and unfair? What if a country's laws are unreasonable and harsh? What if our law enforcement officers are cruel and oppress the innocent, either in search of a bribe, or out of the egregious exercise of power to feed their egos? What shall we do then? What if we find ourselves living under a Hitler or a Stalin?

This is truly a troubling and deeply puzzling question, and

one that is not easy to answer. It is important to note that it is not a paradox to which Paul would have been a stranger. As Paul wrote these words, the ruler occupying the emperor's palace in Rome was a man by the name of Nero; a man who even today is synonymous with tyranny, extravagance and capricious governance. He was an early persecutor of Christians and Paul himself would later spend years in Nero's prison system. Paul was not writing in some idyllic fairyland of justice, equality and good government. The world he lived in was every bit as brutal, harsh and oppressive as anything we face in the world today. Yet he wrote these words of command to us.

This leads me to the heart of the question. Are these principles absolute? Are there exceptions? Are there times when we should stand up against government authorities? Are there times when our faith in God leads us to civil disobedience and even revolt? This is a troubling question which has often divided churches and Christians. Not long ago I read the biography of Dietrich Bonhoeffer, a pastor and committed believer who lived in Germany under Hitler. It was painful to read how the church was torn apart in their debates and decisions on how to respond to what was happening in their country and in the halls of government. How should Christians respond to such challenges? Dietrich Bonhoeffer was eventually executed after being implicated in a plot to assassinate Hitler. Was he right or was he wrong? This is a very difficult question, and we may not all agree on the answer.

I say this carefully. While I freely admit that I cannot demonstrate it from the text in front of us today, I personally believe that there are times when we not only can disobey civil and governmental authorities, but we must. I believe Scripture itself supports this belief.

Let me take another verse of Scripture as a starting point. It was Jesus himself who made this profound statement: *"Render unto Caesar the things that are Caesar's and unto God the things that are God's."* This much is clear and it falls in line with Paul's teaching here in Romans. But what happens when Caesar oversteps his bounds and demands that which belongs to God? When earthly governments command us to do what is clearly contrary to the will and purpose of God, then, as followers of Christ, we have not only the right but the duty to disobey.

Let me quickly highlight several Scriptural examples. In Exodus 1, Pharaoh, ruler of Egypt, commanded the midwives of Israel to kill all the Israelite baby boys at birth. The Bible tells us in Exodus 1:17 that *"the midwives feared God and did not do as the king of Egypt commanded them, but let the male children live."* God clearly honored their courage and their actions.

In Daniel 3:16-18, three young Jews stood before King Nebuchadnezzar when he commanded them to bow and worship his image. This is what they said: *"O Nebuchadnezzar, we have no need to answer you in this matter. If this be so, our God whom we serve is able to deliver us from the burning fiery furnace, and he will deliver us out of your hand, O king. But if not, be it known to you, O king, that we will not serve your gods or worship the golden image that you have set up."* It was an act of courage and civil disobedience against a king who was demanding what he had no right to demand.

In Daniel 6:10, Daniel heard that the king had signed a decree forbidding prayer to anyone but the king. This is how he responded: *"When Daniel knew that the document had been signed, he went to his house where he had windows in his upper chamber open toward Jerusalem. He got down on his knees three times a day and prayed and gave thanks before his God, as he had done previously."*

In the Book of Acts, the Jewish authorities forbade the apostles from preaching in the name of Jesus. This what they said in Acts 4:18-19: *"But Peter and John answered them, 'Whether it is right in the sight of God to listen to you rather than to God, you must judge, for we cannot but speak of what we have seen and heard.'"* And in Acts 5:29, they spoke even more clearly: *"But Peter and the apostles answered, 'We must obey God rather than men.'"*

The early history of the church also tells us of many followers of Christ who were executed because they refused to bow down and worship the emperor.

Yes, there are exceptions to the principles Paul lays down in Romans 13. God willing, they will be few and far between and, for many of us, this will remain an academic question. But should the time come and we face such a challenge, may God give us the wisdom to see our duty clearly and the courage to do it irrespective of the consequences.

In some ways, this passage leads us to a similar dilemma as the one we faced in the previous chapter. How do we face evil and confront it without becoming evil or engaging in evil actions ourselves? Romans 12 clearly told us not to return evil for evil, but rather to give thought to that which is noble or good in the sight of all men. In laying out that principle of returning good in place of evil and overcoming evil with good in the context of personal ethics and relationships, we should not conclude that this means we must always remain passive in the face of evil. While we should never return evil for evil, there are times when doing good means we must actively stand up to evil. I believe there is a time, for example, for self-defense when we need to defend ourselves physically against assault. There are times to intervene, even with physical force if necessary, to protect the innocent, the weak and the vulnerable from those who would do them harm. There are even times when we are called to be angry, and yet with this caution: *"In your anger, do not sin."* The challenge is, how do we react to such examples of overwhelming evil without becoming evil doers ourselves? That is one of the great tensions and paradoxes of our faith and of our calling. Once again, I pray that such tests will be few and far between, but should we face such tests, may God guide us to find that response which is honorable in the sight of all; one which will enable us to confront evil without becoming evil doers ourselves.

One final word: while such questions are real and painful and should not be taken lightly, let us not allow the exceptional cases to take our eyes off of the far more common challenges of our everyday lives; returning good in place of evil in our personal relationships and discourse as well as respecting and submitting to the various layers of human government that impact our lives on a daily basis. This is my confidence. If we consistently get the everyday choices right, I believe we will be prepared by God's Spirit for the exceptional challenges if and when they come our way.

29

DO YOU KNOW WHAT TIME IT IS?
Romans 13:8-14

When our sons still lived at home, our morning routine followed a very predictable pattern on school mornings. My alarm would go off. I would get up and go to the door of the bedroom of one of our sons and open it. I am not very creative or talkative that early in the morning, so I would usually say the same thing. "Dennis, it's 6:30!" Once I had some acknowledgment that he'd heard me, I would go to the next door and say, "Drew, it's 6:30!"

Why did I say that? Why did they care what time it was? Later on, as our morning routine progressed, if one or the other had not made an appearance on schedule, I might shout up the stairs: "Drew, Dennis, do you know what time it is?"

Why this preoccupation with time in our home in the morning? Time is connected with action, isn't it? Certain times require certain actions. And in a well-used routine, if we know what time it is, we know what actions are required of us.

In the last half of Romans 13, Paul reminds us as Christians what time it is. In doing so, he makes this same assumption; that if we know what time it is, we will know what actions are required. In Romans 13:11, we read: *"Besides this you know the time."* We could render that phrase this way: *"And do this, because you know the time…"*

In this passage, Paul is using this reference to time to build in us **a sense of urgency.** Paul uses three different phrases to emphasize the urgency of his instructions.

In verse 11 he says, *"the hour has come."* Actually he uses the word "already." "The hour is already…" There is something about that word "already" that creates a sense of urgency. In our house in the morning, if we were running behind, I might call out, "It's already 7:15!" In other words, we should already be out the door and in the car. Things are now urgent. There is no more time for waiting or for procrastination.

The second phrase he uses is, *"the night is far gone,"* in verse 12.

This is linked with the third phrase: *"the day is at hand."* The day is almost here.

So, what time is it? We know it is urgent: "The hour is already. The night is far gone. The day is at hand." All of these phrases create a sense of urgency, a sense of hurry; time is passing, time is short, time is almost gone. But what is the hour? What is the day? What time is Paul referring to? He makes it clear in the second half of verse 11: *"For salvation is nearer to us now than when we first believed."*

But wait a minute! I thought we were already saved. I thought that our salvation was a completed transaction when we trusted in Jesus Christ as Savior. I find it helpful to think of salvation as having three tenses; past, present and future. Once again I am going to attach these tenses to three big theological terms.

First of all, our **salvation has a past tense.** We have been saved. This refers to our **justification,** when we were **declared righteous** before God's court based on our belief (faith) in Christ and his atoning sacrifice for our sins. We might also refer to this as our **salvation from the penalty of sin.** This is a completed work. This is why Paul could write in Romans 8:1: *"There is therefore now no condemnation to those who are in Christ Jesus."* The penalty for our sins has been removed.

Secondly, our **salvation has a present tense.** We are being saved. This refers to our **sanctification.** Sanctification is the process by which we are **made righteous** as we are transformed from the inside out by the work of the Holy Spirit who lives in us. We might also refer to this as our **salvation from the power of sin.** Sin no longer reigns over us as we learn to walk in the power of the Spirit.

But there is still a third tense. Our **salvation has a future tense.** We will be saved. This refers to our **glorification,** when we will receive our glorified bodies and reign forever with Christ. We might also refer to this as our **salvation from the presence of sin.** All traces of sin and the desires of the flesh will be forever removed when we receive our new bodies which will be like Christ's own resurrected and glorified body.

It is this final and future tense of our salvation to which Paul refers in this verse; this final tense of our salvation that is the culmination of God's entire work of salvation in the believer's life. This is the salvation that is *"nearer to us now than when we first believed."* Of course, none of us knows exactly when that moment shall occur. It can come in two ways. It can come at the glorious return of our Savior to the earth. Or it may come individually when a believer dies and goes immediately into the presence of the Lord. Either way, that time is unknown to us. Either way, we do know this: that day and that hour is nearer now than it was when we first believed. Time is passing.

The passing of time becomes a concern only when it is linked to some kind of action. Flash back to our home in the morning. In Abu Dhabi in those early days, the days off from school and work used to be Thursday and Friday. On a typical Thursday morning, 6:30 came and went, 7:30, 8:30… No alarm, no call at the door, no urgency. It was a day off from school. No action was called for, so the time did not matter.

So having built on Paul's sense of **urgency,** let us look at the **action** that is called for.

Verse 11 opens with the words, *"Besides this you know the time."* This is linked with the previous verses. Translations vary here because the original language in the text literally reads simply *"And this because you know the time…"* He is referring back to his instructions in verses 8-10 and giving them a sense of urgency by noting the passing of time. We might link it up this way, "If you know what time it is, you know what to do…"

So what do we learn in these preceding verses? What action is called for? What is the "this" we will obey if we know the time? In this passage, Paul is painting with a very broad brush. In light of the urgency of passing time, in verses 8-10, we are called to **walk in love.**

Owe no one anything, except to love each other, for the one who loves another has fulfilled the law. For the commandments, "You

243

shall not commit adultery, You shall not murder, You shall not steal,
You shall not covet," and any other commandment, are summed up
in this word: "You shall love your neighbor as yourself." Love does no
wrong to a neighbor; therefore love is the fulfilling of the law.

This teaching both simplifies the law and expands it. It
simplifies the law, because we have difficulty remembering a
whole list of commandments. However, it is easy to remember
this single, all-inclusive commandment; to love your neighbor
as you love yourself. But this teaching also expands the law
because no list of commandments could ever include every
possible human situation or circumstance. It is easy to say,
"There is no commandment against this. I didn't break any laws
or commandments." Maybe not. But was it a loving thing to do?

This is not new teaching. The command to "love your
neighbor as yourself," is originally found in Leviticus 19:18.
In long rabbinical debates, the Jewish teachers had correctly
discerned that this was the most important commandment in the
Law. Jesus himself, when asked which was the most important
commandment, replied, *"You shall love the Lord your God with all*
your heart and with all your soul and with all your mind. This is the
great and first commandment. And a second is like it: You shall love
your neighbor as yourself. On these two commandments depend all
the Law and the Prophets."

In the section of Scripture in front of us, Paul is simply
calling us back to Jesus' own teaching and the teaching of the
Old Testament. When we correctly obey this command, all other
laws become unnecessary. As Paul tells us, the basic premise is
simple. Love, in its simplest definition, does no harm or wrong
to a neighbor. Look at these commands. They are taken from the
second table of the Ten Commandments. The actions prohibited
are a list of ways to harm people. Adultery, murder, stealing,
coveting; all are actions that harm others. True love, genuine
love, does not engage in actions that harm other people. These
are things we will not do if we love our neighbor. Any other
commandment we can think of that impacts our relationships
with other people can be summarized in this one commandment.
"Love your neighbor as you love yourself." Treat him or her the

same way you want to be treated yourself. It is a simple but profound moral and ethical principle.

"Do this," Paul urges us, "because you know the time." As followers of Christ, whose bodies have been placed on the altar as living sacrifices, this is how we are called to live. **Walk in love.** This is what transformed living looks like. This is what happens when we allow the Spirit of God to transform us from the inside out and make us righteous. Walk in love. This is the command that sums up all the other commands. Walk in love. Do it now. Do it, because you know what time it is.

There is another simple command that Paul uses to summarize the kind of life that we are to live if we understand the time. We are to **walk in light.** This is the emphasis of the second paragraph in the text.

"Besides this you know the time, that the hour has come for you to wake from sleep. For salvation is nearer to us now than when we first believed. The night is far gone; the day is at hand. So then let us cast off the works of darkness and put on the armor of light. Let us walk properly as in the daytime, not in orgies and drunkenness, not in sexual immorality and sensuality, not in quarreling and jealousy. But put on the Lord Jesus Christ, and make no provision for the flesh, to gratify its desires."

In this case, Paul is using his language and imagery of knowing the time to double effect. There is the sense of urgency: hour, now, already, almost, nearly. But there is also the imagery of night and day, darkness and light, slumber and wakefulness. In this imagery, the darkness is the night of sin from which we are emerging. Light and day represent the righteousness of Jesus Christ and the life style we are now called to live. As those who are emerging from the night into the day, we are called to wake up from slumber. As the day approaches there are certain things we are to take off; things that belong to the night. There are also certain things we are to put on; things appropriate to the new day that is dawning.

What are the "works of darkness" that we are called to cast off? Paul uses three couplets to describe the kinds of behavior or lifestyle that are no longer appropriate to those of us who belong to the day.

Orgies and drunkenness. These terms together depict a life of over-indulgence and excess; ill discipline, too much food, too much alcohol, party after party with no thought for tomorrow. "Eat, drink and be merry!" is the rallying cry. I am writing this during the height of the Coronavirus pandemic. In the early days of the crisis a debate was raging over whether or not to close the Florida beaches in the midst of spring break. One college-age young man was interviewed and heard to say, "If I get Corona, I get Corona. I am not going to let it stop me from partying!" That is the kind of attitude and action that we are told to cast off. That is behavior that belongs to the night. We are now children of the day.

Sexual immorality and sensuality. Included here are all the sins of a sexual nature, both in thought and action. Sex and sexual relations are a precious gift from God that he intends to be exercised within the boundaries of monogamous marriage. God has not changed his mind about that. The "new normal" is not normal to God, no matter how many people are doing it. Whether it is indulging in internet pornography, premarital sex, extramarital sex, same sex relations or any other departure from God's revealed will, these are behaviors and patterns of thought and action which we are called to cast off. They belong to the night, but now morning has come.

Quarreling and jealousy. The first word in this couplet describes conflict resulting from rivalry or discord. The second one describes an extremely strong feeling of resentment and jealousy. All the common quarrels of life, and the seething emotions that cause them, are included here. How many Christians clear the hurdles posed by the first two categories rather smugly, only to find themselves tripping over this one? It is sad to say, but church fights can turn really nasty. When we Christians get embroiled in a conflict, it seems we can be as mean and vindictive as anyone. Just about the time we wrap our superior standards of personal discipline and sexual morality around us like a pharisaical robe, we turn and blast a fellow believer out of the water for some real or imagined slight or difference of opinion. As the Scripture says to us elsewhere, "Brothers and sisters, these things ought not so to be." Quarreling and jealousy need to go. They belong to the night. "Take them off," we are told. "It's time to wake up and put on the attire appropriate to the new day."

This is what we are to take off. What are we to put on? First we are told to **put on the armor of light.** The word for armor is used to describe all the implements of a soldier; both offensive and defensive. I don't think we should press the image here or try to be too specific. Paul does that elsewhere in Ephesians 6, using this same word. Here Paul is speaking in general terms. Take up and put on all that is appropriate to the day; all that is characteristic of light rather than darkness. Another way of saying this is found in the next verse: *"walk properly as in the daytime."* Don't rush out in your pajamas or nighttime attire. Get dressed for the day.

Paul then summarizes it all in the most powerful and evocative image possible in the final verse. **Put on the Lord Jesus Christ.** This is the most concise and beautiful summary of sanctification in the Bible. *"Put on the Lord Jesus Christ!"* All the character qualities that Jesus himself displayed when he walked on earth – put them on! His love, his humility, his compassion, his holiness, his devotion to prayer, his gentleness, his response to evil. In applying Romans 12:9-21 in a previous chapter, I challenged you to read the passage as a description of the character of Jesus himself. Here we are again. *Put on the Lord Jesus Christ!* He is the ultimate model of walking in the light. A number of years ago, a movement swept across many churches (at least in America). Christians started wearing bracelets or other items with the initials WWJD. What Would Jesus Do? I would affirm that desire. Jesus is indeed our perfect model.

But I would also raise a caution to this movement. If we simply take this as a list of character qualities that we do our best to imitate, then we are making a big mistake. We are doomed to failure. Jesus is a perfect model, but we are woefully unable to imitate him in our own efforts and our own strength. When Paul tells us to "put on the Lord Jesus Christ" I believe there is more involved than just imitating his character. He is telling us to actually "put on the Lord Jesus Christ." You see, the Spirit of

Christ, the Holy Spirit, now lives inside us. We are called to allow him to live out the life of Christ through us as we yield daily to him. Paul describes this in slightly different terms in Galatians 2:20: *"I have been crucified with Christ. It is no longer I who live, but Christ who lives in me. And the life I now live in the flesh I live by faith in the Son of God, who loved me and gave himself for me."*

Do you see that? *"It is not longer I who live, but Christ who lives in me."* I believe that is what Paul has in mind when he tells us to "Put on the Lord Jesus Christ." Our outward behavior begins to resemble the life of Christ because we are submitting to his rule in our hearts and allowing him to live his life through us. Galatians was written to believers who, having been justified by faith in Christ, now thought they could be sanctified by human effort and by trying to keep the law by their own efforts. It is a mistake. We must never separate our desire to emulate Jesus in character from our passion to walk with him in close relationship.

Put on the Lord Jesus Christ. That is what it means to be sanctified, and that is the only way to be sanctified. It is a description of both the goal and the process.

Paul ends with one final caveat or warning: *"and make no provision for the flesh, to gratify its desires."* Do you ever do that? Do you find yourself planning ahead, in some secret area of your heart and mind, for some forbidden indulgence of the old nature? An obvious example of this is the alcoholic who decides to quit drinking, but before he quits, he hides a bottle of his favorite beverage "just in case." What is your Achilles heel of weakness? How do you make allowances for indulging it? I like the quote, (found written in the margin of my study notes): "Stop sin in the planning stages."

Walk in love. Walk in the light. That is our calling. This is the new life we are called to live. This is what sanctification looks like. This is Christian ethics at its most profound and most fundamental level. I doubt that I have said anything in this chapter that you have not heard before. But I want to end by coming back to where we began and the sense of urgency that Paul injects into this passage. I believe many Christians have good intentions. We applaud high standards. We say a hearty

"Amen!" to this kind of teaching. But in our hearts, in our secret lives where no one else can see, we are procrastinators. We are often victims of a deep spiritual inertia. We are like a teenager who doesn't want to get up for school. We desperately cling to the last vestiges of sleep and slumber; one last dream. To us, Paul is calling. Wake up! Don't you know what time it is? *The night is far gone; the day is at hand...cast off the works of darkness and put on the armor of light. Put on the Lord Jesus Christ.*

30

MAKING A LIST AND CHECKING IT TWICE
Romans 14:1-15:13 (Part 1)

In this chapter, I want to discuss lists. Lists play an important part in our lives. We make shopping lists, to do lists, and packing lists. I want to discuss a particular kind of list. It is an internal list that we carry around in our hearts and minds. I suppose it is a kind of "to do" list, although in most cases it is more of a "not to do" list. I will explain what I mean in just a moment.

How shall we then live? That is the broad topic that Paul is addressing in the last 5 chapters of the Book of Romans. In light of our justification by faith; in light of what Christ did for us on the cross by offering himself as the atoning sacrifice for our sins (which is the topic of the first 11 chapters of Romans); how shall we now live? What is a Christian lifestyle? How shall we behave?

Paul has already given us some very clear and solid instructions. Each of us is to present our body to God as a living sacrifice. Paul instructed us to use our gifts to serve the body of Christ. He told us how to respond to our enemies. He showed us how to relate to governing authorities. He told us to love our neighbors as ourselves. We are to walk in love and walk in the light. In summary, we are told to "put on the Lord Jesus Christ."

So we have already received a wealth of instruction to digest and apply. But there is still much left unsaid about the details of daily life. How should a Christian dress? What should he eat or drink? What leisure activities are permitted and which ones excluded? What occupations are permissible and which ones are taboo? As followers of the Lord Jesus Christ, we all make a multitude of decisions daily which are simply not covered in the Bible. To help us sort through that daily maze, most of us carry within us a sort of internal list of things that we believe are right or wrong; things we do and things we will not do, based on our convictions. This list is not written down, but it is there in our minds and in our consciences. It wields a large influence over our daily behavior.

The passage we are considering is found in Romans 14:1 through 15:13, and if you have not done so already, I encourage you to read the passage through.

We are going to spend two chapters on this passage and this topic; a kind of Part 1 and Part 2. In this chapter, we will discuss **Making Our Lists.** In the following chapter we will talk about **What Happens When Our Lists Collide.**

We need to think clearly about our lists and how we arrive at them. As we begin to define the list we are talking about, I need to make one thing abundantly clear at the outset. We are not including in our discussion those matters about which God has clearly spoken. I believe all Christians should carry in their hearts and consciences another list; a list of God's clear instructions or commands. About these, there should be no debate. We are not given discretion in these areas. When the Bible says clearly, "Thou shalt not steal," we are not left to make up our own minds about whether or not we should shop-lift to fill our Christmas gift list. When the Bible tells us to stop lying and speak the truth, we are not at liberty to decide whether this applies to us or not. When the Scripture clearly spells out God's standards on matters of sexual morality, that is not an invitation to debate. They are commands to be obeyed. Where God, through the Scriptures, has clearly spoken, we have only two choices; obey or disobey. We are not free to alter, ignore or delete God's clear instructions. But, there are a host of other matters about which Scripture is silent. Either there are no specific guidelines, or the guidelines are ambiguous and open to different interpretations. Let me give you two examples of these kinds of issues from the passage in front of us.

Let's read Romans 14:2: *"One person believes he may eat anything, while the weak person eats only vegetables."*

Meat versus vegetables. To eat or not to eat, that is the question. What is a Christian diet? Why was this an issue in the early church? First, let me say that this was not a question of health or nutrition. It was a religious question, and scholars believe that this issue may have arisen from two possible sources.

First, Paul may have been addressing Jewish concerns about food that was clean or unclean, kosher or not kosher. Remember, in Paul's day, strict observant Jews refused to even eat with Gentiles at least in part to preserve their dietary, old-covenant standards of purity. Now there were Gentiles and Jews together in the church of Jesus Christ. Imagine a shared meal; a kind of first century church potluck. What was kosher? What wasn't? What could a strictly-raised Jew who was now a follower of Christ eat or not eat? Since many of the dietary distinctions applied to types of animals and meat, the safest path for a Jewish believer who wanted to remain kosher would have been to eat vegetables only.

But there is another issue that Paul may have had in mind. This is one he also addresses in his first letter to the Corinthians. It relates to animals or meat that had been offered to the pagan idols of the day. Such animals were often given to the pagan priests, who would slaughter the animal ceremonially, burn part of it, keep part of it, and then the rest might show up for sale in the local meat market. Was it OK to eat such meat or not? Once again, the safest route was to stick to the vegetables.

A second issue brought up by Paul is found in the first part of verse 5: *"One person esteems one day as better than another, while another esteems all days alike."* This is most probably a reference to Sabbath keeping or to the Jewish feast days or festivals. Should these be observed or not? There were differences of opinion in the early church.

What are some modern examples of such issues? I have lived almost 70 years in the context of Christian communities, and I can think of a long list of issues which have been debated during that time period: women wearing head coverings in church, wearing jewelry or make-up, going to movies (especially in the cinema), dancing, drinking alcohol, using tobacco in any form, allowable activities on Sunday. Gambling was clearly off-limits, but what about using dice or playing cards in games, or even going to the horse races? Dress standards and standards of hair and personal grooming were often a lively topic of discussion, and I might go on and on. The list is more or less endless. What I have found fascinating is that the list often differed dramatically from one denomination to another and from one part of the US to another. This was even more apparent during my 25 years living in Abu Dhabi and serving in a church with members who came from more than 60 different countries!

So, in this maze of conflicting voices and opinions, how shall we proceed? Let me share four points with you to begin our discussion.

1. There is no divinely mandated list.

Many of us carry the presupposition that even if it is not revealed in Scripture, there is still a list somewhere in the heart and mind of God; that if we have the mind of Christ, we will know what is on that list and what is not and that it will be the same list for every true follower of Christ.

Once again, let me say plainly. Where God has spoken, yes, his command applies to all. But where he has not spoken or where the Bible is unclear, then there is no universal list. Within this domain something can truly be right for one person and wrong for another.

Consider these verses:

"I know and am persuaded in the Lord Jesus that nothing is unclean in itself, but it is unclean for anyone who thinks it unclean." (Romans 14:14) In other words, Paul is saying, there are things he can eat with a clear conscience, but if another Christian were to eat the same thing, for him it would be wrong. Romans 14:23 continues in a similar vein. *"But whoever has doubts is condemned if he eats, because the eating is not from faith. For whatever does not proceed from faith is sin."*

There is no divinely mandated list. Certain things can be wrong for one believer and right for another. I have found that this can be particularly difficult for some people to accept. They want everything to be in black and white without debate. I was once counseling a young woman who had served as a missionary among a particular tribe of people. She came to me one day with a very finely made, small leather pouch someone had given her as a gift. She treasured it, not only because of its workmanship, but because of the friendship of the person who gave it to her. Another missionary had seen it and told her that it was an article attached to the animistic charms practiced by the tribe. If she kept it she was inviting a demonic influence into her life. She brought it to me and asked me what she should do. I attempted to lead her into a discussion of the object's meaning to her, but she became upset. She did not want a discussion. She was very black and white in her thinking. She wanted me to give her a clear answer, label it right or wrong, and tell her what to do. She did not want to live with any ambiguity. In her case, I believe she probably needed to destroy the article because of the doubt that had been raised in her mind. But I do not think that same answer would apply to everyone.

What are some of the reasons for the differences? I believe they are based on the differences of the meaning of certain objects and actions. That meaning can vary from person to person. For a converted idol worshipper, meat offered to idols had a certain meaning. For a converted Jew, to eat pork still didn't feel right. There are differences in culture and religious backgrounds. There are also differences in experience; for a recovering alcoholic or for someone raised in an alcoholic home, taking a drink takes on a different meaning than it does for someone else. So, because of that diversity in our backgrounds and experiences, there is no divinely-mandated list.

2. There is no direct correlation between the strength of one's faith and the length of one's list.

Does a longer list of taboos or "not to dos" make a person more spiritual and Christ-like? The Pharisees would certainly have endorsed this kind of thinking. But Paul makes it clear that this is not the case. Consider verse 2 again: *"One person believes he may eat anything, while the weak person eats only vegetables."* Here it is clearly the person with the longer list ("I don't eat meat") who is regarded as the weaker brother. On the other hand, I would certainly not advocate that we swing to the other extreme and conclude that it is the believer with the shortest list who has the strongest faith. This would send us in the wrong direction as well. There is no direct correlation between the strength of one's faith and the length of one's list.

3. The believer's list may change over time.

I do not have a particular verse for this, but I think the implication is clear. Certainly the early church and even Paul himself would have gone through some evolution as their understanding of Scripture and the new covenant grew. I believe we must remain open to evaluating our lists as we gain new light from Scripture and from interaction with believers and cultures. I would suggest that we need to be willing to add items to our list as well as to delete them as we grow in faith and in our sensitivity to the leading of the Holy Spirit in all areas of life. While it is important to have a list, I also believe it is necessary and healthy to check our lists from time to time. Be willing to step back on occasion and analyze your convictions. Where did they come from? What is cultural and what is Scriptural? Are there Biblical principles involved, or is it simply a matter of social norms in the Christian sub-culture?

4. Strength of faith is demonstrated by living in a manner that is consistent with one's personal convictions.

I believe this is the most important principle to be found in this section. Rómans 14:5-8 says this:

"One person esteems one day as better than another, while another esteems all days alike. Each one should be fully convinced in his own mind. The one who observes the day, observes it in honor of the Lord. The one who eats, eats in honor of the Lord, since he gives thanks to God, while the one who abstains, abstains in honor of the Lord and gives thanks to God. For none of us lives to himself, and none of us dies to himself. For if we live, we live to the Lord, and if we die, we die to the Lord. So then, whether we live or whether we die, we are the Lord's."

Whatever we do or don't do should be for the Lord and in his honor. These verses represent a beautiful summary of the attitude of a living sacrifice. Whether we live or whether we die, we belong to the Lord and we should be doing what we do for him. If we abstain from doing something, we should abstain for the Lord and for his honor. In both cases we should do so, giving thanks to God.

In verse 14, Paul says, *"I know and am persuaded in the Lord Jesus that nothing is unclean in itself, but it is unclean for anyone who thinks it unclean."*

The NIV translates that "fully convinced." As one who is "fully convinced" that he can eat anything he was ready and able to live by that conviction. But for the one who is convinced that something is unclean he needs to live by his conviction and not eat. Verses 22-23 summarize the matter plainly. *"The faith that you have, keep between yourself and God. Blessed is the one who has no reason to pass judgment on himself for what he approves. 23 But whoever has doubts is condemned if he eats, because the eating is not from faith. For whatever does not proceed from faith is sin."*

Live by your own faith and convictions before God. You are blessed if you do not condemn yourself for what you allow yourself to do. Keep a clear conscience between yourself and God – and that means living by the convictions of your own experience and conscience. The film "Chariots of Fire" is a powerful example of this kind of faith and testimony. Eric Liddell, the son of Scottish missionaries, spent his early years in China. As a university student in Scotland, he blossomed into a world class runner and began training for the 100-meter dash in the 1924 Olympics. Several months before the Games, the schedule of events was released, showing that the heats for the 100-meter race were to take place on a Sunday. As a committed Christian, Eric held a strong conviction that there were certain activities that were appropriate on a Sunday and certain activities that were not. Running in a race was not among the list of appropriate activities. Eric made up his mind. Because of his convictions, he withdrew his name from the 100-meter competition, his strongest event. He decided instead to train for the 400-meter event; a race that did not favor his raw speed and in which he had little experience – but he would not be required to run on Sunday. As Eric lined up for the final race, someone pressed a slip of paper into his hands. On it were written the words from 1 Samuel 2:30, *"Those who honour me I will honour.*" Liddell ran with that piece of paper in his hand and not only won the race but broke the existing world record. We may or may not agree with Eric's list or share his convictions regarding Sabbath keeping, but he was a man with the courage of his convictions. He did what he did for the glory of God, and God honored him for it. I don't know about you, but I want to live like that.

Let me conclude briefly. I hope no one is going away with the idea that having a "not to do" list is a bad thing. You need a list, just like I need a list, and we need to live according to our lists. We are desperately vulnerable and defenseless if we go through life without convictions, making every decision based on what people around us are doing. Without such a list, every behavioral decision can become an exhausting crisis of conscience. It is wise to have a clear sense of conviction of what you will do and what you won't, of where you will go and where you will not. Make your list under the guidance of the Holy Spirit, based on where you are right now in your walk with God. Then live by those convictions. That is the path of blessing. That is the path to a clear conscience before God.

This, then, raises the question: What happens when your list differs from my list? What happens when lists collide? That will be the topic of the next chapter.

31

WHEN LISTS COLLIDE
Romans 14:1-15:13 (Part 2)

I was walking to school one day on my way to the seminary, carrying my briefcase filled with theology textbooks, when an older man stopped me on the street corner. He thrust a printed brochure or flyer into my hand. I paused, looked down, and saw that it was a Gospel tract. So I stopped, introduced myself, and told the man that I was also a Christian and studying to be a pastor. I commended him for his zeal and his evangelistic effort, and we had several moments of good fellowship.

Then his eyes narrowed as he looked at me, and he said, "If you're a Christian, how come you look like that?" Now, I need to pause here and give a brief description of myself. This was the 1970's; the era of hippies, long hair, beards, beads, bell-bottom trousers and paisley shirts. By the standards of the day, I was actually dressed rather conservatively. But my hair (which I had back then) covered my ears and curled over my collar. I didn't wear a full beard, but I did have beautiful, long bushy sideburns that swept up and joined my mustache, making me look somewhat like a general from the American Civil War era. My new friend on the street corner continued to zero in. "Long hair and long whiskers are a sign of rebellion. Real Christians shouldn't look like that. They should be clean cut, well groomed and neat looking. You can't serve the Lord looking like that!" And so our brief moments of Christian fellowship came to a rather abrupt end.

That is an amusing, yet rather sad and far too common story of what can happen **when lists collide;** when Christians disagree about what constitutes Christian behavior, appearance or life style.

Let me set our context once again. This is the second of two chapters taken from Romans 14 and 15. Paul is talking about what I have been calling our Christian "to do" lists and "not to do" lists. I will emphasize again what I said in the previous chapter; that there are actually two lists. There is a list of things about which God has spoken very clearly and given clear commands or directives. "Thou shalt," and "Thou shalt not…" In these matters there should be no debate. God has spoken and we must obey. But there are many other issues about which we have no specific word from the Lord, or where there are differences of opinion and interpretation. Within that grey area of ambiguity, different Christians have different ideas of what is right and what is wrong, and of what constitutes Christian behavior and a Christian life-style.

In Romans 14:1, Paul talks about "quarreling over opinions." The NIV translates this "disputable matters." This is the arena of discussion in these two chapters. In the previous chapter, we talked about "making our lists." We need to have convictions and to live by our convictions if we desire to live with a clear conscience before God. But what happens when our lists collide; when we have differences of opinion with other believers?

If you have ever watched a TV show or a movie of a crime or undercover operation in which timing is essential, there often comes a time when one of the characters will say, "Let's synchronize our watches." Christians often spend a great deal of time and energy trying to "synchronize our lists." In that effort, I have both bad news and good news. The bad news is **we will never succeed**. As we found out in the previous chapter, that is because there is no divinely mandated, "one size fits all" list. Because of our different backgrounds and experiences, and because of the different meanings and symbolism of different activities and articles, there are some things that can actually be right for one person, but wrong for another. Our lists can vary dramatically from one person to another, from one church to another and from region to region.

I remember the well-known pastor and Bible teacher, Stuart Briscoe, sharing an amusing story to illustrate this point. Christians in a church denomination in Europe had been receiving disturbing reports about the worldliness of their churches in America. They decided to send a delegation to investigate and see if these reports were true. When the delegation returned, they made their report. "Yes," they said. "The stories are true. Christians in America have become very worldly and loose in their standards. Many of the women dress inappropriately, even in church. Some even wear slacks and pant suits to church and they wear lots of jewelry. The men drive flashy and extravagant cars. They engage in many forms of worldly entertainment on the Sabbath." As they shared their report, the list of failings became longer and longer, and they became so distraught and saddened by what they were saying that they began to weep. They shed great tears, and the tears ran down their faces and down their cigars and dripped into their beer!

We will never succeed at synchronizing our lists because there is no divinely sanctioned master list for all followers of Christ. That can be confusing. It can be particularly confusing for our children at times. I remember when we first moved to Abu Dhabi. We had been living and working within a relatively conservative Christian subculture on the West Coast of the US. We hadn't been in Abu Dhabi very long when a family in the church invited us to join them for dinner at a nice restaurant. As the waiter came around to take our order, we ordered Coke and Diet Coke. Our hosts ordered wine to go with their meal. As we got in our car to go home after the evening was over, our younger son, who was about 10 at the time, leaned over from the back seat and said, "I thought they were Christians!"

So that's the bad news. There is no master list. That can be confusing. The good news, though, is that **we don't have to synchronize our lists** to enjoy fellowship and harmony in the family of God if we will follow the principles and priorities laid out in this passage.

If we can't synchronize our lists, how do we get along with people who have lists that are different from ours? In answer to that question, we can summarize Paul's teaching in this text in the following three points.

1. Take the perspective of a fellow servant: stop judging.

In Romans 14:1-3, we read: *"As for the one who is weak in faith, welcome him, but not to quarrel over opinions. One person believes he may eat anything, while the weak person eats only vegetables. Let not the one who eats despise the one who abstains, and let not the one who abstains pass judgment on the one who eats, for God has welcomed him."*

When we get into the business of comparing ours lists with others, we find that there are two groups of people. There are people with longer lists than ours, and there are also people with shorter lists than ours. The natural human tendency is to label these people. Those people with longer lists than ours – well, they are legalists. Those with shorter lists than ours are guilty of loose living. In fact we might even question whether they are "real" Christians at all. Verse 3 warns against this tendency with two different words: "despise" and "pass judgment." We tend to "despise" or look down on those with an over scrupulous conscience (at least by the standards of our list) and to "pass judgment" or condemn those whose conscience allows them to do things we cannot. Either way, when we enter into judgment, fellowship is broken.

In verse 4, Paul tells us why this needs to end. He reminds us to recognize our position as fellow servants. *"Who are you to pass judgment on the servant of another? It is before his own master that he stands or falls. And he will be upheld, for the Lord is able to make him stand."*

Our fellow Christians aren't our servants. They do not answer to us. God has not given us the job of sitting in judgment over them. They serve the Lord. He is their master, just as he is our master. He will do the evaluating and the judging. This does not mean that others always do the right thing. It does mean that we are not the judge of whether they are right or wrong. That is not our job. That is God's prerogative, not ours.

Paul goes on to expand on this point in verses 10-13a: *"Why do you pass judgment on your brother? Or you, why do you despise your brother? For we will all stand before the judgment seat of God; for it is written, 'As I live, says the Lord, every knee shall bow to me, and every tongue shall confess to God.' So then each of us will give an account of himself to God. Therefore let us not pass judgment on one another any longer..."*

Stop judging! Why? Because we are not the judges. God is the judge. We will each give an account of ourselves to God. I would point out that this reality (that we shall all one day give an account) gives us two reasons for not judging our fellow servants. First of all, such judging is unnecessary. God has the task of judging well in hand. If a fellow servant is violating his own list and even God's own standard of right and wrong, he will answer to God for that, not to us. Don't forget that God is the perfect, righteous, holy judge. We must also be careful not to judge because we remember that we too are servants who will give an account to God. And one thing we may have to answer for is our own critical spirit and judgmental attitude toward others. Remember Jesus' words in the Sermon on the Mount, "Judge not, lest you be judged." Remember the perspective of the fellow servant and **stop judging!**

At this point, it would be easy to draw a wrong conclusion, and swing to an un-Biblical extreme. I might conclude that I am a law unto myself and that I am free to form my own convictions before God, make my list and live by my list without any thought for the effects of my actions on others around me. But we must balance the first point of this chapter with the second point.

2. Remember the priority of love: start loving!

We must recognize that we live in a community. Within this community our actions do have an effect on those around us. Let's follow Paul's thought as we read, beginning in verse 13:

"Therefore let us not pass judgment on one another any longer, but rather decide never to put a stumbling block or hindrance in the way of a brother. I know and am persuaded in the Lord Jesus that nothing is unclean in itself, but it is unclean for anyone who thinks it unclean. For if your brother is grieved by what you eat, you are no longer walking in love. By what you eat, do not destroy the one for whom Christ died. So do not let what you regard as good be spoken of as evil. For the kingdom of God is not a matter of eating and drinking but of righteousness and peace and joy in the

Holy Spirit. Whoever thus serves Christ is acceptable to God and approved by men. So then let us pursue what makes for peace and for mutual upbuilding. Do not, for the sake of food, destroy the work of God. Everything is indeed clean, but it is wrong for anyone to make another stumble by what he eats. It is good not to eat meat or drink wine or do anything that causes your brother to stumble."

There are two Christian values at play in these chapters and in this discussion on lists. They are the value of Christian liberty and the value of Christ-like love. Christian liberty might be defined as the freedom to form our own opinions and convictions on matters on which the Bible has not clearly spoken, and then to live by those convictions. We are "free from the law" and at liberty to walk according to the directions of the indwelling Spirit of Christ. That is one value we've been discussing. But there is another value that Paul brings into the discussion. That is the value of Christ-like love. Here is the point that Paul is making in this paragraph. In the hierarchy of Christian values, **love trumps liberty.** Christ-like love should triumph over the exercise of our liberty if and when these two values are in conflict.

While this is a very important point, I do need to clear up one thing before we proceed. Verse 15 states that, *"if your brother is grieved by what you eat, you are no longer walking in love."* Who is the offended brother and how far must I go to appease him? Let's go back to my "friend" on the street corner. Was he offended or "grieved" by my long hair and sideburns? Should I have rushed to a barber for a shave and a hair-cut to avoid offending him? Let's follow Paul's logic carefully. He is choosing his words very carefully. Verse 13 speaks of putting a *"stumbling block or hindrance in the way of a brother."* If we follow Paul's reasoning, it is not the brother with strong convictions or strong opinions who is in view here. It is the weak brother; the brother with doubts, the brother who is not sure of what is right or wrong. How might I cause him to stumble? Let's take Paul's example of eating meat. I may be convinced that it is OK to eat meat, but my weaker brother has doubts. He sees me eating, and concludes that he is also free to eat. But when he eats, he eats doubtfully and violates his own conscience. He has been led into sin by my example.

Was my friend on the street corner going to be tempted to grow long side-burns and hair because he saw how good I looked!? No! He had no doubts. He had strong opinions. So the matter of offending him or grieving him, in the sense of leading him astray, simply did not arise. I believe this is an important distinction to make. There are some Christians with strong opinions who believe that their list is synonymous with God's list. Such Christians seem to make a career out of "being offended" by other Christians. If we try to bend our lives and conform to their lists, the whole community of believers becomes hostage to the believer with the longest list. We truly are enslaved to a new kind of legalism. It is the legalism of "what will people think?"

This is not what Paul is saying. He is speaking of the weaker brother who might be led into sin by violating his more sensitive conscience. In such cases, the principle is clear. Love takes precedence over liberty. We need to be willing to limit our liberty so that we will not lead our brother astray. In the hierarchy of Christian values, Christ-like love trumps Christian liberty. As Paul summarizes in Romans 15:1-4, *"We who are strong have an obligation to bear with the failings of the weak, and not to please ourselves. Let each of us please his neighbor for his good, to build him up. For Christ did not please himself, but as it is written, 'The reproaches of those who reproached you fell on me.' For whatever was written in former days was written for our instruction, that through endurance and through the encouragement of the Scriptures we might have hope."*

If we will maintain the perspective of a fellow servant and stop judging each other, and if we are willing to limit our liberty for the higher priority of love, then we will arrive at the final point I want to make.

3. Experience the power of unity: stand together!

Romans 15:5-7 says, *"May the God of endurance and encouragement grant you to live in such harmony with one another, in accord with Christ Jesus, that together you may with one voice glorify the God and Father of our Lord Jesus Christ. Therefore welcome one another as Christ has welcomed you, for the glory of God."*

Living in harmony. The NIV translates this as "a spirit of unity." There is an important principle of Christian unity here. We don't have to agree about everything to be unified or to experience harmony. Did you know that? We don't even have to share the same lists to experience unity. In spite of our differences, we can welcome one another as Christ has welcomed us for the glory of God. We don't have to sing in unison, but we do have to sing in harmony. When we do, our voices blend into one magnificent voice to glorify the God and Father of our Lord Jesus Christ.

This was an amazing aspect of what God was doing in the first century church. He was bringing Jews and Gentiles together into one Body. In fact, many of the issues Paul has addressed in these chapters were based on differences between Jews and Gentiles. Paul highlights this now with a series of Old Testament quotes:

"For I tell you that Christ became a servant to the circumcised to show God's truthfulness, in order to confirm the promises given to the patriarchs, and in order that the Gentiles might glorify God for his mercy. As it is written,

'Therefore I will praise you among the Gentiles, and sing to your name.'

And again it is said,
'Rejoice, O Gentiles, with his people.'
And again,
'Praise the Lord, all you Gentiles, and let all the peoples extol him.'

And again Isaiah says,
'The root of Jesse will come, even he who arises to rule the Gentiles; in him will the Gentiles hope.'"

These are all Old Testament passages that prophesied that God would one day fling open the doors of his kingdom to the Gentiles and that Gentiles with Jews would together glorify God for his mercy. I love that phrase: *Rejoice, O Gentiles, with his people.* Jews and Gentiles together! That unity was now being expressed in the New Testament church. But for such unity to be experienced and demonstrated, they had to figure out what to do about their different lists.

For us the distinctions are not between Jews and Gentiles. But we do come from many different backgrounds, and among us there is indeed a wide diversity of lists. Such differences of opinion can, and often do, cause divisions among us. But they don't need to, if we are prepared to walk in the power of the Holy Spirit and practice the truths of this passage: **Stop judging! Start loving! Stand together!**

32

A GODLY AMBITION
Romans 15:14-21

Are you an ambitious person? As Christians, we might be tempted to recoil and say, "Of course not!" We tend to shy away from that word "ambition." It sounds rather fleshly, worldly, and man-driven. And often it is! The Bible warns us against something called "selfish ambition." Philippians 2:3 warns us to *"do nothing from selfish ambition or conceit."*

But such a warning does not mean that we as Christians should be passive and without ambition. There is another kind of ambition. We might call this "godly ambition." So I ask again. Are you an ambitious person, filled with godly ambition?

We are moving into the final section of the Book of Romans. We have completed the teaching section of this great epistle. Paul has concluded his treatise on the Gospel, and the rest of chapter 15 and chapter 16 will be taken up with personal notes and information on his plans for the future and a proposed visit to Rome. Nonetheless, even from his personal notes we can learn some valuable lessons. One of the things we learn is that Paul was an ambitious man. He was filled with godly ambition. He writes in Romans 15:20, *"and thus I make it my ambition..."*

What was Paul's ambition? At this point, his answer should not surprise us: *"and thus I make it my ambition to preach the gospel..."* This has been Paul's subject and preoccupation from the opening sentence of this letter. In Romans 1:1 Paul opens his letter by introducing himself as, *"Paul, a servant of Christ Jesus, called to be an apostle, <u>set apart for the gospel of God...</u>"*

This "gospel of God" to which Paul had devoted his life is found in its most condensed form in Romans 3:24-25. It is the good news that we can be, *"...justified by his grace as a gift through the redemption that is in Christ Jesus, whom God put forward as a propitiation by his blood, to be received by faith."*

The entire gospel is found in this sentence, so rich in theological language; Justification, grace, redemption, propitiation, and the blood of Jesus Christ. This is the gospel message distilled into its most concentrated and essential elements. Jesus Christ shed his blood on the cross as the sacrifice that satisfied the wrath of God against our sins. Consequently, we can now be justified (declared righteous) before God by grace, as a free gift. All we have to do is to receive this gift by faith.

We are nearing the end of our journey through the Book of Romans. As we come to the end of our voyage, I sincerely hope that we have all grown in our knowledge and understanding of Romans and of the gospel. But there is a more pressing concern. Now that we have grown in our knowledge of the gospel, what shall we do with this knowledge that we have acquired? What shall we do with the gospel message?

I believe the gospel calls urgently for three responses. First, **the gospel is something to believe.** This is the first and most essential matter that is pressed upon us in the Book of Romans. It is the simple and fundamental question: Is this good news true? Do you believe it? Earlier, I made the point that there was an important division of labor between myself, the writer, and you, the readers. My task has been to explain Paul's words (God's words) as clearly and accurately as I could. I have sought to do that. In reliance on the guidance and anointing of the Holy Spirit, I have brought every effort and skill at my disposal to present the truths of the gospel and the Book of Romans to you chapter after chapter. But there is another part of the contract that only you can fulfill. That is believing it. Believing is something I, the writer, cannot do for you. It is something your pastor cannot do for you. It is something your parents cannot do for you. It is something your teacher or your Christian friends cannot do for you. It is something only you can do. It is the 18 inches the gospel must travel from your head to your heart when you say with genuine faith and conviction: **"I believe."** This is when the power of the gospel is released. As Paul told us in Romans 1:16:

"For I am not ashamed of the gospel, for it is the power of God for salvation to <u>everyone who believes</u>..."

It is not enough to understand the Gospel. We must believe it! Belief is more than intellectual assent. It is more than nodding our heads to say, "I agree. That makes sense." It is a transfer of trust. It is putting our weight down on the finished work of Christ on the cross. The gospel is, first of all, something to be believed. Do you believe it? If the gospel is true, then your eternal destiny is riding on your answer to that question.

But the gospel is more than something to be believed. The gospel is also **something to be lived.** In fact, the one thing that Paul has made clear in this letter is the fact that it is impossible to genuinely believe the gospel, to believe in Jesus Christ as Savior, and yet remain unchanged. If the gospel is true, and if we genuinely believe it, our lives will be transformed.

This is the point that Paul made in Romans 6:1-4: *"What shall we say then? Are we to continue in sin that grace may abound? By no means! How can we who died to sin still live in it? Do you not know that all of us who have been baptized into Christ Jesus were baptized into his death? We were buried therefore with him by baptism into death, in order that, just as Christ was raised from the dead by the glory of the Father, we too might walk in newness of life."*

The gospel changes us. Faith in Christ changes us. We are given a new heart. The Holy Spirit comes to live in us. We are called to "walk in newness of life." As we present our bodies as living sacrifices, the Spirit of God transforms us from the inside out by renewing our minds. We think differently, and in turn, our thoughts, words and actions are transformed. It doesn't happen all at once. It is a process that takes place over time. We may have times of rapid growth and times of slow growth, stagnation, or even backsliding as we hinder the Spirit's working by quenching him or grieving him. But the clear teaching of Scripture is that we will be changed and transformed. If there is no transformation of life, then there is a serious question as to whether genuine faith is present. **The gospel is something to be lived.**

But we are not quite finished. And this is where we come to the question with which we began this message. It is the question of godly ambition. The gospel is something to be believed. The gospel is something to be lived. Lastly, **the gospel is something to be proclaimed.** This was Paul's sacred, holy and godly ambition. Listen to the language and imagery he uses to explain this holy calling in Romans 15:15-21.

"But on some points I have written to you very boldly by way of reminder, because of the grace given me by God to be a minister of Christ Jesus to the Gentiles in the priestly service of the gospel of God, so that the offering of the Gentiles may be acceptable, sanctified by the Holy Spirit. In Christ Jesus, then, I have reason to be proud of my work for God. For I will not venture to speak of anything except what Christ has accomplished through me to bring the Gentiles to obedience—by word and deed, by the power of signs and wonders, by the power of the Spirit of God—so that from Jerusalem and all the way around to Illyricum I have fulfilled the ministry of the gospel of Christ; and thus I make it my ambition to preach the gospel, not where Christ has already been named, lest I build on someone else's foundation, but as it is written, 'Those who have never been told of him will see, and those who have never heard will understand.'"

Now, there are some things in this passage that are unique to Paul and his role as an Apostle, and more specifically, as an Apostle to the Gentiles. However, the imagery he uses can be applied to all of us as followers of Christ. Paul pictures himself as a priest serving God in the temple. As a priest, Paul is placing a sacrifice on the altar. His offerings on the altar are the people who have come to Christ through his ministry; in Paul's case, they were the Gentiles to whom he had been uniquely called to minister. His prayer is that his offering will be accepted and pleasing to God.

I believe that we can all have that same godly ambition, which is to offer our service to God and his gospel. Paul's ambition and his calling were specifically stated. As he says: *"I make it my ambition to preach the gospel, not where Christ has already been named, lest I build on someone else's foundation."*

Not all of us are called and gifted to do frontier or pioneer evangelism. But I believe that all of us are called to serve as priests before God and to offer our service to him and to the gospel.

One of the primary ways we can do that is by sharing the gospel message with the people around us. How could it be otherwise? How could we possibly know this good news, genuinely believe it, experience its transforming power in our lives…and then keep it to ourselves?

Again I ask, are you an ambitious person? If so, are your ambitions godly ambitions? Let me tell you about two friends of mine who, I believe represent the highest form of godly ambition. For security purposes, let's call them Elijah and Elisha. We met Elijah when we were living in Abu Dhabi. He was the first believer in his Hindu family and in his village. He was working as a house cleaner to send money back to his family in India. As we got to know him, we recognized in him a real passion for the gospel. He had led his entire family (siblings and parents) to faith. He had a dream of one day studying to become a pastor. The church was able to facilitate that dream and sponsored him through four years of Bible College. Following Bible College, he and his wife and two children went back to his village to plant a church. My wife and I visited there after a few years to encourage them in the ministry. We found a thriving but tiny church on the bend of a road to nowhere. But Elijah had bigger dreams. On that same visit, we met Elisha, Elijah's teen age son. He also had a desire to serve the Lord. After completing high school, he went to Bible College and participated in several internships to gain ministry experience. Meanwhile the ministry continued to grow, from one church to 4 to 10 and more. Preaching points and prayer cells grew into churches as the network grew. Buildings were built and a school was established. The ministry was thriving as more and more people came to faith in Christ. Elisha and his family joined Elijah in the ministry. Still the dream expanded. Each time I visited, there was more to see, more churches to visit, more buildings to dedicate, and more people to baptize. I've lost track of the statistics, but their latest dream/ambition is staggering. The ministry organization they have established has set a goal: 100,000 believers, 1000 churches, and 100 pastor training centers by 2030! Now that's godly ambition! Yet both Elijah and Elisha remain humble and God-dependent in the undertaking.

What are your ambitions? What are mine? We are not all called or gifted like the Apostle Paul, or like Elijah and Elisha. That being said, there is a place for ambition in the life of every believer; ambition that is centered on the spread of the gospel and the growth of Christ's kingdom within our sphere of influence. The gospel is something to be believed. It is something to be lived. It is something to be proclaimed.

33

THE LONE RANGER IS A MYTH
Romans 15:22-16:27

One of my favorite comic book heroes when I was a boy was the "Lone Ranger." He was a mysterious character. He wore a mask and rode a white horse. No one knew where he stayed or where he came from, but he had a way of riding onto the scene at just the right moment to rescue people from their troubles. At the conclusion of each episode or story, he would call out to his horse, "Hi ho, Silver. Away!" as he rode into the sunset, leaving the people he had rescued to exclaim, "Who was that masked man?"

One of the essential aspects of his persona was captured in that word, "Lone." This was in contrast and an exception to the other part of his label – Ranger. The Rangers were a law-keeping force in the region. The Rangers worked and rode and fought as a group. But, with the exception of his faithful companion, Tonto, the Lone Ranger rode and fought alone.

The title of this final chapter is "The Lone Ranger Is a Myth." While the Lone Ranger may be an OK character in a comic book or a TV show, I want to stress that he makes a very poor model for the Christian life. Unfortunately, there are some who attempt to live the Christian life as a kind of Lone Ranger. Their rallying cry is, "Just Jesus and me." With God as a kind of faithful Tonto, or companion to help out occasionally when needed, they live out their faith in isolation from other believers.

Such thinking is all too common. I had an interesting experience some years ago while living in Abu Dhabi. I was invited to a reception at the British Ambassador's residence for the official introduction of Reverend Andy Thompson's book on the history of Christianity in the UAE. The guest of honor at the occasion was a member of the British royal family. During the informal discussion, comments were made praising the UAE government for their tolerance for Christians in giving us land for church buildings and allowing us to gather and worship openly. In the middle of the discussion, the guest of honor interjected with a question. "Why do Christians have to get together?" he asked. "After all, isn't religion simply a private matter between each individual and God?"

Such thinking (and acting) is absolutely contradictory to the clear teaching and example of Scripture. If you read the New Testament carefully, you cannot escape the clear conclusion that the Christian life was never intended to be lived as a solitary existence. We are called to live out our Christian faith in community and in relationship with other believers. There is a common expression on TV when someone displays some extraordinary talent or performs some daring stunt: "Don't try this at home!" I think it would be appropriate to adapt that expression relative to the Christian life as it has been described in the entirety of Romans, and especially in the final chapters: "Don't try this alone!"

This comes out very clearly in the last chapter and a half of the Book of Romans. The theme that stands out to me in this section is simply this: **Believers need each other.** In the previous chapters of Romans, we have already clearly established that the believer needs God. We need the righteousness of God which comes by faith in Jesus Christ if we want to be justified, and we need the power of the indwelling Holy Spirit of God if we desire to be sanctified. But in this closing section of Romans, we also see that **we need each other.**

This last section of Paul's letter would be easy to skip over. Paul has finished teaching and he is being personal. He is talking about his plans, giving prayer requests, and greeting his friends. But as noted in the previous chapter, we can learn some valuable lessons by just listening to Paul being personal. One thing we learn is that Paul was vitally and deeply involved in the lives of other Christians. Paul was no Lone Ranger! And it was not a one-sided relationship, in which Paul did all the giving and teaching. We also see Paul drawing on, enjoying and being strengthened by these mutual relationships and friendships.

As I read through these verses with this theme in mind, I find that there are at least five needs that are met in the context of relationships with other Christians. We might present these as five answers to the question the prince raised: Why do Christians need to get together?

1. The need for mutual instruction.

For this one, we are going to dip back into Romans 15:14: *"I myself am satisfied about you, my brothers, that you yourselves are full of goodness, filled with all knowledge and <u>able to instruct one another.</u>"*

Notice that underlined section. This sentence uses what is called a reciprocal pronoun, which is translated "one another." It is at the heart of what we mean when we use the word "mutual." It is the opposite of one-way. It is two-way; back and forth; you to me and me to you and back again. Paul writes to the Roman believers and says that while, in one sense, he has fulfilled his Apostolic responsibility in writing to them, in another sense, they were not dependent on his coming, because they were able to teach or instruct one another.

The word "instruct" is not the word for formal, class-room teaching. It focuses on application of the truth to our lives, not just theories and fine-sounding ideas. There are people in the church with a special gift for teaching, but we all have the ability and responsibility to instruct one another. Because we all need this kind of two-way, mutual interaction with the truths of God's Word, we need each other. That is also why we all need more than just the Sunday gatherings of the church, as powerful as they are. We need to be in relationships with each other in which we speak the truth into one another's lives. It begins in the home and in the family. This is the same word that is used in Ephesians 6:4 where Paul exhorts fathers to bring their children up in the *"nurture and instruction of the Lord."* However, it extends beyond our nuclear families to our spiritual family. Notice that Paul addresses his readers in this verse as "brothers." We are spiritual siblings in the family of God and we have a need to be engaged in mutual instruction.

2. The need for mutual sharing of resources.

This is practically illustrated in Romans 15:25-29: *"At present, however, I am going to Jerusalem bringing aid to the saints. For Macedonia and Achaia have been pleased to make some contribution for the poor among the saints at Jerusalem. For they were pleased to do it, and indeed they owe it to them. For if the Gentiles have come to share in their spiritual blessings, they ought also to be of service to them in material blessings. When therefore I have completed this and have delivered to them what has been collected, I will leave for Spain by way of you. I know that when I come to you I will come in the fullness of the blessing of Christ."*

Paul is speaking here about a collection that is talked about in the Book of Acts, in which the Gentile churches in what is now Greece and Turkey took up a collection for the suffering Jewish believers in Judea and Jerusalem. This illustrates not only the importance of Christian compassion, but the mutuality of sharing resources within the Body of Christ. The Gentile church received spiritual blessings from the Jewish church, and in turn they shared material blessings with the Jewish church. It is not so apparent in the English translations, but the word "contribution" in verse 26 and the word "to share" in verse 27 are the same in the original Greek, and it is the word "koinonia" that is often translated "fellowship." During my years as pastor in Abu Dhabi, we took a special offering every month. It was called a "fellowship offering," which we used to meet financial and compassion needs within the church family. It was a practical expression of true fellowship.

Paul expands on this in talking about this same offering in 2 Corinthians 8:13-15: *"For I do not mean that others should be eased and you burdened, but that as a matter of fairness your abundance at the present time should supply their need, so that their abundance may supply your need, that there may be fairness. As it is written, 'Whoever gathered much had nothing left over, and whoever gathered little had no lack.'"*

Can you see the mutuality of sharing expressed there? It is a sharing of what one has to meet the needs of someone who does not have. Do you have a spiritual ability? Give it. Do you have financial resources? Give them. Do you have time or energy? Give them. Be alert to needs within the family of God and share what you have to meet those needs. At the same time, remain open to receiving from others and allowing them to meet your needs as well.

3. The need for mutual prayer.

In Romans 15:30-32, Paul says: *"I appeal to you, brothers, by our Lord Jesus Christ and by the love of the Spirit, to strive together with me in your prayers to God on my behalf, that I may be delivered from the unbelievers in Judea, and that my service for Jerusalem may be acceptable to the saints so that by God's will I may come to you with joy and be refreshed in your company."*

Paul began the Book of Romans in chapter 1, verses 9-10 by telling the Roman believers that he was praying for them: *"For God is my witness, whom I serve with my spirit in the gospel of his Son, that without ceasing I mention you always in my prayers, asking that somehow by God's will I may now at last succeed in coming to you."*

Now, in chapter 15, Paul asks the Roman Christians to pray for him. Once again, we see this mutuality; the need to pray for one another. We also see that in both cases these prayers are made within the will of God. *"That by God's will I may come..."* Paul says. I am reminded of the Lord's Prayer: *"Thy will be done..."* I am also reminded of Romans 12:2, in which the outcome of placing ourselves as living sacrifices on the altar is that we will test and approve *"the will of God which is good and acceptable and perfect."* If we are to fully experience the will of God in our lives, we need to pray and we need to pray for each other.

I am struck by the strong vocabulary Paul uses to describe prayer here in Romans 15:30: *"...strive together with me in your prayers..."* The Greek word is a compound word that begins with the preposition "with." It is another word that expresses fellowship, sharing and mutuality. The second part of the word expresses intense struggle, effort or competition. It comes from the root word for the arena in which the wrestling matches of the day were contested. It shows us that prayer is hard work. It is a struggle. It is competition against the forces of darkness as we labor with God to see his will fulfilled in our lives. But we don't just labor with God. We are called to labor with one another in mutual prayer.

One of the vital ministries of any church is the ministry of prayer. While many churches have a structure for corporate prayer and hold meetings devoted to prayer, it is my experience that prayer is most effective when it is incorporated into every phase and facet of our lives and in the life of the church. I appreciate the message on the poster I once saw: "Be aware that at any point in the proceedings, a prayer meeting may break out." Mutual prayer. We need it. Let's do it. Let's do more of it. It is one of the reasons we need each other. It is one of the answers the question: Why do Christians need to get together? But of course, the beauty of prayer is that it overcomes time and space. We can pray for each other even when we are not physically together. Even when separated by miles, oceans and continents, we can meet together at the throne of grace and pray for one another.

4. The need for mutual affection.

I really wasn't quite sure how to word this one. I could have used the phrase "mutual love," but really "love" is the summary of everything we are covering in this chapter. What I am trying to express is the need for deep personal friendships and affection for one another.

In Romans 16:1-16, Paul goes through a long list of personal greetings and in so doing he reveals himself as a man who cared about other people as human beings. It is interesting that, while Paul had never personally visited Rome or the church in Rome, he knew many of its members; people he had met on his journeys who were now living in the capital of the empire.

Here is a sampling of these greetings:

Romans 16:3-4: *"Greet Prisca and Aquila, my fellow workers in Christ Jesus, who risked their necks for my life, to whom not only I give thanks but all the churches of the Gentiles give thanks as well."*

Romans 16:5-9: *"Greet also the church in their house. Greet my beloved Epaenetus, who was the first convert to Christ in Asia. Greet Mary, who has worked hard for you. Greet Andronicus and Junia, my kinsmen and my fellow prisoners. They are well known to the apostles, and they were in Christ before me. Greet Ampliatus, my beloved in the Lord. Greet Urbanus, our fellow worker in Christ, and my beloved Stachys."*

Romans 16:12-13: *"Greet those workers in the Lord, Tryphaena and Tryphosa. Greet the beloved Persis, who has worked hard in the Lord. Greet Rufus, chosen in the Lord; also his mother, who has been a mother to me as well."*

As we read these greetings, a picture emerges of a man with strong personal relationships. He called people by name and made some personal comment. He cared about people and they clearly cared about him. They were family.

What about your church? Is it a family? It becomes more difficult as a church grows larger. It is harder to remember names and put them with the right faces. The reality is that we can't know everyone. That is why it so urgent that we break the church down into smaller groups and settings and make the big church small through Life Groups, Bible studies and one-on-one discipleship and friendships. It is also why the time together in the foyer or the fellowship hall, or wherever people gather after the service, is a vital part of our church life. Don't rush away. Stay. Visit. Meet your friends. Make new friends. We need each other. We need the mutual friendship and caring that the church can provide.

5. The need for mutual protection.

Unfortunately, all is not rosy all the time in the church. Problems arise. There are enemies both without and within. Paul makes mention of this in Romans 16:17-18:

"I appeal to you, brothers, to watch out for those who cause divisions and create obstacles contrary to the doctrine that you have been taught; avoid them. For such persons do not serve our Lord Christ, but their own appetites, and by smooth talk and flattery they deceive the hearts of the naive."

Enemies to our unity and to our doctrine abound. The Bible is clear that such enemies and challenges will multiply as we approach the end of the age. We must "watch out" and warn and protect one another.

During my years living in Africa, we had many encounters with Africa's wild animals. One species we saw frequently was the baboon. It's not a particularly attractive species. However, they have one trait that I admire; that is their loyalty to each other and the way they protect one another. They live in family groups, and it is almost impossible to take them by surprise, because there are always a few lookouts posted. When they spot danger or a possible threat, the lookouts will call a warning to the others. The mothers with the young ones are quickly rushed to safety, while the stronger ones bring up the rear to defend against an attack.

So it should be with us as Christians. As individuals we are all vulnerable: prey to our own weaknesses; prone to misunderstanding; prone to distort things and get things out of perspective and out of balance; even susceptible to being led astray. We need to be part of a watchful group, ready to protect one another. We need each other.

As we meet one another's needs in the ways we have been describing, we can expect certain results.

First, **we can expect collective victory over Satan.**

Romans 16:19-20 tells us: *"For your obedience is known to all, so that I rejoice over you, but I want you to be wise as to what is good and innocent as to what is evil. The God of peace will soon crush Satan under your feet."*

Satan defeated. Satan crushed under our feet. Isn't that a great promise and a great image? But as we read that, we need to keep in mind that the pronoun "your" in verse 20 is plural. This is a collective victory. We won't win this victory by being lots of "lone rangers."

Secondly, **we will experience refreshing rest.**

This is one of the reasons Paul looked forward to visiting the church in Rome. He refers to it in Romans 15:24: *"I hope to see you in passing as I go to Spain, and to be helped on my journey there by you, once I have enjoyed your company for a while."*

The image Paul uses here is that of eating a meal or drinking a refreshing drink until one is satisfied or full.

In verse 32 he says, *"so that by God's will I may come to you with joy and be refreshed in your company."*

The word refreshed literally speaks of being rested. Do you enjoy getting together with other Christians? Do you leave Sunday services feeling refreshed, encouraged, and strengthened? Do you look forward to your small fellowship group? During our time in Abu Dhabi as people prepared to depart (we had lots of coming and going in our international congregation) many came to tell me that without our church and particularly without their small fellowship group and the support and encouragement they received, they would not have made it through their time in Abu Dhabi. Those same people frequently described the church as "an oasis in the desert." I was always encouraged to hear that. It meant that we were fulfilling our calling to be a family; the family of God in Abu Dhabi.

Fellow believers, **we need each other**. Don't try to make it on your own. God isn't looking for Lone Rangers. He created us for fellowship with him and for fellowship with one another.

Well, we've done it! We have reached the end of our journey through the Book of Romans! To conclude, Paul directs one last word of praise and benediction toward heaven. In this letter he has been expounding on what he has referred to as the gospel of God. Now he directs his praise to the God of the gospel.

"Now to him who is able to strengthen you according to my gospel and the preaching of Jesus Christ, according to the revelation of the mystery that was kept secret for long ages but has now been disclosed and through the prophetic writings has been made known to all nations, according to the command of the eternal God, to bring about the obedience of faith— to the only wise God be glory forevermore through Jesus Christ!"

And everyone said, *"Amen!"*

Romans: An Outline

One of the challenges of such a lengthy letter and study is that it is easy to lose track of where we've been and where we are going; to miss the forest for the trees. This is especially true in the study of Romans. In the Introduction, I made reference to my first serious exposure to Romans in a Bible class when I was in high school. One of the first things our teacher, Mr. Hendry, did was to give us an outline for the letter and require us to memorize it. While I don't remember the details or headings in his outline, the basic structure of the book has remained with me. Here is my understanding of the broad bones of that structure.

- **Introduction to the Gospel: 1:1-17**
- **Righteousness Needed (Condemnation): 1:18-3:20**
- **Righteousness Provided (Justification through Redemption): 3:21-5:21**
- **First Detour: Does justification by faith encourage a life of continued sinning? 6**
- **Second Detour: What about the Law? 7**
- **Righteousness Applied (Sanctification; Life in the Spirit): 8**
- **Third Detour: What about the Jews? 9-11**
- **How Shall We Then Live? 12-16.**

Even as I reproduce this outline, however, I am reminded of the limitations of outlines. While helpful, they can send a wrong message that matters of content can be contained in airtight compartments. Paul (and most of the Scripture writers) did not think or write according to an outline. Even my use of the word "detour" can be misleading. A pastor friend of mine prefers to use the analogy of a braided river, in which multiple streams can depart from the main river and rejoin it at unexpected points, all flowing together to reinforce the message. So the text itself may not be as precise and orderly as an outline might indicate. However, I find that there is still value in identifying the main themes and the sections in which they are developed. I hope you find it helpful.

SUGGESTED DISCUSSION QUESTIONS FOR SMALL GROUP BIBLE STUDIES

CHAPTER 1
Romans 1:1-17

1. What do you hope to get out of this study on the Book of Romans?
2. Based on what he wrote in Romans 1:1-17, how did Paul feel about "the gospel?"
3. What do we learn about the identity of Jesus from these verses? Is it necessary to believe these things about Jesus in order to be a true Christian and experience the "salvation" Paul speaks about in verse 16? Why or why not? Do you agree or disagree with the statement: "Jesus is the Gospel?"
4. The chapter describes the word "ashamed" as a combination of disappointment and embarrassment when something or someone we have trusted or relied on does not fulfill their promise. Can you share an anecdote of a time you experienced that emotion? What is Paul saying when he says he is "not ashamed" of the Gospel? Can you say the same thing?
5. What is the link between faith/belief and the power of God in the Gospel?

CHAPTER 2
Romans 1:18-32

1. This is the first in a series of three chapters titled "Who Needs the Gospel?" In describing the person standing before God's court in the first Case Study, the author used the word "pagan" and gave the following dictionary definition: "1. A follower of a polytheistic religion. 2. One who has little or no religion and who delights in sensual pleasures and material goods; an irreligious or hedonistic person." How does this definition match Paul's description of the group presented in Romans 1:18-32?
2. What possible defense might this person use when standing before God's court?
3. Will the defense of "ignorance" stand up in God's court?

Why or why not? What does Paul have to say on the subject?

4. What sources of knowledge about God are available to the "pagan?" What can he discover about God from these sources?

5. Three times in this passage, Paul uses the phrase "God turned them over..." Where are these references found? What did "God turn them over" to? What do we learn from this?

6. "In God's courtroom, each individual will be judged based on what he did with the knowledge he had." Do you agree or disagree with this statement? Do you think this is a fair standard? What does this mean for the person in the remotest part of the jungle? What does this mean for us?

7. Is there anything you have heard in this message or discovered in this passage that is new to you or which surprised you? What questions does the passage leave unanswered?

CHAPTER 3
Romans 2:1-16

1. In this second court case before God's court, the defendant is identified as "the moral man." What are some of the ways in which this person might complete this sentence: "I will be OK because..."

2. How would you describe the concept of "grading on the curve?" Do you think God will grade on the curve? Why is the answer to this question important?

3. According to this passage, what will be the basis or standard for God's judgment?

4. Does Paul propose "salvation by works" in verse 7 and 10? Why or why not?

5. How common is "the moral man's" reasoning in our world today? What implications does this have for sharing our faith?

CHAPTER 4
Romans 2:17-3:20

1. Read Romans 2:17-20. This is a description of the religious confidence of the Jews in Paul's audience. There is another version of this in Paul's personal testimony in Philippians 3:4-6. Try to paraphrase this kind of religious confidence as

it applies to the religious groups or people with whom you are most familiar.

2. Do you think God is "anti-religion?" Why or why not?
3. Why is the word "religion" and "religious" often associated with hypocrisy and pride?
4. Read Matthew 5:20 and Luke 18:9-14. What is the warning here for the man who relies on his religion for his righteous position before God? How does this relate to Romans 2:17-29?
5. In his conclusion, the author stated that "the message of God's coming judgment is part of the Gospel message." He based the statement on Romans 2:16. What do you think he meant by that? Do you agree or disagree? What are the implications when churches and preachers ignore this truth?
6. Based on our study so far in Romans, who needs the Gospel?

CHAPTER 5
Romans 3:21-31

1. "Romans 3:21-31 contains the most complete and comprehensive summary of the legal, logical and theological foundations of the Christian faith contained anywhere in Scripture." Do you agree with this statement? Why or why not?
2. What is man's dilemma? (Summary of thoughts from the first three chapters of Romans)
3. What was God's dilemma? (Clue: look at verse 26)
4. How did God solve both man's dilemma and his own?
5. What is man's part in the solution?
6. Have you been "justified freely by his grace?" As a group, you may want to take some time sharing how and when that happened for you individually, or discuss what is holding you back from taking that step.

CHAPTER 6
Romans 4

1. Take a few minutes together to review the main points of the first 3 chapters of the Book of Romans.

2. See how many times you can find the words "credited" or "counted" in Romans 4. Discuss the concept and its significance to Paul's reasoning in the chapter.
3. The author referred to verse 5 as a truly radical verse. Do you agree or disagree? Why? How might you use this verse to share the Gospel with a person who is a member of a religion that depends on a works-based righteousness?
4. Abraham is referred to as the father of those who have faith. How is our faith the same as Abraham's and how is it different? Use Abraham's story and example to discuss the following: the nature of faith, the object of faith, and the content of faith.

CHAPTER 7
Romans 5:1-5

1. What does the phrase "peace with God" mean to you? Discuss the difference between "a state of peace" and "a sense of peace." How are they different? How are they related?
2. How would you engage a follower of another religion who told you that he had "found peace" when he embraced his religious beliefs?
3. What do you think "the hope of the glory of God" means? What is your picture or vision of life in eternity? Where did you acquire it? How does it relate to this phrase? Do we have to wait until the next life to experience the glory of God?
4. How does being justified by faith influence our response to the difficulties of life now? Can you give examples of how suffering has produced endurance in you?
5. Do you believe God loves you? How do you know? When have you felt most aware of God's love?

CHAPTER 8
Romans 5:6-11

1. What is your favorite love story from the world of fiction?
2. Describe the attributes of those loved and why they were loved (from your "favorites" above)?
3. The first point in this chapter is: "Could there be any less

likely candidates for love?" How is God's love in this passage a contrast to the love stories you've been describing?

4. Pick out the descriptions of the human race found in this passage. Do you agree with this depiction? How does it compare with the way the human race typically views itself?

5. How did God demonstrate his love? When did he do it? Why is this significant and how does it demonstrate the attribute of grace?

6. "The death of Christ on the cross proves that we were worth dying for." Do you agree with this statement? Why or why not?

7. What are some of the benefits we receive from God's love (listed in this passage)?

8. Spend some time in prayer "rejoicing in God" for your salvation.

CHAPTER 9
Romans 5:12-21

1. After reading this passage, what do you find most puzzling or troubling and why?

2. Can you give any examples in which a community or group is held liable for the actions of one person? Are there any parallels between your example and the concepts Paul presents in this passage?

3. The author interpreted the phrase "for all sinned" at the end of verse 12 as referring to the entire human race participating in some way in the sin of Adam and therefore suffering the same consequences. Do you agree with this interpretation? Can you suggest any alternative interpretation?

4. Verse 14 describes Adam as "a pattern of the one to come" (the word is "type"). In what sense is Adam a type of Christ?

5. What did we inherit from Adam?

6. What do we inherit from Christ?

7. Meditate on verse 21, and then express your thoughts in a time of prayer together.

CHAPTER 10

Romans 6:1-11

1. Do you think the Gospel message of **salvation by grace through faith** encourages Christians today to continue in a life of sin, or to treat sin in their lives rather casually? (Give the reasons for your answer and discuss the matter together.)
2. How does the truth of the believer's union with Christ counteract this erroneous thinking?
3. Is the reality of the believer's union with Christ a new teaching for you?
4. How does the act of water baptism symbolize the spiritual realities of the Christian's new identity in Christ?
5. Discuss what it means to "reckon yourself to be dead to sin but alive to God in Christ Jesus." How would it make a difference in your life this coming week?
6. Memorize Romans 6:2 together and discuss how to use it to counteract temptation.

CHAPTER 11
Romans 6:12-14

1. From this chapter, how would you distinguish between the definitions of "justification" and "sanctification?" Based on these definitions and if Romans 4:5 is true ("God justifies the wicked") how would you answer the question: Does the doctrine of justification by faith make sanctification unnecessary?
2. Think of a situation in history (or current events!) in which an old ruler has been deposed and a nation must now reckon with the new reality of a new ruler. What analogies can we draw from these situations that might help us understand what Paul is calling for in Romans 6:12-14?
3. Why is "reckoning" an important part of this process?
4. The author used the hand and tongue as examples of body "members" that can be either instruments of wickedness or instruments of righteousness. Pick some other parts of the human body and use your imaginations to picture them in either a negative or positive role.
5. In the message we discover that the verb form in the second

part of verse 13 ("Offer yourselves to God...") suggests one-time, urgent action. Why do you think Paul uses this tense rather than one that requires every day, on-going, continuous action? What implications can you draw from this?

6. Spend a time of prayer together reflecting on what you have learned in Romans 6:12-14.

CHAPTER 12
Romans 6:15-23

1. 1. Imagine this multiple-choice question on an exam:
   I want to be...
   > **a. a slave to sin**
   > **b. a slave to God**

2. Do you like the way this question is worded? What are some possible options (c or d) that people (yourself included!) might like to add? Read Romans 6:16. Are these really the only two options? (Discuss)

3. If there are only two options, what are the implications for the choices we make every day?

4. How does this reality address the question Paul raises in Romans 6:15?

5. Reread the entire chapter 6 of Romans. What are you taking away from this chapter?

CHAPTER 13
Romans 7:1-6

1. Put yourself in the sandals of a devout Jew in the first century who has just read the first 5 chapters of Romans. What might he/she be feeling/thinking/questioning?

2. How do the first 6 verses of Romans 7 address some of those concerns?

3. Does the argument from the "law of marriage" clarify or confuse the issue for you? Discuss the reasons for your answer.

4. Read v. 4 and the phrase "to belong to another." What does it mean to you to "belong" to Christ?

5. What do you think it means to "bear fruit to God?" In what ways would you like to see that happen in your life?

CHAPTER 14
Romans 7:7-13

1. How does Paul's description and understanding of sin and human nature in these verses contrast with popular understanding today?
2. Why doesn't the law solve the problem?
3. What is the law's role? Can you explain and/or give examples of how this works?
4. The author used several illustrations in the chapter (the snake on the beach, the snake in the house, the broom and the dirt floor, the plumb line). Which one did you find the most helpful and why?

CHAPTER 15
Romans 7:14-25

1. What part of his life experience (pre-conversion or present reality) do you think Paul is describing in Romans 7:14-25? What are the pros and cons of your answer? (Compare the descriptive statements in this passage with some of the things that Paul said in Romans 6.)
2. What are the pros and cons of the alternative position?
3. Compare and contrast Paul's words in Galatians 5 with Romans 7. How are they the same? How are they different?
4. What are the implications and applications of the two different interpretations?

CHAPTER 16
Romans 8:1-4

1. Describe your thoughts, feelings, and experience in the days and weeks immediately after you trusted in Christ as Savior. (Note: If you accepted Christ when you were very young, you may have difficulty doing this. That's OK! Also, this question may raise the question in your mind as to whether you have actually taken this step. Feel free to share this with your group as well and discuss it with them.)
2. In this chapter, justification is defined as "declared righteous" and sanctification as "made righteous." Discuss the distinction between these two words and concepts. What

happens when we fail to understand the distinction? Which one comes first? What happens when we confuse the order in our understanding?

3. In the chapter, the author summarized the wonderful truths of justification in the phrase "I am in Christ" and the truths of our sanctification in the phrase, "Christ is in me." Do you find this distinction helpful? Why or why not? What are some things that are true of us since we are "in Christ?" (Note: you may need to do some reviewing of earlier chapters of Romans to answer this.) What are the implications of the reality that "Christ (his Spirit) is in me?" (Note: Galatians 2:20 may be a helpful parallel verse to consider.)

CHAPTER 17
Romans 8:5-17

1. Based on the previous chapter on Romans 8:1-4, how would you explain what it means to be "in Christ Jesus?" What doctrine does this phrase incorporate?

2. In the rest of this section, Paul now develops another exciting reality: "Christ is in you." What does that mean? (See v. 9-10.) What doctrine does this phrase emphasize?

3. How is the Christian's mind set/world view different from that of the person who does not follow Christ? (Feel free to give your own experience and opinion as well as considering the statements in verses 5-8.)

4. The author made the statement that the times that he is most certain that he is a child of God is when he sins. What do you think he meant by that? Do you agree or disagree? What do you think it means to be "led by the Spirit?"

5. Discuss your feelings and reactions to verses 15-16.

CHAPTER 18
Romans 8:18-27

1. Who are the three different "groaners" found in this passage?

2. The author also identifies three different kinds of groaning. What are they?

3. Give examples of "the whole creation groaning." What is the

link between the creation's groaning and the Fall of man in the Garden of Eden?

4. Give some examples of a "groan of anticipation."

5. What is creation looking forward to and why is that significant? What do we as believers have to look forward to? What are you particularly looking forward to when you get your new body?

6. Discuss your thoughts, feelings and reactions to the Holy Spirit's groan of assistance as described in verses 26-27.

CHAPTER 19
Romans 8:28-30

1. The middle of Romans 8:28 contains a wonderful reassurance ("all things work together for good"). To whom does this promise/assurance apply? Why is this important to understand?

2. Do you think these descriptions in verse 28 apply to all true followers of Christ or only a special category of Christian? Give reasons for your answer.

3. When tying verse 28 to verses 29-30, the chapter made four propositional statements of Biblical truth. Read each one and discuss your reactions to it: (agree, disagree, uncomfortable, reassured, etc.)
   - Salvation is God's work from beginning to end.
   - What God starts, he finishes.
   - God's purpose for his children is to make us like Christ.
   - God has a plan to fulfill his purpose and everything that happens to us fits into that plan.

4. How does understanding the context of Romans 8:28 influence your understanding of the verse and its promise? Does this perspective give you a greater or lesser degree of comfort as you face difficult circumstances in life?

CHAPTER 20
Romans 8:31-39

1. Think back to your childhood. What was your greatest fear?

2. In this chapter, the author makes the statement, "The world is a dangerous place." What are some of those dangers? Which

ones do you find the most frightening?

3. Read Romans 8:31-39 together. How does this passage address our fears?

4. How is the theology of our justification (verses 33-34) the ultimate answer to our fears?

5. Do you think this passage teaches that nothing bad will ever happen to us as Christians? (Support your answer – from life and Scripture.) What does it promise?

6. What do you think it means to be "more than conquerors?" (v. 37). Can you give any examples from your experience, or people you have known?

CHAPTER 21
Romans 9:1-29

1. What do you find most puzzling and/or troubling in this passage?

2. How does Paul address the question: Has God's Word failed?

3. How does Paul answer the question: Is there injustice with God?

4. How does Paul answer the question: Why does God still find fault?

5. Which of these answers satisfy you? Which do not?

6. When asked how he reconciled the doctrine of God's sovereignty with the doctrine of man's responsibility, Charles Spurgeon answered, "I never try to reconcile friends." What do you think he meant? Do you agree or disagree?

CHAPTER 22
Romans 9:30-10:13

1. In this chapter, the author identifies the Jews' error as pursuing "the road of DIY righteousness." What does DIY stand for? In your opinion, how common is this error – especially among religious people? Are Christians (church goers) prone to the same error?

2. What are the marks of someone pursuing this road?

3. "It doesn't matter what you believe, as long as you are sincere and do your best." Do you agree or disagree? Why? How do

you think Paul would answer the question? Do you think there really is a right road and a wrong road to get to heaven?

4. How would you describe the "road of faith righteousness?" What must a person believe to follow this road?

5. What do you think Paul is getting at by his reference to the heart and the mouth in Romans 10:9-10?

6. What road are you on? Describe how and when you began your journey on this road.

CHAPTER 23
Romans 10:14-21

1. As a group, share together your background and experiences in sharing your faith: what training you have had, what types of outreach efforts you have been involved in, negative and positive experiences, and present participation.

2. Read Romans 9:3 and discuss your reaction to Paul's words.

3. Has God given you a particular burden for any particular category of people or people group? Any particular individuals in your life?

4. Do you agree with the statement: "Most people want to accept Christ. They just don't know how." Why or why not?

5. "Successful witnessing is sharing Christ in the power of the Holy Spirit and leaving the results to God." There are three parts to that statement. Take them apart and discuss why it is important to keep each part in mind.

6. How different is the situation in the world (and in churches) today from the situation William Carey faced when he wrote his book <u>An Enquiry into the Obligations of Christians</u>?

CHAPTER 24
Romans 11

Begin by reading the chapter aloud together and pray, asking God's Spirit to help you understand the truths it contains.

1. The author declared this to be the most difficult chapter in the Book of Romans. Do you agree? Why or why not?

2. What do you find the most confusing and/or troubling aspect of this chapter? Why?

3. Why is the doctrine of divine election so controversial? How do you personally reconcile it with the doctrine of human responsibility?

4. Is there a future in God's plan for Israel as a race/nation? What passages in this chapter relate to that question? What other passages of Scripture might you go to in researching this question?

5. Can believers who have been truly saved lose their salvation? How does the parable of the olive tree and the warnings in this passage reflect on this argument? What other Scriptures would you go to in researching this question?

   Remember: If there are different opinions in your group, practice disagreeing without becoming disagreeable!

6. While there is much here that puzzles us and upon which we might disagree, the author concludes the message with three application points that we can all agree on: What are they?

CHAPTER 25
Romans 12:1-2

1. "In view of God's mercies..." How does this phrase capture the essence of the Gospel message as presented by Paul in the first 8 chapters of Romans?

2. What images does the phrase "living sacrifice" create in your mind?

3. Why do you think Paul focuses on our bodies? How does this verse relate to Romans 6:12-14?

4. In his message, the author used his tooth brush as an illustration of something holy. What did you learn from this? What other everyday objects do you have that are "holy?"

5. "This is real worship," could be a paraphrase of the final phrase of Romans 12:1. Do you agree or disagree? How does this compare or contrast with the emphasis on worship in churches today?

6. The verb "to offer" is in a tense describing a point-in-time action or event. Discuss the implications of this in your understanding of verse 1.

7. "Stop being conformed to this world!" What changes have

you made in your lifestyle since becoming a follower of Christ? Discuss some ways that the world pressures us to conform to its standards and values.

8. "Be transformed!" How is the metaphor of "metamorphosis" helpful in understanding the process of sanctification?

9. What is the role of our minds in the process of sanctification? Read Romans 6:1-11 and note the references to "know" and "consider." What do we know? How does this knowledge relate to the renewal of our minds?

10. Read the following verses which refer to the will of God: John 4:34, John 6:38, Ephesians 3:17-21, 1 Thessalonians 4:3, 1 Peter 2:15-17, and 1 Peter 4:2. Based on these verses, what is the will of God? What does it mean to "live for the will of God?"

CHAPTER 26
Romans 12:3-8

1. In this very first paragraph of instructions on Christian living, Paul introduces the subject of Christian service and spiritual gifts. Why is that significant?

2. In the chapter, the author traces his experiences with the subject of spiritual gifts and various seminars and workshops on the topic. What has your experience been with teaching, books or seminars on spiritual gifts? What has been helpful? What has not been helpful?

3. The author calls himself a minimalist on this subject. What does he mean by that? Do you find his approach disappointing/refreshing/a relief/ insightful/other? Explain your answer.

4. This message summarizes the central truth of this paragraph into two basic facts: **We are one. We are different.** What are the implications of these two basic facts? How does the analogy of the human body help us understand what he is saying? How does this safeguard us against pride and competition?

5. What is the "Nike philosophy of spiritual gifts?" Do you agree with it?

6. As a group, share together your journeys in discovering your gifts and areas of ministry/service in the church. (You may be just beginning the journey, be on the way, or have a fully developed sense of your gifts and ministry – share honestly where you are and how you got there, what you found helpful, etc.)

7. Pray together as you consider making new commitments to service in the kingdom of God.

CHAPTER 27
Romans 12:9-21

1. What are some ways in which you have experienced the battle of good against evil in the past week?

2. As you read through the passage, isolate the commands that apply to relationships with other believers. Which ones do you find easy to obey? Which ones do you find difficult? How have you been tested in this area during the past month?

3. Verse 11-12 describes attitudes and strategies necessary for victory in the struggle. Which commands do you find easy to obey? Which ones do you find difficult? How have you been tested in this area during the past month?

4. The last section of the paragraph gives us instructions for how to respond to people who wish us (or actually do us) harm. The author refers to this as "upside down" or "unnatural" living. Why? Do you think these commands are practical in the "real world?" Why or why not?

5. How does "repaying evil with evil" make us vulnerable and cause us to be "overcome by evil?" Can you give examples (from your own or other's experience)? How does returning good for evil reverse this and allow us to "overcome evil with good." Can you give examples?

6. For practical examples of this principle at work, consider Jesus' teaching in Matthew 5:38-48. How do these examples help us understand Paul's teaching in Romans 12?

7. Read the entire passage again, considering it as a description of the life of Christ. How did he live out these principles?

8. Share some ways in which you expect to experience the battle

of good against evil in the coming week, and pray together that God will enable you to be victorious and "overcome evil with good."

CHAPTER 28
Romans 13:1-7

1. Read Romans 13:1-7 together. Do you find this passage easy or difficult to understand and obey? Why?
2. Three times, Paul refers to rulers as "God's servants". What specific tasks has he entrusted to them? (There are at least 3 mentioned in the passage).
3. From your experience, what is the general attitude among Christians toward Christians being in politics or government? How should this passage affect our attitude?
4. Discuss and give examples of what it means to, "Pay to all what is owed to them: taxes...revenue...respect...honor."
5. Do you agree with the author that in spite of the apparent "black and white" statements in this passage, there are times when conscience requires believers to disobey government laws and government officials? Discuss the reasons for your answer.
6. Spend some time together fulfilling the command of 1 Timothy 2:1-3 by praying for the rulers of our country.

CHAPTER 29
Romans 13:8-14

1. "Love does no wrong to a neighbor; therefore love is the fulfilling of the law." (Romans 13:10). In the chapter, the author states that this both simplifies and expands the law. What did he mean by that? In what ways does this simplify the law? In what ways does it expand the law?
2. Share examples of ways that you have (or should have) applied this during the past week? What are some ways you may need to apply this principle in the coming week?
3. Romans 13:11-12 contains a number of references to time and the urgency of passing time? What is the time Paul refers to? Why does this lend an urgency to his teaching?
4. In Romans 13:13, Paul lists 3 categories of behavior that he

labels "works of darkness." What are they? Give examples of behavior that fit under each category. What other types of behavior might be listed as works of darkness?

5. What does it mean to "put on the Lord Jesus Christ?" What are some ways we can do that?

6. Give some examples of ways we as Christians might "make provision for the flesh?"

7. Think (and share together) some of the challenges you anticipate in the coming week. Spend some time praying for one another and the week ahead as you seek to "put on the Lord Jesus Christ."

CHAPTER 30
Romans 14:1-15:13

1. In this chapter, the author discusses our internal list of "not to dos": types of activities or behaviors that we choose not to engage in. But, he distinguishes between matters on which God has clearly spoken and what Paul refers to as "opinions" or "doubtful matters" in Romans 14:1. Give some examples of matters about which the Bible is clear.

2. In the passage, Paul gives two examples of "matters of opinion" in verse 2 and verse 5. What are they? Why do you think there were differences of opinion on these matters? How can the same behavior be sin for one Christian but not for another? Is this an example of situation ethics?

3. Give examples of "matters of opinion" which come from your upbringing and Christian background. How have attitudes in general changed toward these matters within the Christian community during your lifetime? Do you think these changes are good or bad? How have your opinions changed or evolved (if they have)?

4. One of the points in this chapter states that: "There is no divinely mandated list." Do you agree or disagree? Why?

5. Should we discard our lists altogether? Discuss the value (and dangers) of having a list based on personal convictions.

CHAPTER 31
Romans 14:1-15:13 (again)

1. In this chapter, the author talks about what happens "when lists collide"; when Christians disagree about what constitutes right and wrong behavior and standards for Christians. Share together some of those issues about which Christians disagree from your experience and background in the church. How were these issues typically handled? What was the result?

2. In the first point in the chapter, we are commanded to "stop judging." What verses in the text make this point? How does taking the perspective of a fellow servant help us obey this command? How does remembering that we shall all one day give account to God motivate us to stop judging one another?

3. How would you define Christian liberty? What does the author mean when he writes: "Christ-like love trumps Christian liberty in the hierarchy of values?" Can you give some examples of this principle in action?

4. This chapter makes a distinction between acting in love toward a weaker brother and placating a strongly-opinionated believer with a longer list. Do you agree? Why or why not? Why is this an important distinction?

5. How would you describe the difference between singing in unison and singing in harmony on our "lists?" In the early church, the primary differences in lists occurred between Jews and Gentiles. Where do the differences now lie in your experience? How can we maintain harmony in spite of our differences? What is the result when we do?

CHAPTER 32
Romans 15:14-21

1. This chapter is titled: "A Godly Ambition." Should Christians be ambitious? Why or why not? How would you distinguish between "godly ambition" and "selfish ambition" (Philippians 2:3)?

2. In this message, we look at 3 responses called for by the gospel. What are they? As you read this book and participated in these studies, how have you responded to the gospel? Have

you made any new responses? Renewed previous ones? How has your life been impacted?

3. What ambition does Paul refer to in this passage (Romans 15:14-21)? What word picture does he use to describe his ambition? (Think altar and priest.) What is unique about Paul's ambition? What should be universal (to all believers)?

CHAPTER 33
Romans 15:22-16:27

1. In this chapter, the author quoted a question posed by a member of the British royal family: "Why do Christians have to get together? After all, isn't religion simply a private matter between each individual and God?" Do you agree or disagree? Why? In your experience how common is this kind of thinking?

2. The chapter lists five needs that are met by Christians meeting together. Review them together.

3. As you look at this list, which of these areas is your church doing well? Which ones not so well? Are you part of the problem or part of the solution? How can you do better?